Hidden Biscuits

Hidden Biscuits

Tales of Deep South Revivals Told by Heart

Audrey Ward

Foreword by
Fred Craddock

RESOURCE *Publications* · Eugene, Oregon

HIDDEN BISCUITS
Tales of Deep South Revivals Told by Heart

Resource Publications
An Imprint of Wipf and Stock Publishers
199 W. 8th Ave., Suite 3
Eugene, OR 97401

www.wipfandstock.com

ISBN 13: 978-1-4982-0925-0
Manufactured in the U.S.A.

Illustrations copyright © 2013 by Beth Whybrow Leeds
The author has sought all copyrights for music.

"At the End of the Trail" by Charles Wycuff, © 1946 Lovely Name (ASCAP) (adm. At CapitolCMGPublishing.com) All rights reserved. Used by permission.

"It Took a Miracle" (excerpt) by John W. Peterson ©1948 John W. Peterson Company. Used by Permission. All rights reserved.

"Room At The Cross For You" (excerpt) by Ira F. Stanphill. Copyright © 1946 New Spring Publishing Inc (ASCAP) (adm. At CapitolCMGPublishing.com). All rights reserved. Used by permission.

"Got Any Rivers" by Oscar G. Eliason. Copyright © 1945 New Spring Publishing Inc. (ASCAP) (adm. At CapitolCMGPublishing.com) All rights reserved. Used by permission.

"Suppertime" by Ira F. Stanphill. Copyright © 1950 New Spring Publishing Inc. (ASCAP) (adm. At CapitolCMGPublishing.com) All rights reserved. Used by permission.

"Just Keep On Praying" by Chalvar A. Gabriel. Copyright © 1931 New Spring Publishing Inc (ASCAP) (adm. At CapitolCMGPublishing.com) All rights reserved. Used by permission.

"This World Is Not My Home" by J. R. Baxter. Copyright © 1946 Bridge Building Music (BMI) (adm. At CapitolCMGPublishing.com) All rights reserved. Used by permission.

"In Passing" by Lisel Mueller, from *Alive Together*, Copyright © 1986. 1991. 1992, 1994, 1995, 1996 by Lisel Mueller. Used by permission of Louisiana State University Press.

Chronicle of the 20th Century, Chronicle Publications, Inc: Editor, Clifton Daniel: Unless otherwise noted, all information regarding specific years comes from this volume.

For Doris, Bill, and Althea

We were together.

Contents

Foreword

I CAN THINK OF no better way both to honor Audrey's request that I write a foreword and to serve the reader of this unusual account than to offer an interpretation of Audrey's own expression "told by heart."

These stories are *told*, that is, they arose in and come from an oral culture, not a script culture. Audrey herself lived the years of these stories in an oral world in which words were not read but were spoken, were heard, were passed along or were stored in silence. You will hear in the pages that follow not only Audrey's voice but many voices. These voices will sing, shout, cry, moan, scream, pray, whisper, confess, deny, promise, and lie, sometimes as weightless as a rumor, sometimes as heavy as the Word of God. After all, most of these stories have their setting in Pentecostal Holiness revival meetings where, to the uninitiated, everything seems an exaggeration. Some of you will recognize the several dialects of the rural areas of the southeastern United States. If you are familiar with these ways of talking, then read slowly and enjoy the sounds. If you are not familiar with these dialects, then read slowly and hum; soon you won't need to translate.

But in these pages you will hear more than human voices. In an oral world the ear is alert to many sounds, all of which are respected, so prepare yourself. A rooster crows, a dog barks, a factory whistle gathers and dismisses, a church bell summons, a passing train makes many sounds but keeps its secrets about whence and whither, an irreverent motorcycle interrupts all other sounds, and a grinding truck proves to be all honk and no delivery. But seldom does one hear the cracking of the spine of a new book being opened. When all is said and done, for many of the folk in these stories there is only one book, the Holy Bible, King James Version. They love to gather, they love to sing, they love to pray, but when the Evangelist mounts the pulpit and opens the Holy Book of warnings and promises, they love to listen. They have only one question: Is there any word from the Lord? If there is, darkness is scattered and light shines on these bone-tired communities, sometimes enough to last until revival time next year.

And, says Audrey, these stories are told "by heart." Although "by heart" is sometimes used as synonymous with "from memory," as in "the students recited the Gettysburg Address by heart," but such is not the meaning here. These stories were not memorized, learned by rote, or repeated exactly. Rather they have been appropriated body, mind, and soul so that it would be more true to say she could not forget them than to say she was able to remember them. But let's be fair, Audrey is not engaged in an exercise of excessive inwardness with no concern for verifiability. On the contrary, it is important to her to tell the truth about her life.

If you have reservations, prepare to shed them. Audrey is very aware of the distances between her life now and her life as a child. More than fifty years have passed; she is in Northern California, not Alabama and adjoining states; she is educated, in attendance at lectures and concerts, not rural revivals and prayer meetings; she is an ordained minister of the United Methodist Church, not a child singer of Gospel songs in the Pentecostal Assembly of God. To overcome these and other distances she revisited the scenes of her childhood, aided by her father's maps and notes on the itineraries of Evangelist Bill Skondeen and family. She conversed with her sister Althea. And she had that most priceless resource for quickening the memory, her father Bill's sermon notes. Audrey will tell her stories by heart, but she will tell the truth.

But even without these clarifying and verifying resources, Audrey's stories told by heart could make a claim to authenticity. How so? An extraordinary memory? No. I refer to the vivid, striking, moving, impressing, indelible nature of her childhood experiences. Audrey was not another child attending church with her family; she was *in church* 24/7, in revival services, in the family's travel trailer, parked or on the road. Audrey not only attended her father's revivals, she participated in them, her father's helper, singing, playing an instrument, testifying. Educators remind us that participants in an event remember far more than those who only observe. And keep in mind that the church of her childhood was the Pentecostal Assembly of God, a church whose services are vivid in sight and sound and movement. Members laugh, cry, moan, shout, dance, kneel, fall down, pass out. Undomesticated Pentecostalism is a total engagement with the Holy Spirit. Zeal for God, for Jesus, for the Holy Spirit, is all consuming. The experience of God is not mediated; it is direct and immediate. Add to this the fact that the leader is her father, a strong, mesmerizing preacher, and you will not ask if Audrey could remember after fifty years. How could she forget?

And let us remember the music, the Pentecostal house is filled with music. Old Gospel songs, familiar to the worshipers, start the motion and stir emotions. They release the wind and fire of God. Tired spirits stir, tired hands clap, tired feet dance, tears laugh and laughter weeps. Who knows the power of music? A tune will come when words cannot. A song can break through the dark silence of dementia. Music transports the soul to places where the worshipers remember tomorrow and hope for yesterday. All this and more is going on and Audrey is in the midst of it. As you hear her stories, notice how often she breaks into song. She cannot help it; after all these years these songs are on her soundtrack. Grace covers sins and joy chases sorrow away, at least for the night and hopefully until revival time next year.

A few years ago I was host to a filming crew in our area to make a documentary on Appalachian religion. They were a team of five, all young, all from New York, and all first-time visitors to Southern Appalachia. Their early questions made it clear that they expected to encounter only one kind of religion, white, Protestant Pentecostalism. By the end of day one, their expectations were modified, but they continued to ask about snake handling, speaking in tongues, and being killed in the Spirit. On the third day, I introduced them to a Pentecostal Holiness Church of God pastor who welcomed them, addressed their questions, and invited them to their worship service that evening. They accepted the invitation, and it was evident they were not disappointed. Curiosity melted into respect, with a touch of awe. At one point, we had to take a break from filming because one of the crew became quite emotional and shaken. The crew chief asked me to speak with her, which I did. She regained her composure and apologized. I assured her there was no need. Can you continue?

Yes.

What happened?

I don't know. I was baptized Roman Catholic but I haven't attended for years. In fact, since college days I have been rather cynical about all churches. I guess I was not prepared for this.

Prepared for what?

I never realized anyone could believe as deeply, as strongly as these people.

When Audrey says these stories are "told by heart," she has my full attention.

Fred B. Craddock

Cherry Log, GA

Acknowledgments

THIS BOOK WOULD NOT have happened without Dr. Fred Craddock's saying, "When are you going to write about your family, Audrey?" The chairs had been pushed back from the lunch table during a Cherry Log, Georgia, preaching seminar. I rationalized and stuttered about already doing three thousand miles of research, *um . . . well, you know.* But Craddock fervently wanted the record of a country preacher and the people who heard him so he didn't let me slide away from the idea quite that easily: *Hidden Biscuits: Tales of Deep South Revivals Told by Heart* is the result.

Fred Craddock read every word. I can never express my gratitude and awe at his unwavering resolve in seeing the project through. Appreciation, too, for Julie Jabaly who keeps things in place at the Craddock Center.

Deborah and Jerry Ulrich are always shelter in my world and during this time they've provided their home, transportation, encouragement, solace and sheer delight every time I landed at ATL on my way to and from Cherry Log. Also, Trisha and Jack Senterfitt, incomparable hosts in Cherry Log; Granny Annie—Annie Lee Hardee Tate—gives of whatever she has whenever she's on the Mountain in Morganton. Y'all are the greatest!

Bob Bearden, Mary Kay Simmons, Linc King, and all of my interfaith prayer group in San Francisco have been ever present whether near or far away. The Wednesday Writers in Berkeley, with Elizabeth Fishel, prodded, pushed and encouraged the first chapter into life during that initial, daunting year and I appreciate every one of you.

Thanks to Kaian for a place to write and a fine job of editing before I sent each chapter off to Cherry Log for Fred's approval. Joan Eddy gave me guidelines, and readers Anne Anderson, Judith Stone, Wendy Weller, and Patti Brown provided questions and tips.

Beth Leeds, Illustrator; Jennifer Garden, Bluestocking Press; Sharon Dawson and Sean Deffenbauch, photographers; Faith Whitmore for interviews and David Moon-Wainwright with video and tech help: thank you, every one.

Plus all of the above, the congregation of the United Methodist Church in St. Helena has been more than generous with my time and energy for trips to Georgia and for the writing, itself. These beautiful people enhance my everyday life by their quiet patience and always, enthusiastic support. In short, they're full of grace like Christians are meant to be.

Editors at Resource Publishing have proved to be ever present in resolving my queries. I take to heart *blessings* in the way Matthew Wimer signs off. Shannon Carter's aid and empathy came at a most critical time; she's quick to respond and goes far beyond accomplishing professional details.

To Althea, my sister, and her husband, Al, I owe a large debt in this writing. Our long discussions as well as her astonishing memory and attention to detail have been sustaining.

And to Tamara, Julie and Sam, you are my favorite cheerleaders: I love you. These are tales for you and your children's lives, too.

Audrey Ward

November 2014

Saint Helena, CA

Fred Brenning Craddock

30 April 1928—6 March 2015

He saw through our pretensions, compelled us to go deeper, and used small words and stories to deliver stunning revelations.

Dr. Fred Craddock, born on a farm in East Tennessee, came to inhabit the world of higher education with astonishing grace and brilliance, yet his heart never left the people of Appalachia: in his retirement, he established the Craddock Center in Cherry Log, Georgia, for children who have few opportunities.

Fred traveled red dirt roads with Jesus.

What a man.

Audrey Ward

12 March 2015

St. Helena, California

Introduction

Arrivals

> *. . . in the highways,*
> *in the hedges,*
> *I'll be somewhere*
> *workin' for my lord . . .*

TRAIN DOORS SLID OPEN, echoing voices announcing the Florida Zephyr's being received into that giant clam shell Grand Central Station, and a barely seventeen-year-old girl feeling no bigger than a grain of sand was swept onto the platform into the rush, heat, and noise of arrival. Something happened to me in that lurch forward: ecstasy. Without words, a sudden clarity that New York, where so many broadcasts originate, was where I belonged even though at the time I was only headed up the Hudson River to Nyack Missionary College.

There were years I forgot about that voracious young girl. The event that awakened me was seeing the Pearsall Sisters sing "In the Highways" at a Southern street meeting in the film *Oh Brother, Where Art Thou?* I came of age in the Deep South and "Highways" was a song I sang with all my heart though my mother would have been accompanying me with an accordion rather than a guitar. Most of the time we performed in simple, scruffy churches that had no glass "winder" panes, but only boards fit into openings that were pushed out during warm weather.

Ten months after I saw the film, I traveled to those red dirt roads, gripping the map my father provided for me when I asked for the history of our travels. Just like his sermon notes, he wrote the list of towns in a 5x7 spiral notebook and sent it along with a letter and a United States map that did not yet include Hawaii or Alaska. The orange highlighting pen he motioned over the routes directed me to spots on and off the highway, but what I was looking for was that spirited young girl and her true religion I remembered that surpasses anything I have found in church since then. OK, maybe not religion, but a well-founded yet curious faith that's unrestrained by creeds. The kind of faith you feel around for in the dark.

An older sister and I, along with our Pentecostal Assemblies of God preacher daddy and musical mother—all living in an 18' trailer, our only home—worked for the Lord by day and were lulled to sleep by crickets at night. We loved the mostly Appalachian people of those revivals.

Hard as they labored with little reward, they found their solace in the backwoods Pentecostal churches where we ministered, calling each other *sister* and *brother* for the warmth and connection of family. Revival lifted them into the gifts of the early church, the book of Acts, when the Spirit filled praying people with *fire from on high* and they spoke in the language of their heaven.

Bill Skondeen was driven by news of the Azusa Street Revival in Los Angeles back in the early 1900s when the Holy Spirit fell and people began speaking in tongues. Participants in the Azusa Street Revival were immigrants, laborers with whom my father identified, living on the wrong side of town. By those facts they were also free of the restraints of upscale society's inhibitions. The Azusa Street Revival cracked open religion's window and beamed in belonging for people who were often shunned and too often shamed. Pentecostal churches popped up all over the map, extending the Azusa Street message everywhere in the United States. But the Jesus-enriched soil of the South may have proven the most fertile for growth.

My one year of public high school after our family settled in Orlando and an additional two semesters of junior college—I was too young at fifteen to be admitted to the dorms in New York—served me well in gearing up my inquisitive nature. And I've used it, living in France, studying abroad, and as an ordained pastor of United Methodist Churches in Northern California. But *audacious* was born as the *Spark Plug*—my father's name for me—singing revival nights.

Those sweet gatherings we experienced from 1945 to 1956 no longer exist, now sifted through leaves of a backwoods reality that incorporates television and the internet, homogenizing speech and making instant all messages. That's why I'm telling you this.

Hidden Biscuits: Tales of Deep South Revivals Told by Heart is about meaning among members of devoted communities hidden from society and reaching beyond lives that could only be endured. Although the years described here define our context in the outer world, our family wasn't out there. We were sequestered in pine-fringed woods hung with kudzu vines, hearing about that larger civilization by way of brief clips from a shortwave radio's news.

Welcome to these pages and into the lives of good country people you've never met but will always remember. Welcome to their undaunted hope and spiritual practice; the comfort of their imagination and their kinships of faith, gathering to bless and to heal each other as they listen for the Word. For me the word was, indeed, made flesh.

I came of age on these highways, confusing my daddy the Preacher with God the Father, and experiencing what matters in the midst of it all. So I ask you to listen to the child. This is her story.

Grove Hill, Alabama 1947
Way Out

- *A Baby Boom year.*
- *Life magazine declares in an April 7 editorial, "Materialism and science worship are in full retreat . . ." and the "trend is toward God, all right."*
- *President Harry Truman warns against inflating fears of Communist Russia, but still, the Cold War between the USSR and the US heats up. The CIA is formed.*
- *The US Congress investigates communism in the film industry. Joe McCarthy's House Un-American Activities Committee interrogates movie insiders; ten Hollywood executives are blacklisted this year alone.*
- *Billy Graham, aged 29, escalates from being the featured preacher for Youth for Christ rallies to organizing a citywide evangelistic campaign in his hometown of Charlotte, North Carolina.*
- *Again on the move are the rugged Irish, Scotch, Polish, plus a few French immigrants who moved into remote areas of Appalachia during the eighteenth and nineteenth centuries. An unruly lot, they managed to be just out of reach of British law and negotiated life with the Cherokee Nation, but they could not negotiate with the crushing poverty of the Great Depression in 1929; they migrate to the industrialized north in search of factory jobs.[1]*
- *The less adventurous filter into the familiar comfort of the backwoods in Georgia, Alabama, and Mississippi as sharecroppers or workers in cotton*

---

1. Jeff Biggers, *United States of Appalachia* (Emeryville, CA: Shoemaker & Hoard, 2006), see esp. chs. 2 and 6.

gins, paper mills, and, after WWII, clothing factories. Reading and writing are luxuries. Few have cars or trucks.

- *These Appalachian folk are especially drawn to the Pentecostal variety of Holiness churches. These are humble churches of less than sixty congregants, though a tent or brush arbor can attract double that number.*

- *Audrey Skondeen is five years old.*

MAPS ARE THE FIRST things I learned to read, but no map has the road to Sister Irene's house on it. Her front yard tells a difference easy to recognize. Daddy says you have to be alert to see what's being said—the real story's staring right at you without words—and this house says *somebody's quit.*

No porch or walkway and no shade trees or grass. Just beat down stray weeds and hard red dirt right up to the torn screen door. Weathered boards are slightly off kilter and some window panes replaced by cardboard. Pitiful place seems tired of standing in the South Alabama heat. Makes our little trailer parked in the pine grove next to the church house look real good.

Daddy worries the car over the last rut and lurches to a dusty, unsettled stop. Mama, our manners guide, dips her head toward the back seat, "Now girls, we're guests in this home. It's a privilege to be here with these good folks."

Usually she adds *Lord bless their hearts*, but the car's rushed by children with Sister Irene in tow, wiping her hands against a skirt that's lost most of its flower print to the scrub board and wash tub. Her two eldest hang back, leaning against each side of the doorway, watching. The girl's lanky body, head tipped, forming her own question mark. The boy's arms crossed over his chest, shoulders square, reporting for duty.

We're here to have dinner on the last Saturday of the Grove Hill Revival Meeting. When people bother themselves to put dinner on for the Preacher, it's a reckoning day. Daddy never lets us forget that in general folks don't kill a chicken for their own meal and that's why we have to respect their cooking by eating every bit we take on our plates.

Summer in the South means *revivals*. That's how we landed in Sister Irene's front yard. Revival stirs new excitement into old time religion. Local pastors hope to convert sinners into church members, besides save them from hell and eternal damnation.

After crops are planted and fireflies light up the night, people start looking for a traveling evangelist. Heat beats down all day on hard working folk and revival nights spell r-e-l-i-e-f.

Together, our family is called an *Evangelistic Team*. A preacher Daddy who plays fiddle in the country and violin in town, an all-purpose musical Mama who reads the notes for our singing as well as follows along with us on accordion or piano, and two girls. One girl named Althea who's almost eleven and plays the vibra harp. And Audrey, that's me, I'm almost six, old enough to sing and lead the kids in choruses. We've been on the road for Jesus since I was three.

What Billy Graham does in the city in stadiums, we're doing in the country in cement block churches like the one here in Grove Hill. Other towns use brush arbors—standing frames made of rough pine with cut limbs and bushes over them—some folks call them "bush arbors." Or maybe a tent is raised up for a church house, and that's fine, too.

A preacher has to get people's attention for a revival meeting to happen 'cause nobody'll show up the second night if he doesn't. Music puts them in the mood to *listen* to a preacher, both music by the team the evangelist brings and songs the congregation sings. Sometimes when a particular tune strikes just right, we sing it every night.

With our Team, you can count on heart stirring music—led by the *Spark Plug*, that's how Daddy introduces me—and soul tested preaching. And on the last Sunday, guaranteed! An all day Sing with dinner on the ground.

My aunt and uncle live in San Francisco and we'd call dinner on the ground a picnic there. It's simple fare. But here all the cooks show off just short of the sin of pride.

Food stays out of the way of ants on long, warped gray boards stretching between two pine trees at the side of the church. Those boards tell tales of homemade bread and butter pickles, scalloped corn or potatoes, macaroni and cheese, chopped greens with ham hocks, black eye peas, snap beans, succotash, ambrosia, ham, and fried chicken. Plus coconut layer cake, pecan pie and peach cobbler. Banana pudding's my favorite. Vanilla wafers and ripe bananas bathed in smooth, creamy custard, touched just enough with toasty marshmallow meringue. Anybody can see why folks get happy when revival comes to town.

Sister Irene's mill bus leaves her at the church house early for service every night so we have time to talk. Right off, she wants to know about traveling: How'd we get to this here church house? Don't being on the road wear you plumb to death?

Revival meetings begin on Wednesday when churches have midweek prayer meeting and they end on the second Sunday unless the Holy Ghost takes hold. Then we might stay longer if there's time to tarry before we have to be at the next stop.

From our last revival in Bessemer, Alabama, Daddy's map directed us back toward Mississippi, but we delayed traveling a day: tornado warnings were blasting out of our radio. No fooling around with tornadoes. Irene just nods and says, "Have mercy," only it sounds more like, *Ha' mussy*.

Sure enough, even after the delay, we follow a tornado right down Highway 43 from Tuscaloosa. Looked as if an angry Goliath was stomping along just ahead, pulling trees up by their roots and tossing them aside, leaving pieces of pine trees twisted like corkscrews. The sky was hanging close, dark and damp. The air smothering and still. Waiting. Scared of the giant's return.

Right after that we ran into Halloween even though it's June, driving through mossy swamps on Lake Demopolis. Rickety little houses and trailers perched way up on stilts look as if they're trying to get away.

My companion on the church house steps listens like I'm telling a mystery. Says she ain't never been to nary a one a these here places.

Finally, a tall cool pecan grove gave us relief and fields of cotton raised their tight-fisted tufts in salute to our car pulling our trailer along the road. We were glad to be near Grove Hill.

The town's name points to a grove of oak trees. Lumber and cotton tell the story here—saw mill, lumber yard, grist mill, cotton gin, cotton seed oil mill, cotton warehouse—plus the paper mill where Sister Irene works. Before we see a paper mill, we can smell it, like that abandoned nest full of eggs rotting in Miller's hay barn. You can never mistake such a stink.

This is the county seat, too. Proof is a one room courthouse on Court Street. A bee hive busy-ness marks the one room post office next to the general store. The filling station serves transportation *with* tires and a blacksmith serves transportation *without* tires.

Grove Hill provides local folks with necessities and help on Highway 84, right between two rivers, the Tombigbee before the Mississippi state line and to the east, the Alabama. Sister Irene's paper mill with its smoking stacks and confusion of tin roofs appears just across the Alabama River. On a sorry day, breezes float in from that direction with smells that make you want to lose your dinner.

And Sister Irene's bus? That thing looks like it rolled over and over in the dark yellow gray smoke expelled from those smoking stacks. The mill bus hauls workers up and down these back roads. As ugly acting as it is ugly looking, too. Just dumps Irene off and keeps going. Leaves her there in a cloud of dust. Slumped, she resembles one of those army surplus duffle bags not quite full. But I can tell she's used to it. *Don't make no difference.* That's what her body says.

She carries a small burlap sack that holds her bit to eat and a tin cup. That first night, I saw her from the trailer window while I was eating my supper and watching as she drew cool water from the well to fill her cup. Irene ate alone on the front stoop of the church house.

The next evening I go out to draw some water, letting down the little tin bucket on the rope. She smiles her sweet straight-lipped smile, like the corners of her mouth lost their lift.

Her warm dark eyes talk to me along with her words, "Honeygirl I heared ya las night! Shor can sang!" Nobody's here yet. It'll be a while before the Spark Plug has to start the crowd singing.

"I love to sing!" I answer, taking her words as an invitation to sit down beside her, hugging my knees, looking up into her narrow H of a face, mouth straight across. When she says the word "honey" the gold in those brown eyes finds me. I add, "And you know what?"

Seems like this might be best to whisper, "I love school best of all." I'm not sure if loving kindergarten *maybe* more than Jesus is a sin. Probably.

The furrows in her brow deepen and she straightens her back, hunched as she is over her supper sack in her lap, tips her head to one side, "How you goin a school, chile?"

"*Calvert*. Comes in a box at the General Delivery window, Post Office? Mama says first grade will be here in a month. That's thirty-one days, but it might be a little longer." A silence that feels crowded takes over and I wonder if I said something wrong. *School*. Mama says I have to be careful not to brag about school. Then the people huddled in Irene's silence begin to show up.

"Jolene's m'bigirl. Tha chile can do bout ever thang a reckin. They's some at's quicker. Made iss here lil sack, ain a cute?" grinning a wider straight line and lifting the little burlap supper sack for my inspection. "Wesley's a oldess boy." She pauses, gazing back out at the road as if the bus is still there. That bus carries a lot more worries than it does workers.

Folks say true things to me. When I hear them talk to other people, they chatter on and on about weather, who's here and who isn't. But when we talk, I can hear their hearts in between the words.

A strand of Irene's hair escaping the tie back hints of the gold I see flash in her eyes, "Jolene, she can read, mmmhmm. She reads me some." Nodding, Irene sits straighter when she mentions Jolene. "They's a lil ole li berry close by a generl store? She gots a memmership. Card with'r name on it."

I saw that library—looks like a tiny brick house—in Grove Hill. Has a sprawling oak tree out back like a tree angel spreading her wings for protection.

"But them two bigguns, they ain gotime fer no schoolin. Not no more."

What matters more than school. I'm trying to imagine, when she explains about their children having to farm, "Auvr chirrun haf a take up a work. Ellis, m'maan? Jus cain do no more." There's quiet again except for the low stuttering hum of the crickets, their sad song. Shadows are coming in and they miss the sun. "Plantin feed corn, plowin. Feller in Mobile . . . thass a thang."

"He owns your place?" I ask about the man in Mobile. Mama and Daddy talk about sharecroppers. *No way to get ahead*, that's what Daddy says.

Irene nods and takes a sip of water from her tin cup. "Specially now. Afore Ellis . . . afore his legs's gone iss better. Course."

"His legs . . ." I begin.

"At shuga thang . . . been had it fer no tellin how long, but neva knowd nothin til . . . whussat word . . ." She shakes her head. Her voice shifts into a sigh. Stalled.

"Diabetes?" I've heard that sugar word when Mama and Daddy talk about how people eat. All wrong, according to them. Too much fat back. Too much sugar. *Diabetes* always means big trouble. She nods and shrugs, helpless.

Irene tells me about the paper mill. A place that nibbles on the workers and drains their color, too. Just a little so nobody notices. I said the mill stinks, didn't I? *Bad breath.* But I try not to act ugly about it. After all, she has to go there again in the morning. Anyhow, Sister Irene says she talks to Jesus while she works.

"When do you have time for that?"

"Honeygirl, talkin a Jayzus don take no time! Iss here machine . . ."

"You work a *machine*?"

She shakes her head, agreeing in a negative way, and says, "At thang wuks me—keepn wood mov-in thruit." I offer to get her some more water—I love rolling the bucket down to the water—and she thanks me. When I return, she finishes, "Could take m'han, m'arm. Seen a happ'n afore. Pays a mine at thang." Silence sits with us a few minutes while the summer evening breathes through the pine trees.

Irene adds, "Jayzus heps me. By m'side ala time." She turns her head away, and up, as if something really interesting nests in the treetops. But the sound of her voice, crackly and soft like tissue paper being crushed, makes my eyes smart. She turns back to me and smiles, this time a little moist at the edges, "Jayzus. He keeps me sangin."

Sister Irene—other people call her Sister Pridemore, actually they say it more like *Pridemer* but she says I can call her Irene—wants her family to meet us. This means a whole lot. She raised up her nerve enough to invite us to dinner on the last Saturday night we're here.

When folks invite us to dinner I know it's not about food or eating. It's about putting our feet under their table, seeing what they see and hearing what they hear everyday. Some cooks want to show off, naturally. But everybody does their best when the Evangelist comes to their house. Mama and Daddy take every chance to remind Althea and me what a privilege it is to be a guest.

That title for Daddy, *Evangelist*, means somebody who brings good news. Most everybody says it's about the men who traveled with Jesus and wrote the Gospels, Mark, Luke, Matthew and John, but I can see it's a lot bigger than that. Daddy likes being called *Evangelist* better than *Preacher* or even his own name.

Truth is, his name's kind of a problem. Skondeen. People are curious. "Eyetalian?" Daddy laughs and says, "Oh sure, *Skondini!*" The spelling is not the same as in the "Motherland" as he calls it, but the origin is Ukrainian. And that means *Russian* and that means *never tell anyone*.

"We seen yer pichers afore y'all come, down to a store at a cross road? At fiddle an wheeze box, an whass at thang, big bells-rangin thang?" Irene says. "Vibra harp?"
"Thassit!"

Sister Irene's talking about the hazy photograph on the 8x10-inch flier at the General Store in Grove Hill. When we drove into town asking directions to the Holiness church, the owner of the store recognized Daddy from that poster.

Brother Mobley, the pastor here, posted it weeks before we arrived. Daddy said to Mama after he was back in the car, "Lord have mercy. Right up there next to the carnival poster, Doris, comin in July to the fair grounds. Brother Mobley sure put this revival at the right time."

"Bless his heart!" Evangelists book revivals a year in advance, maybe when Daddy meets a pastor at camp meeting. Or, he arranges a time in the future with a local preacher who visits our revival when we're near his town.

This week, a pastor and his wife from Mobile came to see us. If he liked what he heard, he'll invite us to his church a month or two from now or next summer. Mama keeps track of every pastor in the address book and marks the dates in pencil on the calendar inside the closet door.

There's not much else happening in these parts besides that carnival and the county fair in August. Television's just a rumor. Even radios aren't guaranteed.

There's no electricity out here in the backwoods. Just along the main roads. Good thing the Grove Hill church is on one of those roads or the vibra harp couldn't run the rotators under its flat metal keys. That's what makes the wavy chiming sound when Althea strikes them with her mallets, the sounds Sister Irene loves so much.

Night after night Irene comes, the lines on her face crimped with too many cares. Her shoulders, strained, even though the fabric of her web like dress seems weightless as the soft night air settling around us.

People gather, catching up with each other's news, fanning with cardboard ovals advertising the funeral home in Thomasville fixed on flat wooden sticks for handles. The other side of the fan has the Good Shepherd leading his sheep beside still waters. My favorite one, though, shows Jesus with children all around him. Children of every color in the world.

Folks watch for our family to step out of the trailer, parked close to the rough cement block church house in the grove of pine trees. By a quarter of seven, it's time to tune up the instruments, daddy's violin with mama's accordion. Mama reckons the old upright piano here hasn't been tuned since the turn of the century.

Althea's just tall enough to reach across her vibra harp but she makes it sound real sweet. That "bells rangin thang" as Irene calls it plays as a perfect toy for a musical girl like my big sister. She hears music "by ear" without notes to follow.

Mama and Althea resemble each other, quiet, musical. Kind, too, except when my sister gives me a dirty look for something I probably didn't even do. And if I should try out a bad word—saying *gosh* or *shut-up*—Mama doesn't hesitate. She sticks a whole bar of Ivory in my mouth and washes it out as if it was full of mud.

Their fine, light brown hair—Mama's and Althea's—matches each other's, too, with a slight wave. Not a problem like my dark unruly curls. Mama tries hard to control my hair. It's a job. I try hard not to give her any reason to have to control me, too. Being Good, which means never acting peevish or sassing *even* to my sister isn't just for company, it's all the time. That includes fidgeting or not paying attention in church. The code is when Daddy says, "Help us Lord," I better snap out of whatever I'm doing because if he has to say it a third time, there'll be a whipping later on. With his belt. Believe you me, Behaving's a job that wears a body out.

My hair's dark like my Daddy's, but his has more waves than curls. When I was little, only three years old, I used to sit on his shoulders while he studied, combing his hair down instead of back and telling him I was going to make him into a woman. I'm too old for that now. He smoothes it out with Hess's Hair Milk so it's easier to comb. We all have blue eyes, only Daddy's are the color you see in a blue jay's wing.

One night, just before church started I was reaching for a fan I saw down under a bench and I heard two women talking about Daddy behind their hands.

"Lawdy mercy, at air vangliss shor is hansome! Em blue eyes!"

"Em sholers, enough fer *two* vilins!"

"Mmmmmm, hmmmm. Praeze Jayzus he's preachin a gospel! Coulda bin in *pitchers*."

Now how would Holiness women know about moving pictures and their idols? They probably have some old *Silver Screen* magazines hidden in a pie cupboard. We don't go to worldly places like picture shows.

I didn't tell Mama and Daddy. They'd be disgusted.

When everybody's finally gathered, it gets close in the church house. We're glad for the fans with fifty people or more packed into what feels like one big cement block. A wooden platform at the front has a railing hung in faded blue velvet. Looks like somebody cut up some drapes they found at Salvation Army in Mobile. The pulpit and the altar down in front of the railing are hacked out of the same pine forest as the straight-back hard benches. "Winders" are long planks that fit an open space, no glass to them. Unhooked, they're pushed out on poles into the open air.

Daddy fires up the evening's singtime, saying, "We stole this vibra harp," motioning with the violin in his hand toward Althea, quickly adding, "Praise the Lord!" so they'll know it's not for real, "'Stead of being a tool of the devil, played in bars for drinkin and carousin our girl's playin for the Lord." Shouts break out all over the place.

"Thankya Jayzus!"

"Prayziz Naame!"

Lord one, Devil nothing. Revival's off and running.

Sister Irene calls out "Numba eight." The number pronounced *southern* in two or three parts. Words themselves become music in these parts. It beats all. "Numba eight, *He Keeps Me a Sangin*." We only use the hymnal *Victory Songs 4* to identify the song by the page numbers, then we sing by heart. Or by shape, Mama says the shape of the notes tell what the sound is and everybody knows them all.

I stand on a chair near the pulpit to cue up the singing. Wearing the sky blue dress Mama just made me with a wide ruffle at the hem feels special, as if I'm standing in the window of the General Store advertising yard goods and patterns. I almost giggle, but instead I smile real big and raise my hands then give the downbeat.

Mama's fast with a chord from the accordion. Daddy takes his violin from under his arm and fiddles to the tune. Althea runs the mallets from one end of the vibra harp to the other.

Standing, clapping her hands, the music revs Irene all through. As the words, *Jesus, Jesus, Jesus, sweetest name I know, Fills my every longing; keeps me sing-ing as I go,* flood her body, she sways like a willow branch in a breeze and her face begins to unfold. With the verse, the frown that tugs at her mouth fades away:

> *There's within my heart a melody*
> *Jesus whispers sweet and loow*
> *Fear not I am with thee*
> *Peace be still*
> *In all of life's ebb and flow.*

Singing always stirs people to say a few words, that's testimony time.

Tonight, Mary Watford visits us from Franklin, a few miles over the Alabama River. She pastors Faith Chapel, the only woman I know who's licensed to preach by the Assemlies of God like Daddy. "Praise auvr Savior! Folks, He sa faithful. I come to hear 'Vangeliss *Skon*dee cause my soul's hungry for the *Word*. This here Preacher, he digs on down an finds a truth. Feeds m' soul ever time. Hal u u! Y'alls sangin? Cain't be no better sangin up in Glory!" They're prompted to take time out for shouting when anybody mentions *Glory* which is another name for *Heaven*.

When Sister Irene testifies, she always stands up and says the same thing: "Don't know what ahdo thout a Lawd. Keeps me a sangin. Puts at meldy in m' heart! Jayzus? He's m'life! Yass He's m'life." She sits down, head bobbing.

Mama and Daddy sing a duet that I only know by the name Castles. Everybody asks for it over and over:

> *Some build their castles in Ireland*
> *Some build their castles in Spain*
> *But I'll build my castle in heaven,*
> *Where there's sunshine and no rain . . .*

I see rapture on faces when Castles is being sung. Enchantment. Not a person here's been to Ireland or Spain, but they figure on making it to heaven. Jesus said, "A sower went out to sow. And as he sowed, some seed fell along the footpath; and the birds came and ate it up . . ." I recognize this parable from the thirteenth chapter of Matthew. First, the Preacher, white shirt sleeves rolled up, blue and red striped tie pulled loose, slips in some bad news:

> Jesus isn't talkin' about how *many* seeds, now, is he.
> We're worryin about the numbers when
> we should be *prayin.*"
> Tell me, have you had any answer to your *worries*?
> Moses didn't pray for Success:
> "God forgive their Sin; if not, *blot my name out.*"

Preachers can always count on Moses to bring up shouting. Whenever his name's mentioned people get on up as if they're headed out for the Promised Land.

> We got too many numbers up on the tote board . . .
> Statistics are idols!

"Idols" is a troubling word in a Holiness church. They're forbidden under all circumstances.

> How many in Sunday School?
> How many saved?
> has turned many a preacher,
> a faithful sower,
> into a *premature reaper.*

The Preacher raises the tempo,

> It's not no *number* of seeds,
> it's the *wonder* of a *single seed*!
> *Here's* your evidence for that fool that says there's no God!

Now he's down off the platform, preaching on the move, up the aisle and back to the front again.

> But I don't have to *defend* God.
> Somebody asked that great preacher Spurgeon,
> "Why don't you write a book in defense of the Bible?"
> and Spurgeon answered,
> "The Bible is like a lion in a cage.
> You just let him out and he'll take care of himself."
> *Amen?*
> And when these professors try to cram their doctrines of evolution
> saying we come from monkeys, say to them

"Don't say *we* say *I*!"

"Yasssss Lorrd!"

Flares of laughter go up. Shouts of approval shoot sparks out into the night past the light bulbs dangling from the ceiling. One man lifts up off his bench with both hands raised, his full face blushing cheer, then motions one hand toward the preacher and shouts, "Go ownow—preachit!" Sits down.

Tell me please—where did the little watermelon seed get its wisdom?
Put him in the ground—after a few days
he takes off his black coat and goes to work.
Knows how to get red color, sugar, all the ingredients.
To me a seed of whatever it may be is a greatest miracle.

The Preacher's rolling up a sleeve that's fallen, acting the part of that busy seed as he paces the platform. Smiling, even laughing, Sister Irene takes in every word. Then the preacher comes closer, bending over the railing. A husky loud whisper, like a mystery unfolding.

Why won't some of those seeds grow?
Our hearts need attention.
Need to be plowed up, that's
why revivals often come after
great *calamity or sorrow*.
God has to plow our fields up before they are open
to receive seed.
What's *your* sorrow? What's in your
heart that *needs attention* . . .

First, a nod, then slender fingers rise to shield Irene's face. Words used on sharecroppers are worse than on Negroes, seems like. Never been so bad, no help for it. Called shiftless and no good all his life and now Ellis with no legs. Pitiful shame, that's what.

Daddy says I'm his eyes. I stand next to him before or while I'm singing and pay attention 'cause he depends on me to notice what's going on with folks. Sometimes what I see makes my throat hurt. Irene there, her face crumpled as a used up Kleenex.

She's smarter than she thinks she is; I ask Jesus to help her see that. And maybe even give her a chance to learn reading. Daddy glances my way and I go up to sing *Softly and Tenderly*, for the altar call.

Come home, come home,
You who are weary come home . . .

Earnestly, tenderly Jesus is pleading . . .

People head toward the altar all kinds of ways. Some, purposeful, marching toward a confrontation. Others drift forward more slowly, looking for a place to land. Late comers, then, timid, unsure if they really have to be there but worried that maybe they do.

Their prayers match them. Shouting demands to an old deaf God. Tearful pleadings to a Good Shepherd. Whimpering needs meant for sweet baby Jesus and maybe for his Mama, too, though we never mention her. Most of them out loud. Except, of course, prayers of the ones who are 'slain in the spirit' lying straight out on the floor, silent in a reverent kind of nap. It's no wonder folks think of prayers as going *up*. So many voices, words, pleas and tears crowd this small space, there's nowhere else to go.

Sister Irene sinks to her knees at the bench where she's sitting. Elbows on the seat, her head sheltered by her arms, hands clasped above. Shoulders sagging at first. Tears flowing, she lets everything loose.

I don't know how or when, but something starts to shift for Sister Irene. The heaviness she carries slides out of sight. I can tell by the lift of her shoulders, the relief in her face as she stands to sing the closing song. Irene tunes up that little song in her heart. And for tonight, that's enough.

We go out singing:

Love lifted me! When nothing else could help, Love lifted me!

No time to linger. Out in the country, roosters keep the clock. Now it's 8:30 and a rooster's call at four or five AM comes mighty early. The last sight I have of Sister Irene stays with me. She's waving, "See yall tamorry," braced with her back against the cab of the flatbed hauling truck of Brother and Sister Patterson. They take Irene as far as her mailbox. She walks the rest of the way.

On Saturday there isn't an evening service. Everybody's preparing for Sunday, at least that's what they say. Nobody mentions the Grand Ole Opry on the radio. I overheard Billy Dees down at the store say with a little nod, "M'Pa, he got a radio, mail order? Folks come on ova t'auvr yard Satiddy night. Yeah, comes on foot, by mule. It's a sight! Listens ona radio t'a Gran Ole Opry. Pa, he has a bat-ries all heat up inna oven? Makin shor they charged. Ready a go!" He nods again, pride beaming in a good way all over his freckled face.

Even the store closes at noon. And today the promised dinner at Irene's house is finally here. I'm surprised she put up enough nerve to ask Mama if we can come out to her place. When strangers visit, like the pastor and his wife from Mobile, Irene keeps her eyes on the ground. Never says "Howdy, how y'all doin!" or anything. The visitors got out of their car looking important, his polished brown hair slicked back like a healing preacher, and her all powdery and pink. Irene put her head down and moved out of their way fast as she could.

"But Mama, how can she feed us dinner when she hardly has enough herself? Scrawny sausage and old cornbread she eats for supper every night." *Dinner* refers to a main meal at midday.

"Don't you worry, Lord makes a way where there is no way." Mama's answer as always. But by the shadow that flits across her pale blue eyes, I'd say she worries, too. She adds, "Besides, dinner isn't about food. It's about fellowship."

The way to Irene's house is through the woods up more than one path ruined by rains. No fixing year after year. A hodgepodge stand of battered mail boxes mark the way for the last turn. Some are tin loaf-shaped boxes, others, rectangular wood. One painted red, the rest plain, weatherbeaten, the posts they rely on repaired with odd chunks. All, anchored to a sweet gum tree trunk.

Sister Irene says she talks to Jesus all the way home, walking this road in the dark after the ride from Pattersons. So does Daddy and it's not even dark.

"Help us, Jesus, help us. This road'll bring a car to rack and ruin." Daddy bears down on the steering wheel to iron out the ruts.

The price of our '41 DeSoto—has to be heavy enough to pull a trailer—is earned slow and hard. The cheapest DeSoto is $895 new, now that they've started making them again. No cars were made during the war. Ours is second hand, anyhow. Daddy made a deal with a man in Miami last January.

We're out of the woods and in sight of Irene's house soon enough. Old hound dog lounging at the step near the big kids in the doorway hardly raises his head. "Woof." That's it. Back to his nap.

Sister Irene's oldest girl is thirteen, Jolene, maybe three inches taller than Irene. Tawny skin stretched over high cheek bones and her hair a long dark swirl. Even the army drab sack she's wearing looks good hung over her long arms and legs.

Wesley's nearly twelve. Stocky and proud, his skin browned and freckled, his hair blond from life in the fields. He handles his pa's wheelchair in and out the back door over a makeshift build-up of what appears to be broken cinder blocks. Sister Irene gives his arm a little pat and says, "Look at em muscles!"

Fried chicken piled in three battered pie tins anchor the table end to end, set on a green striped shower curtain—table cloth—over slightly uneven boards on two saw horses. The gravy's pan, big spoon hanging to one side, seems to be mid stir. Mustard chop greens with fat back, mound up in two big cereal bowls and I kinda wonder if the juice might leak from a crack in one of them. Black-eye peas fill a cook pan missing the handle, and cornbread and biscuits rest in scraps of faded feed sack cloth in lidless Christmas cookie tins.

I spy banana or sliced canned pineapple sandwiches piled high on a bent up baking pan, too. This layout spells feast for sure.

We arrange ourselves on benches around the table at each place where there's a fork and a plate, some look like Melmac, but dull colors and beat up pretty bad, others are tin. Ellis, the man of the house, wheels himself up to the head of the table with a "Hey ya'll it's timeta eat!" What a swagger, as if he never even thought of having legs, who needs'em? Man works a big show.

Shirlene, the middle child about my size, thin, wispy hair that seems to float around her head, mostly stares through eyes the color of weak tea, but I can't tell at what. "She don't talk much," her big sister offers, "but she picked em flow'rs." A canning jar jammed full of dandelions plus one big oak leaf hydrangea blossom that grows wild in the woods adorns the table right in front of Sister Irene.

Lulamae, "she us named Lurene, but it neva did took," looks like a tomboy twin to the youngest boy, Willis, about four, both little miniatures of the older boy, Wesley. We're an odd fit here, kind of like the mailboxes.

Ellis—I don't know if he's "brother" or not, that's for a man who's saved—says, "Preach, whynt chu do us ablessin."

"Lord, Lord, thank you, thank you, thank you. Jesus bless these good people, these children, and especially the hands that prepared this food. Help us Lord so we're ready, yes Lord! We wanta be ready to feast in heaven with You some day." I can tell Daddy put that word "ready" in there cause he's not sure about Ellis and the saved part either.

Daddy's blessing finishes with a strong *Amen*, when there's a chuckle from the host, "Preach," he says, crinkling the brown stain in the corner of his mouth, "Iss ere *womon*?" jerking his head, shaggy dark mane following like a used mop, in Sister Irene's direction, "She's akind a grabaholt a sumpn an she don neva letigo." He laughs, "liketa drive me plum crazy."

Jolene repeats his coloring, not his attitude.

Daddy looks at him, interested, and says, "Well. Lord knows our hearts."

Ellis isn't finished. "But she don't neva come home w'no frown fr'm yer preachin, no she don't," adding another laugh that doesn't sound the least bit happy.

Daddy follows that with a "Praise the Lord!" And turns to Jolene, "Please pass the biscuits," his eyes engaging, smiling big. He motions to the tin where they're folded into the scrap of feedsack cloth, I recognize the print from the Lee's hen house where I gathered eggs earlier in the week.

A worry look crosses Jolene's face as if she's not too sure she wants to hand them over even as she does. Maybe she's just shy. Anybody can see she keeps the family together when their mama's at the paper mill.

My biggest job is to be polite about dinner because what I really like most of all are the banana sandwiches made with white slice-bread and Miracle Whip. We never get to eat anything like that at home. But they've been working hard since early morning and I don't want to hurt their feelings by not eating their cooking. So I take a skinny chicken leg, some blackeye peas, and chop greens. A biscuit, too, but it tastes like sand from a riverbed so that turns into a quick nibble. I'm pretty good at making a mess of what I don't eat, spreading it around.

Two little piglets squeal beneath the table, competing for crumbs dropped for them by Lulamae and Willis, giggling like crazy all the while. Baby chicks join us, too, their new feathers tickling my ankles. Through cracks between the floorboards we can hear muttering sounds from old hens foraging under the house, our dinner music.

Jolene has Sister Irene's eyes. The honey color runs warm when she looks pleased, like Daddy asking for biscuits a third time.

Another pie tin heaped with Moon Pies appears after our meal, welcomed by yelps and squeals. It's a sight, those big round chocolate or vanilla covered cookies filled with marshmallow. Best thing they could think of, for sure. I choose a vanilla one, saying I'll eat it for my supper, knowing Mama and Daddy will only allow one bite before it's tossed out as trash.

After dinner, at my request Jolene shows me to the outhouse in the woods. Kudzu vines crochet dark green covers like tea cozies for the bushes and trees. She waits for me, talking so I won't be scared in there by myself I reckon. But the door doesn't really close, plus, I can see her through big cracks. Besides, I'm used to creaky outhouses with ragged old Sears catalogues and corn cobs stacked by the hole in the bench.

"A sneaks outta sleepin when a hear Ma tippytoe'n affer *revival*?" It's just the one room with beds or pallets lined up. She goes on, a hint of privilege sneaking into her voice. "Ma n me, we sits all hugged up ahine a wood stove whispern . . . Pa gits bent real bad if is sleep's ruint." As she talks, the sun flirts with her hair, winking copper glints in the dark waves.

"But Ma, she tells me all bout yall's sangin? An at lil bells thang." We laugh as if it's the best secret. She plucks a clump of pine needles and rubs them between her palms so a tiny perfume goes with us as we head back to the house.

Suddenly I ask, inspired, "You know who you remind me of?" She gives me a quick, surprised look as we poke our way past blackberry vines sprung from new growth. "Pocahontas—the Indian princess?—I saw her picture in a book at that library house in town." We can't carry any books besides the ones for school in the trailer. Libraries spell pure luxury for me.

We laugh while I protest that it's true. *It's really true.*

She says around the giggles, "Welllll, now ahm jus gonna haffa look at Pokeyhannas up, ain ah!"

Before we go, Daddy wants us to sing a song. He chooses it on account of the man, here, Ellis. Mama gives us the starting note, then Althea, Mama, and I sing harmony:

Lord, lay some soul upon my heart
And love that soul through me
And may I faithfully do my part
To win that soul for thee.

Sister Irene wants her children front and center in the church house tomorrow, our last Sunday, "Ya'll gotta pray!" She can count on me.

At first we're all quiet in the car, windows down to the steamy mid-afternoon heat. We need a thundershower and the sky says we'll get one real soon. Holding on, we jolt along, sometimes the car jumping sideways. Althea breaks the silence, "Mama, what tasted rotten in the cornbread?"

"Biscuits, too," I murmur.

"Well, I'm guessing the milk that was supposed to be clabbered was rotten, instead. Gravy had the same taste. Bless their hearts."

Daddy's concentrating on driving, not listening. But in the turn onto the main dirt road at the mail boxes, his face begins to brighten, "Those good people set me t' thinkin, Doris," Mama responds with a nod in his direction, "we're all *Americans*. At that table?" His voice trails off. When he says "American," that means he's thinking about his Homeland, the Ukraine. "Different, of course, and . . . don't know bout the man's soul." Mama waits to hear what he has on his mind, "But thank the Lord, there's a Bible in that house. I saw it. Pitiful, maybe, like everything else, but there's a Bible. They have the Word." Daddy worries that people in Russia aren't allowed to have Bibles.

Mama shakes her head, "Lord help them. Hard living, Bill, and those precious children."

"But Doris, they have a *chance*. That girl, Jolene? She's a smart one, I can see that. She can *think*, why she . . ."

Mama interrupts him, unusual for her, but she's anxious to start praying, "Lord, Lord. Lord have mercy." I think what Daddy wanted to say about Jolene was, "She doesn't miss a thing."

Just as we pull into the church-house yard, the rain descends, straight down, in a five minute *Amen*! for the day. Pastor Mobley, eyes buried in a laughing *heh heh* kind of chuckling face—looking as if he stuffed his shirt front too full of blessings—and his wife, Nellie, are here to bring a new batch of fans from the funeral home so we dash into the church.

When they hear where we had dinner, Nellie straightens up as well as she can, large bosoms swathed in a drape of yellow flowered feed sack dressing, and starts talking, "She's sa faith-ful, Sista Pridemer? Ever weekday air's a meetin. Cain get here a Sunday. Only when at bus letser off?" She shifts closer to Mama, using a fan over her small, tight O of a mouth to say in a lower voice, "It's at maan." Her sand colored eyes darken, and she nods in a knowing way. She's probably been to the beauty parlor Emmy Tuttle operates in her living room, having acquired a few rows of pin curls in her hair—tied with a remnant of the same feed sack as her dress—to be sprung forth in all its glory for tomorrow.

Mama asks what she means and Sister Mobley sighs, "He us always liquer-lazy, ats what we calls'm here. *Liquerlazy*. It's talk, y'know, talk at he makes is own?" After she lets that sink in she adds, "An they's some at's common law," raising her eyebrows. Mama tells me later when I ask, that "common law" means they weren't married in church.

Trouble is, Nellie can't stop. "A speck at perty girl Jolene gonna be inna simler fix t'er ma," the tight O pursing into a dried prune, "some nogood wandas up at dirt path an taker outta ther," nodding agreement with her own opinion.

Back inside the trailer Daddy empties his pockets—usually he puts his change up on top of the front set of drawers, but this time it's on the table—and at least five biscuits, one by one, appear. I noticed that Daddy kept taking one biscuit after another, raving about Irene and Jolene being such fine cooks. Now at the sight of his stash, not one of us says a word. I still don't know how he did it.

Daddy does good news tricky sometimes. It started me to wondering: If Jolene had said, *Preacha, see canya make em biscuits fitten ta eat,* he couldn't have done a thing. But by slipping them into his pockets real careful like, they took on their own secret Jesus powers. Those biscuits gave Jolene a good feeling about herself whether they were any good or not. Not everybody who's saved is at the altar.

Of course some people might say Daddy fibbed about the biscuits, not eating them and all. But hooray and hallelujah! for the way he treated Jolene. She didn't hear him preach, but I can tell by how he paid her attention that he thinks she's first-rate.

All day that last Sunday of revival in Grove Hill I kept looking for Sister Irene. When she and the children don't show up in the morning, I thought, well maybe in time for dinner on the ground. But sorting through the crowd lined up around the tables of food, they couldn't be found.

Back in the church house during afternoon Sing, Sister Annie Lee begins *The Lion of Judah*, shaking her tambourine with everybody joining in, shouting the words over and over again. One round, happy man bounces up and down with his arms pumping in time as if he's preaching it as he sings:

The Lion of Judah will break every chain
And give to us the Victory again and again.

But I wasn't singing. From my front row seat I was staring out the window, determined that Sister Irene and Jolene would appear when, what do you know! The Lord, that ferocious *Lion of Judah* came roaring into sight instead. The Lion strutted tall as the trees lining the rutted lane right up to Sister Irene's house. Ellis hissed, startled—unbelievers don't recognize the *Lord*—and before he could dive for the bushes, the Lion brushed him out of the way with His giant velvet paw. But Judah's Lion bowed low in front of Sister Irene and Jolene so they could scramble up on His plush back to ride in majesty back to the Sing at the church house.

Satisfying as my way of seeing was, Jolene and her Ma didn't find a way out to the church house that day. And we prayed, too. The Bible says, "if any two of you shall agree in prayer *it shall be done*." What goes wrong I don't know. The Lion of Judah has to be more powerful than a puny, irritating husband, doesn't He?

2

Enterprise, Alabama 1947

In the Dark

- *The world is increasingly Red: Rumania's King Michael is forced to abdicate by Soviet-supported Communists on December 31, 1947.*

- *Communists stage a coup against the Czech regime toppling the government and attempting to seize control.*

- *President Truman proposes the second largest peace-time budget in US History (39.6 billion), citing European Reconstruction following the end of WWII.*

- *State of Israel comes into existence and is under attack from the north, east and south attempting to force it into extinction.*

- *The Academy Award for Best Picture for the first time goes to a film that is not American, but British: Hamlet.*

- *Alfred Kinsey, a professor from the University of Indiana, publishes a report called "Sexual Behavior of the Human Male," considered scandalous by academia.*

- *Christian Dior's "New Look" demands more fabric production to maintain, in short supply after WWII both in Europe and in the US; factories spring up in the economically oppressed southern United States.*

- *Enterprise, Alabama, where the Skondeen family is in revival, prides itself on its resourcefulness, Deep South friendliness, and progressive attitude.*

SOUNDS OF A COMMOTION during the altar call get my attention. It's no wonder there's disturbance after the Lord heated up the air tonight—leftovers from a suffocating day—and the Preacher heated up the church house through the power of the Holy Ghost. Now, somewhere out in the dark the clang of a truck bed being stomped—maybe jumped off?—then rustling. But all I can see are pinpoints of flashing light from fireflies even though we've raised up the windows far as they'll go.

Well now. Here comes the commotion. Donny Johnson, thumping up the front steps in his battered cowboy boots, rushing the open double doors. Wiping his eyes with the back of his hand, he heads down the aisle toward the altar. "Thankya! *Lawd*" and, "Ooooh *Jayzus—thankya* now!"

"*Hal-luuu.*"

At first sight of him people start up glory shouts, arms directed toward heaven, some waving. One woman jumps into the aisle right in back of him and turns a complete circle, shooting her arms up and down, joy dancing before the Lord, "Ohhh yas—Mer-cy! Mercy—iss boy's acomin home!"

But Donny stops mid-way. A sudden lull takes the crowd. He reaches up in a deliberate motion and unrolls something out of his t-shirt sleeve and pitches a pack of cigarettes outside to his best friend Lester, sitting on the end of a flatbed truck nearest the window. Trucks driven by young folks back up close in before service starts as if they're at the drive in picture show. Lester raises his hand and catches the pack even though he looks brain-dead, his mouth slack, slightly open, the usual hat pushed back on his head. But the shouting takes on new sounds of laughter, clapping, and turns up the volume.

Catching the flying cigarettes brings Lester to, seems like. Still, he just sits there staring as Donny continues up the aisle, dropping to his knees at the altar.

The place breaks open with action close to frenzy. Men swarm up around Donny, praying loud, demanding, "Take ova, Lawd, Oh Lawd, *Lawd Jayzus!* Take im on ova." Brother Wiggins cries out, "We gotta *new*born, Yasssss Jayzus!" tears streaming down his face, he reaches for a kerchief out of his overall's back pocket, the other hand resting on Donny's head. "Hits a sinna here, Jayzus, iss here's a *sinna*! Save im outta hell n *Damnation*! We knowed, yas Lawd, knowed he deserved it, but mercy, Lawd. Mercy! Others look around for somebody else to usher up to the altar.

Clumps of women, heads of silver hair knotted in buns as well as pale blond strands braided, or dark locks, beribboned, all in fervent prayer. "Jayzus, Jayzus, fergive iss here chile ah'knowed he mus be fergive s'much. Make'm one a yorn!"

"Yassss, *Lawd*, one a yer precious chirrun."

Big a sinner as they know Donny to be, they still recognize a child of God. I am glad for that.

Daddy and I are right about this Friday night. Sometimes he'll say to me kind of quiet while there's singing going on, "No sinners here tonight." He's asking a question. He knows I've been watching. If I disagree, and say, "There's some lounging out there on the trucks backed up to the windows? I saw them before church started." He may switch the sermon he was planning to preach right there on the spot.

If you ask Daddy about that, he'll say that he's led by the *Holy Ghost*. That's true. The Holy Ghost points things out to me so I can see the situation.

Tonight when we came in to start the singing I was surprised by Donny and Lester having a smoke, standing on the far side of Lester's pick-up parked out back. They were trying not to be noticed, but I'd recognize Lester's old wreck anywhere. That's when I saw Donny's flat bed truck backed in toward the open windows for a good look at the inside of the church house. He must have arrived real early to get a place like that.

Three pickups and the flat bed truck parked so close make the parking yard appear to be a drive in picture show like the one we ran up on near Birmingham. I can tell you that is a *strange* looking thing. A giant white screen standing out in a field. Spaces for cars in semicircles facing it, lined up inside a chain link fence.

Daddy says as we drive on by pulling the trailer, "Lord! Lord! Lord help us. Another playground for the Devil, Doris." Mama shakes her head and makes the noise she makes with her tongue against the roof of her mouth, five quick sounds, like sweeping sludge off a cement floor, meaning *dirty shame*. That's what I think when I hear it.

So of course, I never say a word to Mama and Daddy about the trucks out there making me feel like we're at the drive in. Difference is, we're the moving picture. Tonight we're entertaining sinners, all of them sitting outside the windows in the dark. But I have to admit that Lester and Donny are the two I least expected to see anywhere near revival.

Granny K told me about Donny and Lester when they came speeding up the road this week, Tuesday afternoon. A cloud of dust like the world's last chance following behind them.

Granny Kathleen lives across the road from the church. Pastor P. D. Creel or his wife, one, or maybe a church lady, I'm not sure, wrote instructions to us a few weeks before we arrived, "*Y'all can fetch a key from Granny K. Lives catty-corner to the church house. Ain no believer, but keeps a eye on things.*"

After we pulled into the pine needle covered dirt yard and Daddy situated the trailer close as he could to the little wooden church house—as usual, no steeple, no crosses or fancy glass—we went to find *Granny* K as most everybody calls her. We always need to open the church right away so we can unload our instruments and hook up our electricity in the trailer.

I liked Granny Kathleen right off. She's hardly taller than I am. Well, she would be if she didn't hunch into a round little ball most of the time. She wears a faded yellow, orange, blue, or red kerchief at her neck, making her dungarees and work shirt look as if she's on her way to the county fair. Her eyes shine like beacons, blue high beams, pure laughter making their way through strands of hair supposed to be gathered in a bun in back. White silvery hair borrowed from angel decorations on a Christmas tree, but with just enough leftovers of young peachy gold strands to give it a shine. Her skin glows that peach color, too, right out of a sky's best sunset.

If I called her *Sister* she'd puff smoke right in my face from a short pipe that fits into the curve of her palm and then she'd laugh up a tornado to blow me away. I'm sure of it. She calls me interesting names when no one else is around, and says things like, "Ah, you, grrrl, a smallest one, yer holdin all a *mis*chief of a goody good fam'ly in yer wee lil angel eyes, now ain cha." We laugh for the longest time, while she picks up her banjo and sets it on her little bowl full of jelly stomach and goes to picking, tucking our secret away inside the music.

Daddy wants her to come *play along with us* at the church some night during revival. But Granny, fixing a look on him that could wither Kudzu vines for miles around, says, "What arrr ya askin, Prrreacha maann? Leave this heerrr churrrch in *cin*derrrs?" She rolls her r's when she's teasing. That's how her mother and father talked, she tells me. "They come here from a M'ral Isle," she says, "m'sef, nevah lay eyes on it."

"Emerald Isle? You mean *Ireland.*" She nods, laying her pipe down and looking out over the railing as if she's envisioning a castle on the far horizon.

Every chance I get, I escape over to her steps when she's picking. If she's playing a tune I know like *Shortnin Bread*, I sing along at the top of my lungs. But Tuesday, she saw Donny's flat bed truck speeding—probably just unloaded the logs he hauls at the sawmill up the road—and she quit picking. Jumped to her feet ready for a fight. Stretching out over the railing, she yelled, "Y'all cut yer motor," shaking her fist after them, "drivin like satan's handyman, ah swan," but I could see they were paying her no mind. Granny K takes responsibility for things around these parts.

"Em boys ain been reared like you," she says, settling back to rocking, one rocker has a *crrreak* when it goes back. Her banjo's forgotten as if the music's been knocked out of her. "Schoolin's over when they legs's long enough to reach em gas peddles." She shakes her head and scrunches her face so the long hairs around her mouth stick straight out. "Donny's Ma run off a Memphis when he's a lil ole thang," pausing to spit into a five pound can that's seen gallons of tobacco juice since it held coffee. "Ain no secert—she us painted up like a fer sale sign when she lit outta here. Perty girl. Donny's right hansome hisself."

"What about his Pa?"

All she says is, "No count." Spits again.

A few days later, I see the boys at the feed store on Main Street, packing sacks of chicken feed out to Lester's beat up no color pickup. Cigarette's dangling from Donny's strong mouth, the kind of mouth you notice, wide and formed in a hard line jaw. Balances out his eyes, as dark a blue as a brewing storm. With Donny Johnson, I guess *turbulence*, like the weatherman on the radio reports, happens often. His blackened brown eyebrows throw down exclamation marks for whatever he has to say and match the heavy hair that falls across his forehead.

Now, Lester, you hardly see at all. Smaller and lighter in his coloring, he only serves as a contrast when he's alongside Donny. His skinny bones to Donny's brawn, his freckles to Donny's tan, his stutter to Donny's easy banter. Lester's ratty straw hat seems stuck to the reddish brown hair. Probably meant to shade him from too much sun but tipped back as it is, fails the job so his nose has a perpetual burn. Hat does make him a little taller, still, Donny could fit Lester under his arm.

Donny's slinging those sacks into the back of Lester's truck like they're tea bags, that's what his body's saying. *Nothing to it and who cares anyhow.*

First time we drove under the railroad trestle and up the main drag in Enterprise, I knew this was going to be a different kind of town. Right there in the middle of the street there's a statue to what they call an "agricultural pest." It doesn't sound exactly that way here, though. More like "ageeculcher." This statue of a Greek lady—I saw one like her in Althea's art history book—stands with arched lights at her feet. And in her hands, raised above her head as if she's holding a torch, squats a giant boll weevill. You can't believe it til you see it.

"H'its a onliest *statue* inna worl ats *ereck* fer a pest." A man whose name turned out to be Wilmer told us that when we asked directions. But first he told us, in answer to daddy's question, that we missed the church house located on the other side of the trestle where the street y's off of the road that goes under the railroad. Wilmer works at the filling station and tickles himself to pieces explaining Enterprise. "Back air pert near thirty fie yars," he nods, his long boney face swelling on the left side with a ball of tobacco which he works side to side while he's talking, "boll weevil come up from Mexco by way a Texis." I picture the little thing with its bags packed hitching a ride, but I'm not laughing. Wilmer's real serious beginning his story.

"Bout wiped us outta *ever* thang. Farmers goin broke. Cotton near shuts down from at air pesky thang. But at don't stop us." He spits a brown stream in the direction of the street, "Folks goes a plantin peanuts ennyhow." He says the statue's to remind people here in Enterprise that they can get past anything that goes wrong. I like that.

"They gone an put uppa banna," I have to think a second before I realize he's saying *banner*, not banana. "An at thang stretch cross iss here street sayin, 'Pull fer Ennerprise er pull out!'"

"Haw!" he guffaws, to clue us in that it's time to laugh. His blue coveralls tell about the grease of every car he's worked on today. Wilmer's so tall and thin I figure the man can slip under a *Radio Flyer* wagon if it needs work.

Boll weevils invade and destroy. Picture perfect for their role: ugly looking according to a sketch at the library. They're so tiny, you can't see them without a magnifying glass. Even though they're supposed to be in the beetle family, beetles would beat them in a beauty contest any day. Gray, scrawny bodies, boll weevils' legs poke out on all sides. Just goes to show, you can make anything look good sculpted in stone.

Words chiseled on the base of the monument read:

> In profound appreciation of the boll weevil and what it has done
> as the herald of prosperity. This monument was erected by the
> citizens of Enterprise, Coffee County, Alabama.

Wilmer, the filling station man, tells us we'll see other grand sights at the Pea River Historical Society, too, but I doubt if we will. Daddy doesn't do sightseeing. He doesn't think God will protect us on the road when we're *fooling around*. Only when we're headed to a revival to save souls or on our way to work, like in Miami during the winter, where he upholsters to pay for the revivals.

Only forty people or so crowd into this little white clapboard church tonight, but they sound mighty powerful. Their singing calls to folks driving by; maybe they'll even come sit out in the churchyard to listen for a while. Enterprise Assembly has windows almost to the ceiling that open wide on summer nights as hot as this one.

"Nearly a hunnert!" folks complain as they gather, fanning.

Two electric fans cool from the corners of the platform—one on top of the piano and the other rigged on a chair next to Althea's vibra harp—pointed outward to the congregation. Daddy makes sure they're in a direction that keeps him out of the breeze they create. There's a center walkway, straight to the door from the pulpit and when he preaches up the aisle he can't be in a draft. When he's sweaty, that'll cause him to lose his voice every time.

But tonight after this altar call, we're focused on Donny Johnson. What do you reckon pulls on him? Could be Daddy preaching Delilah reminds Donny of his Ma.

Delilah had a for sale sign on her, too, and the Philistines bought her right up like she was on end of the season clearance. Samson's head in Delilah's lap?

> What's a *man of God doin* here?
> He's unequally yoked. Careless! *Friendly* with the enemy.
> Philistines found a woman who's the perfect weapon.
> And she's in it for the money. No. Doubt.
> *No love in her.*

Instead of the usual shouting, people are calling on God to "Have mercy!" "Lawd, Lawd, Lawd!"

> Samson's Mama knows he'll be powerful before he's born.
> His Daddy promises God
> no razor will touch his head.
> That boy is told when he's so small he's
> still on mother's milk that
> *his hair* shows God's power in him.
> Strength against their enemy, the Philistines.

Daddy talks about Bible story characters so they're real as your neighbors. Still on the platform as he preaches, he's walking back and forth working himself into the Samson character: First, stepping like the honorable Samson, then strutting like a smart aleck.

> Samson stands tall, a hero to his people.
> He's a judge, he's honored!
> A wild beast roars out to devour him—
> Samson rips him in half with his bare hands.
> Blood on his hands?
> You're anointed! Nothing ordinary about you:
> a Nazirite, Samson. Where's your vows of purity?

Later he finds wild honey in the
carcass, comes home dripping with that honey.
He's something all right.
But he gets too used to being special.
Why, he takes the jawbone of a donkey—think of it—and scatters
a Philistine army all by himself.
Spattered with blood but victorious,
did he forget he's s'posed to be sanctified? Undefiled?
Holy unto the Lord.
Or is he just showin off?
Yeah—he's a big shot—strutting—but wait til you see
how he finishes . . .

"Have mercy! and "Hep us, hep us, hep us!" Laments and out loud worries
ring through the congregation.

Samson's a smart one, all right, makes up
riddles about the beast and the honey:
Out of the eater came
Something to eat.
Out of the strong
Came something sweet.
He stumps the enemy, makes them mad as a nest of hornets!
His riddles outsmart them and just for that, they want to kill him.
Get him out of their way!

In a rough voice the Preacher whispers the words *they want to kill him* into
the microphone. Electricity came in last year and people pride themselves
on amplifying the Preacher. He walks away from the mic, steps down into
the aisle.

And now the Philistines have Delilah.
She names her price. To deliver . . .
The victim . . .
Samson's going to the Valley of Sorek to visit this Delilah
but now don't you think that all the Delilah's are in no *Valley of Sorek*!
No siree, she's planted at every corner, right here in Alabama weeds
of sin parade like lilies. She'll surprise you with that sweet smelling
disguise. As if you're the only man she's ever swayed. *Only man she's*
ever fooled.
What's Samson doing with a woman like Delilah?
"I'm in lovvve"

The Preacher, hands on hips, throws his head back and brays the word love like a donkey, all pitiful like but bragging at the same time. Women in the church house begin to murmur amongst themselves, "Oh Lawdy, ain ah heared at afore!" Others just clap their hands as if saying, "yep, at's it!" That's the way it goes.

God can't clean you up when you're layin in the mud!

The Preacher shouts it out and the people respond, *Aaamaan, na.* "You go on n preach it, Brotha," a bearded man in dungarees, faded blue bandanna stuck in a back pocket, jumps up in his exuberance but quickly sits again, attention focused:

> Delilah *pesters* him for his secret
> she whines, she cries. "You don't love me!"
> Samson teases: *three times*
> he gives her a riddle instead, and when she brings
> the Philistines on him, binding him as he sleeps in her arms,
> he rises up, shakes himself and rips off the ropes as if they're string.
> "I've still got the power," he laughs.
> But she wears him down.
> Delilah's cobra-like sweetness twines around Samson one more time
> with tears. Love! Devotion.
> *It's my hair*
> Samson speaks low as if it's only another seduction.
> But he's the one seduced.

The Preacher's strolling, then at the microphone, speaking quietly. Not a sound from the people on the benches or outside. He begins his prowl up the aisle again, pushed by the story of a man in trouble.

> Samson sleeps and Delilah motions for the waiting Philistines.
> They've got the troublemaker this time,
> cutting his long locks, color of that wild honey.
> Binding him tight.
> And when he wakens this time—this time!—and tries to
> shake himself as before,
> Samson has no Power.
> The Power's Gone . . . *Gone!*
> God's power. Has. Departed. From. Samson.

There is no sound from the people on the benches. The air's gone out of the room.

They put out his eyes with a poker.
The Philistines put out *his eyes*.
Blind, helpless he's tossed into the ring to grind corn at the mill,
day after day going in circles like a mule.

The Evangelist begins a slow circular plod in the space before the altar. Head drooping, hands pushing the grinding wheel.

See what his *compromise with sin* brings him?
Grinding corn for the Philistines.
Such a glorious start, but
look where he is for the finish.
"Where's your God now," his enemies jeer.

Breaking his walking cycle, the Preacher's words, "But the Philistines don't have the last word," bring him back to the mic, whispering:

His hair began to grow.

After that, there's not a breath being taken, seems like. All is quiet except for the distant scratchy moan of crickets out there in the dark. Preacher begins again in a quick, steady voice:

At night, sleepless in the stone house of the prison camp with no eyes,
he don't even see the difference between light and dark.
All he can see is his sin. His arrogance. His pride.

The Preacher's Samson voice wails with,

Weeping, crying out, it's too late. Too Late! To regain his eyes, but,

(said low and dark into the mic)

his hair began to grow.
A young slave boy leads him back to the rounds of grinding corn.
Around and around Samson goes,
"I ain't so smart after all. Forgive me, oh God forgive me!"
He don't even know if he's worth another chance.
But his hair began to grow.

It's like folks don't know this story. They're waiting to find out. Darkness floats around the church house, quiet as midnight, soaking up the tale. Even little kids and babies rock themselves with the rhythm of the words. After that last phrase the Preacher speaks into the mic, he walks up and down the aisle in silence. Then he turns at the altar and begins to increase his volume and rev up his speed.

> The Philistines don't pay any mind to Samson now;
> just bring him out *like a circus act*
> when they're having their games.
> *He's their clown to mock.*
> They taunt the fool,
> everyone of them drunk with wine—they have
> their own brands of white lightening in a Mason jar!
> Ain't nothin new!
> Debauchery on every side.

Mentioning moonshine, Preacher's gone to meddlin now, as they say around here. I have no idea what that word *debauchery* means, but people sure enough shake their heads and cluck their tongues when it's said. Little slave boy leads Samson back to rest between two pillars in the grand pavilion.

Weary now, the Preacher recovers the mic, his head down, speaking slowly, a moving picture of the defeated hero: he places an arm around each pillar. Preacher stretches out both arms in an attitude of being on a cross, head still down, and in a hoarse whisper says,

> Samson prays . . .
> power he showed off all those years on the outside
> inside him now.

Loud, now, one last effort with a rough, crackly voice:

> *Remember me.*
> *Oh God, one more time.*
> *Remember me*
> *One more time!*

His embrace tightens. A crack breaks through the party noise.
The Preacher's voice makes a noise skidding, screeching out of his throat.

> *slikierrrierrrrrrashhackssshh*
> a mighty thunder
> and the pillars are shattered.
> All the Philistines die
> along with Samson.
> (silence)

Crickets echo from the dark outside the windows. Weeping hiccups, snuffles, shush through folks taking Samson in, grasping God's fallen hero restored to Glory. At least Glory sure is the hope. You never know.

Tonight. Tonight!
No matter how you started your life, you can have
a glorious finish.
This night is your One. More. Chance.
It's this very night.
Tonight is your time of salvation.

Every altar call feels as if it's meant for me, too. Prayers are being said all over the room like a hum. Tears sound out, too, sobbing puts in pauses but there's no stopping it. A rustling under the prayers puts in a strange rasp to the muffled cries. Loud kind of sadness that comes up out of broken hearts. Broken for stray children, stray mates, and stray parents, too. Daddy doesn't even have to motion to me, I rise for the altar song. I'm already up at the pulpit and standing on a little step Brother Bees made for me so I can sing into the mic.

> *When my little boy blue*
> *Closed his eyes and went to sleep*
> *He prayed the Lord my soul to keep*

This part always gets me, swallowing and singing slowly keeps me from crying, myself. I have that little slave boy in my mind tonight. Of course I'm wearing my blue dress.

> *And if I die before I wake*
> *The Lord my soul will take*
> *Oh darling mother do not weep.*
> *God bless my Daddy too, for*
> *He s been so kind and true.*
> *Our home dear Lord I know you'll keep.*
> *Then he closed his big blue eyes and went to paradise,*
> *When my little boy blue went to sleep.*

The slave boy, Samson's guide in prison, goes to heaven with Samson, that's what my heart says, not like the Philistines who all go to hell. The Evangelist steps back to the mic and says,

> Maybe you're here tonight living like Samson,
> running from a godly home, but you can't outrun God.
> Or is it that your Pa might as well *be* a Philistine, and
> your Ma's just another Delilah carousin and
> dancin with the devil.

The Preacher's saying that made me catch my breath. I've never before heard him say a thing about a no-count Ma and Pa when he's at the altar.

> But you—*you!*—don't have to be
> another splinter off that block.
> Tonight, you can be new.
> A new man, a new woman.
> You can be born. Again!
> This time into God's family.

Then we hear Donny making that commotion.

Up in my top bunk, sleep doesn't lift me into the stars right away. Samson's whole life reads like a riddle that holds no answer. Couldn't he tell Delilah was after him when she has already tied him down two times?

And I reckon that lion he ripped up came after him with a message, a message from the Lion of Judah. Trying to warn him against the filth he's fooling around with, all those mean women and that mess of murder. Mama calls it "mayhem" which sounds like an even bigger pile of sin. Yep, you might know Samson would tear up the lion who was bringing him a message about disrespect. He should've slept with the sound of the Lion of Judah purring him to sleep instead of Delilah.

That noise Daddy made when the pillars crashed? It sounded an awful lot like the Russian words he talks with his sister in Canada. Aunt Lena. But nobody here knows that. One woman said real quiet like after the service, shaking her head as if she still didn't believe it, "Ah declare a'God amity! Ah could pert near feel a dust from em pillers afallin!"

Sleep only comes when I find the vent that rolls up at the center of the ceiling. There it is, my twinkle-star. At last I hitch my riddles to the stars with no more questions.

In the morning, we're quiet at the breakfast table during our hot Postum in bone china mugs from Aunt Edna and unbreakable bowls full of oatmeal. Our utensils make me laugh to myself—fancy bone china and clunky Melmac—but I don't say anything out loud. When it's busy yet without any words at all, it seems like too much is going on to make a sound.

Daddy does say, "Those cigarettes! Flying out the window!"

And Mama shakes her head as she dishes up the porridge, "Never seen such a thing in all my years," sounding as if she's an old, old woman.

After breakfast, it's the morning news. Daddy and I are going into town before the Post Office closes at noon and I'm anxious to be on our way, but the news always comes first.

"Spy mania," the reporter says through the static, we're out of reach of major stations and Daddy's radio is having trouble bringing in the sound, "is sweeping America." I don't know what that means, exactly. But it's about Russia, so in one way or another it's about us. Most of the spy news, I do know, mentions Wisconsin Senator Joe McCarthy and the House Un-American Activities Committee. This *edition of the news*, as they say, starts with a man named *Chambers* who says he's a spy, and he's accusing a man named Alger Hiss of spying, too.

With a name like Alger Hiss, how did he get a job anyhow? Anybody can tell there's something wrong with that one.

Daddy's on the pull-up seat between the table and the kitchen counter where the radio sits. He bends his head, listening, a dark wave of hair float-ing above his eyes, his ear at the level of the brown-and-gold-weave fabric over the radio's speaker. His right hand's bracing his forehead, the other, holding one of his 5x7-inch sermon notebooks, fingering the wire ring binding. Sometimes he says, *Help us Lord*, a trouble-prayer. That sounds threatening to me because he says it when he's displeased with my behavior in church. Whispering to a kid next to me—though I'm usually sitting next to mama—swinging my legs, or in general not paying close enough mind to what's going on. If he has to say it a third time to get my attention, I know there'll be big trouble.

I can tell it's not good news for our family today or anybody else for that matter. He sits there for a minute during the ad for John Deere tractors. The Sons of the Pioneers singing *Cool Water*, snaps him out of his dark thinking. I can tell there are no lights on in his eyes when his head hangs down after the news.

Besides picking up the mail, we have to give the post office a forward-ing address. Monday morning, we're packing up and pulling out and the mail has to be ready to follow us. It's just the two of us, since Mama's helping Althea practice the vibra harp.

Daddy talks while he drives, "*This world is not my home*." That's a song we sing. "No sirree. We're looking to a better place," still with the news.

"Daddy, you reckon Samson makes a riddle for his hair starting to grow again?"

He glances at me kind of surprised as if he hasn't thought of that. Takes him a minute, "Well, if he does, he keeps his mouth shut," shaking his head,

"Samson's through being a big mouth, thinking he can outsmart the devil in a debate. You can't win that one. Not never."

"No more clues for the Philistines, huh? Samson's done with getting attention . . ." Daddy nods. I keep it up, "I'm sure happy 'bout Donny. Wonder what'll happen to Lester."

"Lester?"

"That's Donny's friend. They were both there last night. I heard them talking. They were smoking, 'course, out in back of the trucks when we first went in to sing." I sat on the side steps while Mama and Daddy tuned up the instruments and I could tell which was Donny because Lester's voice is kind of whiney, plus that stutter even when he's relaxed. "Those two boys are always *up to nothin' decent* according to Granny K. But that's before last night."

Daddy just says, "Thank the Lord for Donny. Lord help him."

"Tossing those cigarettes out the window? That will be the talk of Coffee County."

A big grin spreads across his face as he parks in front of the Enterprise Post Office, "You can count on it," he even chuckles a little, nodding his head. I'm feeling successful as we walk up to the General Delivery window.

But while Daddy's talking to the Post Office man, I spot a wooden box kind of newspaper holder with a slot to put the nickel, just inside the door. *The Enterprise Ledger* headline reads, "Russian Spies Invade U.S." My heart sinks.

As we leave, three men who've been checking their mail boxes in the Post Office, stand at a bench right outside the door. One, rolling a cigarette, props his foot on the bench while his left hand holds the fine paper and the right rolls it tight around the tobacco. Of the other two, a pudgy little thing talks all excited like so his short frame looks like he's jumping around even though he stays in place. He's loud, "'Em Commies's gonna take us all down, a tell yas. We in a heapa trouble!" The third one's bony hip is leaning against the back of the bench, his bib dungarees have been kicking around awhile and the strawpatch substitute for a hat slouches over greasy brown hair streaking his forehead. He takes a draw on his cigarette, grinning, and with a sly look shifts his head back and says, "Ah, Hank, less jus sen em a live in Russia, whatcha say?"

But the fellow who's rolled his tobacco, strikes a match and says through thin lips, lighting the tip of the cigarette, "Yeah . . . Naw! a tell ya what. A gotta tree out ta m' place an a long ole rope!" All three laugh real hard.

Daddy turns his head away from them as if there's somebody coming up the steps; as if they're not saying a thing that interests him. But back in the car parked at the curb in front of them as we drive away we can still hear their laughter. Daddy's face doesn't have a bit of color in it. And I can't think of a thing to distract him.

After dinner, I see Granny K out on her porch. Mama says I can go over, "Just for fifteen minutes. Don't be a pest," of course I immediately think, *boll weevil*. Very ugly. Daddy and Mama are careful about the Evangelist's kids bothering people, but maybe for unbelievers it doesn't matter so much.

Granny K's house outdates most cabins around here. The corrugated tin roof is in a steep slant that sounds happy as a drummer boy at work when it rains. Looks like a saltine cracker box made of pine planks, gray from being whipped by years of winter storms. The porch where we sit is across the wide side of the box. Pink roses looking wild as Granny K, climb all around the rails. It's a sweet thing. She has two purple crepe myrtle trees in the front near the road that are in full bloom right now, their flowers resembling tiny bunches of pulled to a pucker crepe paper.

When I asked about her family, she just says, "Ma died right young. Pa leff me iss here place n ats bout all they is." Yesterday when she began to pick her banjo—it was *She'll Be Comin Round the Mountain*—I came running over to sing, and after that she went into *This World Is Not My Home*. That surprised me. I thought she didn't know a lick about church music.

> *This world is not my home I'm just a passing through*
> *My treasures are laid up Somewhere beyond the blue.*

I sang out on that one and she sang with me. By the last part, I was standing up, tapping in rhythm on the tin drain pipe that comes off the roof into a barrel for catching rain water. She laughed at that. I should say *cackled*.

> *The angels beckon me from*
> *Heaven's open door and I*
> *Can't feel at home in this world any more.*

Afterward, I sat back down on the step. When we caught our breath, I had the nerve to say, "How do you know church songs, Granny?"

"Pays a mind at singin cross a road."

"But you don't go in the church house."

"Na Angel Eyes, I feel yer lil devil startin a peek inta m'bidness." We hooted out some big laughs on that one, then I just kept it up.

"Yep, that's me, your Ma and Pa go to church?"

"Ats a secret," she begins, and I stay quiet because I can see that when she starts putting tobacco into her pipe—which she's doing—that she's fixing to talk a spell. Real thoughtful-like. "Ats a secret ah kep all m'life." *Rock creak rock creak.* She takes a puff, nods. "Folks in these parts don't git it. Mebbe you don't neither?"

"Try me," I invite, even though I'm cautious around other folk's secrets, having a big one of my own.

"Awright, now. It's jus you'n me here a talkin, right?" I nod solemnly. "Ma n Pa-back onna M'ral Isle? They's Catlic. Calls em 'makrl slappers' roun here. An *worse*."

"Our church calls them 'idol worshippers,'" I agree, then race ahead, "But one time when I was a little girl . . ."

Granny interrupts me with a guffaw, "You a lil girl now!"

"I mean really little—just four years old—I'll be six next month. Anyhow, I was taking a walk with my Mama in a real pretty part of town, Savannah? I saw this beautiful lady in a blue gown standing in front of white steps—she had her hands out—like welcoming to her house? I stood in front of her with such a love feeling. But my Mama came up behind me quick as a wink and pulled on my hand, *That's an idol! God says, 'have no graven image!* We walked away from there fast."

"Perty church house, ah reckon."

"Most beautiful—ivory white, tall steeple—and rubies, emeralds and sapphires in the windows. No kidding."

"Wal. Ma n Pa, they figgered they's 'nuf gainst us with they funny way a talkin." She sits still a minute, nodding. Puts her pipe down in the dented hub cap she uses for an ash tray, jumps up and says, "How bout some sweet tea!" Our church conversation is over.

That's the only time I went inside her house. There are just two rooms, the front one for visiting in the winter time that has two rockers and a couple of cane back chairs on a braided rug and a sawed off stump for a table in the middle of them next to a pot-bellied stove. Her bed is over in one corner along the wall that's shared with the other room, the kitchen.

The outhouse is a ways out back I notice, through Nelliemoo's yard. She's Granny's cow and she knows her name, too. Couple of goats and about six chickens and a rooster. The chickens are what worry her when people drive fast. She's afraid the rooster and "his'n ole ladies" won't have enough warning to get out of the way.

Today she's already heard the big news. Her cheeks are never so full of sunshine as when there's something juicy going around. She laughs out loud when she sees me cross the road. "They gone n made some histry las night, Angel Eyes." She takes time out to puff on her pipe, slapping the thigh of her dungarees with her other hand.

"Lawdy mercy, at air Jayzus may be a comin even sooner n ya'll r figurin. Donny Johnson!" She laughs again, "An em flyin cigrettes!"

"Where do you get your news so fast?"

"At air party line!" That's the telephone exchange. Five, six, people share the same line and you just have to know your own ring. On the other hand, if you're curious about the neighborhood news, you listen in to everybody's conversations. "Done heard a preachin five, mebbe six time." She grins a sly smile and squints a little as if to warn me not to re-preach it to her. "*An is hair begin a grow*! whooeee, thass a story fer ya."

"And Donny . . ." I start to say but she's already into a rush of words like her banjo notes piling up on each other when she picks.

"Lordy, Lordy. Ahm hopin at air savin sticks, ats all ah gots ta say."

"So am I. But what about Lester? What'll he do now?"

She's quiet. So quiet it doesn't seem like Granny K. She stops rocking. Then she rests the pipe in the hubcap and reaches for the banjo propped against the rough porch rails in front of her, sits it on her belly, and says, "Ain no tellin."

She goes to picking. Real slow at first, *Little Brown Jug* then it speeds up. Slow part's exciting knowing there's soon to come that cloud cracking lightening she plays.

After my fifteen minutes over the road, I come back to find Mama and Daddy mulling over the calendar. Black letters saying, Get Your Bar B Que at the Opelika Cafe, and below that, one month at a time, big squares for everyday.

"No way to do it." Mama says, her elbows on the table since there's no food in sight. Daddy's on the other side of the table with the map of Alabama.

"Even one day longer don't give us *no* time for travel. Sylacauga's too far. I'll have to tell Brother Creel when he comes around this afternoon." Brother P. D. Creel is the pastor here in Enterprise. He wants us to stay another week.

Sylacauga's the town with the scallops around the bottom of the water tower. It's the sweetest thing to have up high over a town. Sure beats a boll weevil for landmarks. But then I hate to leave Granny K.

Enterprise Assembly has some people who care about how it looks. You can tell by the flower bushes that grow along the sides of the building. Just four o'clocks that aren't much more than weeds, but their yellow or red upside down parasol shaped blossoms twirl together, folding when the sun goes down. They keep on showing up with no attention but somebody had to bother putting them there. That's a good sign. Makes me smile when I see people treat God's house like their own.

Oh, and a chinaberry tree in the center of the five picnic tables out back. Dropping its berries like it does, it's a mess. But the leaf looks like a thick, dark green fern, each leaf, glossy, majestic.

Cement block steps stretch across the front of the church house. Kind of unusual for a poor little church. Double doors open out to give it a welcome feeling. And this last Sunday morning of revival it sure does feel like a welcoming place.

Low and behold, Donny Johnson shows up first thing with his hair wet down and smelling like Ivory soap. He has on a white looking shirt that tried hard but didn't quite get clean at wash time. Ironing doesn't happen.

I'm standing on the front steps as he comes in. His smile is small, face tipped sideways as if he wants to be shy but doesn't know how. "You a lil girl at sang s'sweet th'other night!" he says to me. I just smile back at him.

And you know what he did? He knelt down so as to be on my level, eye to eye, and he said, "Thank ya." Then an odd kind of look, like a rain cloud flitting across his face, "As a kid a wanted a sang. No chance." Shaking his head, then back to smiling. "Thank ya sa much." I couldn't think of a single word, just, "You sure are welcome, Donny."

Then he stands up real straight again. I thought to add what Daddy would say, "We'll all sing in Glory, Donny!" He looked down at me with a crooked one sided smile. Walks carefully, seems like, through the church doors. Stands there, quiet, looking for a place to sit. A brand new citizen of heaven still hunting for his place on earth.

The women bustle about, chattering, when it's time for dinner on the grounds after Sunday School and the morning service. A Sunday School room doubles for a kitchen across the back of the building. They even have an old ice box and when it's a dinner Sunday they plunk in a block of ice they buy at the ice house in Enterprise.

Usually there's dawdling talk and fellowship while dinner's on the way and they take their sweet time getting it arranged. But today, food shows up in minutes.

That back all purpose room opens out to an area around the chinaberry tree. Dishes are put on two of the picnic tables, and the adults sit at the other three tables to eat. After the teen-agers dish up their food they pile onto the backs of the trucks as usual. Little kids take their plates out to the front steps.

"Na hon, you just go on ahead an have you a secont heppin a ham. Plenty a sweet taters, too. Doncha hol back!" church ladies fret over pointing

Donny in the right direction. He let slip that pecan pie's his favorite and Sister Rachel Bees has a hunk cut for him before he can even get to it. Donny'll sure enough bask in a glow of attentive mamas around this church house.

After the kids make short work of eating their portions of chicken legs and potato salad sitting on the front stoop, they start playing tag. That's when I have to go in to rest. Daddy won't tolerate any running around, especially on Sunday. That would be good for at least three "Help Us Lords."

The *Sunday Afternoon Sing*, advertised all around town for weeks, starts up at four o'clock. That gives everybody time to rid the dishes and have a rest under the trees. Folks sit and talk at the tables over cool glasses of sweet tea. Children, tired of tag and *Red Rover, Red Rover*, drift off to loll in the backs of the pickups. I see the Bees family brought their long eared happy dog, Barney. Ollie and Mavis Joy, their two girls, say he was born in their barn. Ollie's resting her head on his back for her nap. Teen-agers take walks in the woods.

Our family goes to the trailer for our quiet spell. Days like this *wear me plum to death*, Daddy says. "Just finish preaching in the mornin then it's singin and shoutin half the afternoon." He sits down in front of the trailer to take off his shoes. "Not to mention all the rich food. My stomach can't take it." Tomorrow he'll only be eating stewed together bread and milk.

Mama signals time to go about half an hour before the music's supposed to begin. Daddy needs time for tuning up the violin with Mama on the accordion. Althea does a few runs end to end on the vibra harp, that's the best way to tell everybody it's time to gather.

Afternoon Sings buzz with a noisy kind of fun. Teens are out in back of the church, getting a group together to sing a special. A blond boy with a mouth harp tries a riff. Another kid about sixteen strums his Gibson guitar, red head bent to hear the tune he's plucking. Girls, of course, make up the admiring fan club for the boys. Except one flouncy one, Lilly Ann, long straight blond hair pale as lemonade, chooses songs from the hymnal, concentrating, then loudly proclaiming the numbers they should be working on. All of them are sitting on top of and around the picnic tables now that the food's been put back in the kitchen or in the icebox.

I'm idly watching them from the back doorway, entertained, waiting for our instruments to finish their tuning. Brother Hadley Simms is going to be in charge of the singing this afternoon. That's a relief for Daddy and me both.

Just about time to start, I see a cloud of dust in the direction of town. I'm thinking it's probably the quartet that promised to come from the Baptist Church. But when it's closer, I recognize Lester's no color pickup.

But he's not the only one—he's leading a parade—a '39 Chevy follows, then a '35 Dodge and three Ford trucks, '37 to '40. I can identify cars from being on the road so much. It's a game I play with myself. Folks must be coming on over after being at other churches this morning, arriving just in time for the music.

It looks like a living red ant hill by the time they're all parked and out of their trucks or rattle trap cars. One of the teen-agers says, "Boy howdy, it's done come 'live. We got us a resrection!" The girls all laugh, of course.

Lester arrives first, giving him the choice of parking places. He turns into the area of the church house yard right in back of Donny's wired to-gether flatbed. It worries me to think that Donny hauls logs to the lumber mill in that thing. Seeing one close up, I understand why I'm scared when I see them on the road, loaded, groaning up a hill just ahead of us.

Lester keeps his truck right near the road so he can make a quick get-away if it doesn't feel good. People do that all the time and sometimes they ease on out of here. He sits there a minute, unsure of what to do. Usually, with Donny, they just blast in together wherever it is.

Donny spots him quick as can be, like he's been waiting, and saunters over. He leans up against the door, arm resting on the top of the truck and his head dipped down to talk through the window. In no time Lester's grin-ning. Donny opens the door and easy as can be, they're both walking over to sit on Donny's flatbed, backs leaning against the cab.

They're ready to listen to the music and watch girls float by in their pastel summer dresses, their hair brushed to a high gloss. But the boys aren't making girl-watching obvious like they did when I saw them in town. They were whistling then, calling out names, "Hey Lula, you lookin goood, Swee-Pea!" And the girls, turning around and around in response, or crossing the street to say *hiiii* drawling it out as if it's a strawberry ice cream cone melting all over.

I see the cigarettes in the pocket of Lester's faded orange and green plaid shirt, long sleeves rolled above the elbow. It's probably the only shirt to his name. Working peanut crops and logging when you don't own the land means you're sitting right on that *poverty line* newsmen talk about. Donny knows how hard the dollars come for buying those cigarettes that's why he threw em on out to his friend. But neither one of them is smoking today. Maybe they're learning respect. Big doses of pride and fear are pushed way back in a corner for Lester to show up at all.

Music swings in with *He Keeps Me Singing*. Time for me to get inside. Brother Simms keeps the crowd's attention with fast choruses, *I've Got the Joy*, and *Love Lifted Me*. Then, Mama, Althea and I harmonize, *The Meeting in the Air*:

You have heard of little Moses in the bullrush You
have heard of fearless David and his sling; You
have heard the story told of dreaming Joseph, and
of Jonah and the whale you often sing . . . By and by
the Lord will surely let us meet them
at the meeting in the air.

You can count on shouting when you sing about all these heroes plus meeting up with them and Jesus, too. Right on time, the cheers begin with the chorus. When folks are thinking of being taken up with Jesus in the Rapture, they just go in that direction: Up. Now! *There is going to be a meeting in the air, In the sweet, sweet by and by, I am going to meet you, meet you over there in that home beyond the sky.*

Mama and Daddy have a request to sing the *Castles* duet now. I can't tell if it's because they sing it together with a sweetness, Daddy's dipping his head toward Mama during their duet, or the actual song that's so popular. Anyhow, I'm free to go back outside. Since we're not in charge of the afternoon Sing, I have more wiggle room. That's unusual, and I did have to use the outhouse. But I'll admit it, I wander around through the parked cars and take time to scratch Barney behind the ears, too.

While I'm perched with Melva Joy on the tailgate of Bees' pick up, Barney slobbering all over me, I hear Sister Betty Jean Wiggins and Sister Darlene Bees, two of Donny's new church mamas, come over—it's near the end of singing—to ask Lester and Donny if they'd like a plate of leftovers from dinner. "Ya'll bein big ole hungry boys, we reckon ya'll need a bite ta keep from starvin?"

I can't help but think that's what Jesus does for people. Helps them want to care for God's little children. No matter how long their legs may be and—as Granny K tells it—even though they already "pass a numba twenny still bein kids." On Jesus' list of what's important children rate first place. Anyhow, I've noticed that when it comes to what makes us cry or what makes us happy, pretty much everybody acts like a little kid.

Daddy's so tired tonight his shoulders sag as if a cotton picking burlap bag plum full weighs down each one of them. I hardly ever see him this weary. There's some talk about how people wish we could "tarry a while longer." But we're telling folks that since we're scheduled to be in Sylacauga, then Wetumpka after that, we'll have to wait to see them again next year, Lord willing. We always add "Lord willing" in case Jesus comes back in the Rapture before then.

Nights like this, the Evangelist doesn't have a minute to sit down. People grab his hand and tell him how much his preaching means to them, even while he's trying to keep tonight's message in mind. It's a hard job, preaching.

Daddy doesn't use any notes except when he studies, so all the words are in his heart when he's up there in front of people. And of course he spends time with his books, taking notes, every day. When he's around big towns like Birmingham or Atlanta, he looks for used book stores. Hymn writers like Wm Frederick Faber or Charles and John Wesley always catch his eye. Stories by Tolstoy, too. And the composers—Bach, Beethoven, Tchaikovsky—count as his best friends. That's how he talks about them. It's as if they live down the street and visit often, they're so real in his mind. We talk. Or I should say, Daddy talks and I listen when it comes to people and books he reads.

As we gather tonight, Daddy plays the violin at first, just starts playing the sweetness of this music and Mama joins in about the second line down. Althea finally figures out what he's playing and she adds a run on the vibra harp.

> It will be worth it all when we see Jesus.
> Our trials will seem so small when we see Him.
> One look at his dear face all troubles will erase,
> so bravely run the race till we see Christ.

The music soothes us, like coming in after a long walk to a cup of cool water and a damp cloth for your face. Second time through, Daddy soars on the strings—sounds of near Mozart for hymns—and I hear people starting at different places, joining in with words. *Our trials will seem so small*; two or three others come in with, *one look at his dear face.* Stronger, more voices, for *all troubles will erase.* There's a swell after that with, *So bravely run the race! Till we see Christ.* Then it's from the top a third time, all, together.

That third time through, the church house overflows their cup full of joy in Jesus. Sister Bees and Brother Dayton Jones raise their hands as they sing, tears *trinkling* down their faces, as they say here. When I'm up on the platform watching the folks enjoying songs about Jesus, I think this must be what heaven's like. You can forget the whole streets of gold idea. Blooming four o'clock bushes, a few chinaberry trees and a purple crepe myrtle at a dinner on the ground, followed by music that sings in your heart all week long makes enough heaven for me. But no body asks me, and that's a good thing. My idea of heaven could get me in trouble by disagreeing with the Bible out loud.

Look at the faces in this church house: Elner Ann Bagley, all fussed up this morning because "My cocnut cake jus ain as high as usul. Jus don seem quite right." But Lester devoured two pieces this evening, happy as can be. Sure enough, the worry crease between her eyes is gone now. Praising Jesus, her face lifts and pinks up like Granny's roses.

Souls being saved, that's why we're here. Mama and Daddy talk to me, to Althea too, all the time about this being the only good reason to be alive. When I'm with people who take care of each other, I can see what they mean. Donny and Lester, loved on right here, right now, besides not going to hell. When I was little I thought it was just about hell.

As the song ends, . . . *till we see Christ*, the voices joining in prayer and giving thanks create uproar so full of Holy Ghost wind and happy noise, the roof raises toward heaven. Just like when a flock of songbirds rise up from a sweet gum tree after they've been serenading the neighborhood, you can't tell where their songs end and the fluttering of their wings begin in that rush of what's happening.

Folks have a mind to tarry, I can tell. Linger with us before we go, but tonight every part of the service is shorter than usual. Besides Daddy and Mama being so worn out, all the people have to meet farm mornings at dawn, or even before dawn. Some have to be ready and at the junction to catch the mill bus for the cotton gin or the peanut processing plant by 6 AM, too.

Soon as I hear the Bible passage for the sermon, I know why *It Will Be Worth It All* started us off tonight: Job 13:5: *Ah, if you would only be silent and let silence be your wisdom.* When Daddy preaches about Job and all his troubles—loses his farm and his family; scrapes at boils all over his body—he stirs in some comfort before he begins. He always comes back to Job's saying of God, *Though he slay me, yet will I trust him.* Maybe he chose this text for the post office incident. Chose it for himself. But the part I like is the very end of Job's story rests in the fact that everything changes when he prays for his friends. And that's the part daddy plays up strong this time.

> Who are you praying for tonight?
> Mother, Father, sister, brother . . .
> neighbors?
> Praying doesn't just change the people we pray for—
> prayer changes us!
> *Hallelujah?*
> Job's life turns around . . . *when he prays.*

Daddy asks me to sing *Lord Lay Some Soul Upon My Heart*, and I hardly have three lines out when Lester's at the double doors, heading toward the altar. But of all things, he stops just as I'm singing, *and may I faithfully do my part to win that soul for thee*, fetches those same cigarettes out of his pocket, and out the window they go! Again. But this time, there's no one to catch them.

Men surge around Lester just like they did around Donny. They bring down the Holy Ghost fire, I tell you.

Then something sweet as fresh honeycomb happens. After I sing, I'm standing in the side door, looking out at the trucks parked in the dark. Some of the young people from the Sing stayed around, so there are four or five more vehicles than usual. But Donny's truck, parked in the same place since morning, sits close-in to the windows. He's bent over, his head in his hands propped against his knees. Doing what he can, praying for Lester no doubt.

He stays like that for a long time it seems, but really only five minutes. Then he wipes his face with his shirttail and steps off the flatbed truck. Slowly, he saunters toward the church house. Spotting the cigarettes on the ground, he smashes them with the heel of his boot, twisting them into the dirt. Walks on in the double front doors toward the altar and kneels at the end of a bench close to Lester.

When the men—Daddy, Brother Bees, Brother Wiggins, Brother Jones and Brother Simms—are tapering off in their fervent prayers, Lester rises to his feet, his face wet. Somebody passes over a kerchief pulled out of a back pocket. Donny gets up, too. There they stand, face to face. Donny reaches out first, putting his right hand on Lester's left shoulder, and Lester reaches up and puts his left hand on Donny's right shoulder. Both, standing there looking at each other maybe a teeny bit embarrassed at first. Then they go to grinning. Great big smiles chock full of sunshine even though it's long after dark. Men crowd around in a circle and commence to praising God. It's something.

Women don't come around at a time like this. They stay in their places and let the men deal with each other. Female Christians keep their fervent prayers to themselves—it's usually about men or wayward boys, anyhow—but they don't hold back a bit when it comes to praying or shouting in general.

First thing Monday while Mama helps Daddy and Althea pack up the vibra harp in the long black case, they let me run across to tell Granny K good-bye. She doesn't seem jovial as usual, but she does say, "Mighty glad at Lesser join up Donny at a altar," nodding. "Em cigrettes! Outta at air winder agin!" She claps her hands and whoops, "Em boys is slap down audacious. Hopin at savin sticks. Kindom a heavn ain neva gonna be a same."

Granny reaches over then and messes up my hair like a lot of people do. I have to admit that sort of disappoints me. I thought she'd be different.

Sometimes I think I should say, "Please don't mess up my hair." But I figure people would just answer, "How can you tell?" So why bother.

She does add, which nobody else does, "Ya devlish lil ole angel!" That's while she's setting my hair on end. Seems like she's acting as if it doesn't matter at all to say goodbye even though we may never meet again this side of heaven. The only other thing she says is that she'll play a send off tune and goes right to it, *She'll Be Comin Round the Mountain*, but she sang "she'll be *goin* round the mountain," this time with her own devlish grin.

I waved out the car window for as long as I could see her. Most folks around the church house think Granny K needs to get saved, but no matter, I'm sure I'll see her in heaven some day.

After Enterprise, something changes. Every time I hear Daddy preach about Samson, used to, I saw Samson with hair the same color as the wild honey he found in that messenger-lion's carcass. But now in my mind he looks a whole lot like Donny Johnson.

3

Scratch Ankle, Alabama 1948

No Fooling

- *A Leap Year.*

- *Mahatma Gandhi, spiritual leader of Indian independence, is assassinated. Pakistan charges India with attempting to systematically wipe out Muslims.*

- *Christians cite Israel's existence as God's will for the "latter years" according to Ezekiel 36–39, pointing to Christ's imminent return.*

- *Grand Ole Opry brings country music and country humor home by way of radio, beginning in 1925 as a commercial for National Life and Accident Insurance Company. Week-ends, their stars travel with tent shows, taking turns on the Saturday night program.*

- *R. J. Reynolds, alone, markets 84 brands of tobacco, a main economic source in the Deep South in the 1940s where it is grown and where it is a pervasive personal habit: Snuff, (powder form) not chewed, a pinch put in back of the lower lip. Loose leaf tobacco (sweetened), plug tobacco (pressed into sheets formed with syrup, cut and wrapped in fine tobacco), and twist tobacco are the most common forms of tobacco used in the rural south. Usually carried in aluminum lined pouches or tins, a bit is tucked between gums and cheek and chewed occasionally to release the nicotine. Unwanted juices are expectorated.*

- *Originally, tobacco was thought to have medicinal value due to the narcotic in nicotine. A saying in Punjab is "He who chews tobacco would live to be a hundred."[1]*

1. *Wikipedia.com*, s.v. "tobacco."

- *Sacred Harp music, since the early 1800s, accounts for the shaped-note hymnals in the South. "Shaped notes" are to choral singing [often unaccompanied], as "bluegrass" is to instrumental music. The famed musicologist and cofounder of American Folksongs, Alan Lomax, refers to "White Spirituals from the Sacred Harp."[2]*

- *"The hymn-books . . . [have] round, square, triangular, and diamond-shaped musical notes. In this easy four-shape system, the eight-note scale is divided into two do-re-mi-fa tetrachords: learning the four basic pitch relationships is all you need to keep you on track—plus listening to your neighbor, of course, who, like everybody else, will be vocalizing very loudly. Anyone who has taken part in a 'Sacred Harp' sing knows how effectively the austere, unsentimental, 'open' harmonies contribute to the euphoria engendered by the enthusiastic shared fortissimos."[3]*

- *Such songbooks, often published by Stamps Baxter, were stacked on top of the piano, or on a bench next to the singers in the country churches where the Skondeen Family serve.*

- *Audrey Skondeen turns six years old.*

RIGHT OFF I HAVE to tell you the real name of this place is *Franklin* or you'll never find it on a map. "Bein' called *Scratch Ankle?* Offends some folk. Pay no mind, m'self—ther's other nicknames, too—like Wetumpka." Sister Mary Watford, the pastor, said when she invited us for the meeting a few months back.

"What's the other name for Wetumpka?" Daddy wonders aloud.

"Slapout."

"*Slapout?*"

"Slapout inna country!" She shakes her head, "Now take Scratch Ankle—some boys just hangin around a school yard?—chiggers got aholt a ther ankles."

A kind Brother sent us directions for getting there:

> *After yall smell a paper factry, pass at on by dont at beet all!!! Turn off a mane road at a overflo well next to a telfone xchange—hits a tin box. Foller iss here road 14, 15 mile on, yall see Faith Chapel, prase His name! Stil standin.*

Says he's better at showing the way than Sister Watford. Besides, she later confides, he's very proud of being able to read and write.

2. Alan Lomax, "White Spirituals from the Sacred Harp," www.newworldrecords.org/linernotes/80205.pdf.

3. Martin Bidney, introduction to *Shaped Notes: Stories of Twentieth Century Georgia*, by Patricia Wilcox (Binghamton, NY: Pageant, 2000).

Not many maps cover this road—the one into the heart of Franklin, Alabama—even the county only refers to it as "Franklin County Road #41." But when Daddy inquired about our directions, the man at the general store in Grove Hill says, "Ya'll headed on over ta Scratch Ankle?" then, "Hey! Ainchu at Vangliss come through these parts a while back?" Splat. Spits at and hits the bucket next to the pot belly stove steadied on bricks, center of the store; good shot.

"That's us!" Daddy nods with a smile that most folks can't do anything about but purely enjoy.

The man's brown rimmed mouth turns up one edge in a half grin, opposite side from the spitting-champ corner, "Y'all goin back inna woods! Betta be ready fer ignernce." He guffaws, giving anybody who's listening a good idea of how *ignernce* sounds. I keep still. "Em peoples, they so eat up from em chiggers, we calls it *Scratch Ankle*." Guffaw number two blows out of him. Daddy, saying, "God Bless you, now," beating an exit, pulling me by the hand.

Crunching over the gravel back to our car and trailer stretched in front of the lone gas pump, Daddy mutters, "Everbody lookin for somebody to look down on. Lord have mercy." Shaking his head, he slides behind the wheel again and I jump into the back seat next to Althea.

"Man in there don't have much respect for Franklin, Doris. *Ignorance*, he says. Over there."

Mama says, "Lord help him." She does that *tsk tsk* with her mouth, the dirty shame sound.

"Yeah. Foolishness, that's what it it is. Talkin foolishness. When a man talks outta his head and not his heart." Daddy's aggravated by foolishness in any form. Mama nods.

Both sides of the road stretch out endless rows of dark green craggy bushes now, but next month, August, the leaves will be brown with white cotton fluff balls floating over their branches. You try picking one of those fluffy clouds? At the end of every pod four sharp thorns await your fingers. Folks picking cotton all day end up with bloody hands, besides sore, bent-over backs from loading up the burlap bags that hang down from their shoulders all the way to the ground. Pick drag dump into a wagon, from sun-up, all day long. But fast as they can. Paid by the bag-full.

"Here it comes," I announce, catching my first whiff of the paper mill, even before irregular smoke stacks and a patchwork of tin roofs rise in our sight. But the Alabama River's low water of late summer invites me to splash and drift on an inner tube, drawing on a smile, as much as the stench of a paper mill pulls at a frown. Comes out even.

Mama's focused on finding the overflow well of our instructions. About that time I spot the telephone exchange, nothing more than a black metal box, like the good Brother said. A pipe extended into the air is the overflow well.

We turn onto a gravelly dirt road, the racket sending up dust giants, but at least it's in repair. Bad roads and the gas gauge trouble me plenty on travel days. Worries grow big and bulky loaded with fire crackers that may or may not go off. And so far I'm not prepared for the explosives I'll find in this revival week.

Trails disappear from a few broken down mailboxes back into the woods, clues that people do live around here. Otherwise, jack rabbits darting out of the underbrush and birds congregating on limbs of pine and sweet gum trees count as all the living creatures we see. There are no telephone or electricity poles, the main road is as far as they go.

Daddy slows the car as a yellow school bus that's lost most of its color rumbles toward us. School's out now, but it doesn't look as if it's for school kids, anyhow. Only the driver—a big hulk of a guy leaning over the wheel— can be seen inside, plus boxes, or shapes that resemble signs of some kind. I kneel to peer out the side window through his and our dust as he comes to a halt before a bank of mail boxes just off the road, honking up a storm. That's a new one. Don't figure it to be a mail truck.

Faith Chapel rests in the curve of the road, backed by trees more lacey looking than what we've seen along the way. Pine, live oak, hickory and sweet gum trees jostle for position, with something that resembles wild grape vines stringing them together. No kudzu, with its dark heavy leaves creeping over and smothering everything in sight.

An accidental half moon driveway made of red dirt—tracks from feet, hooves and vehicles—introduces the front of the white washed cement block church house. You have to wonder where the people come from, though.

We roll in just past dinnertime. Ate our loaf of wheat bread and bologna plus carrot and celery sticks on the road beneath a giant pecan tree. It's a Tuesday, about two o'clock. But by 3:30, the place begins to get busy, not what we're expecting. Sister Watford tells us they're here after their shift at the mill or farm chores to help raise a tent. I've never seen a spectacle like this before now.

Men start showing up from all directions, out of the woods on foot or by mule; a bunch of them arrive on the flat bed of a truck still scrappy with leavings of bark and tufts of pine needles from the day's haul to the paper mill, plus two more guys in a pick up with only one door on the passenger side wired shut.

The tent rolls in on another flatbed truck, as Mama says, "My stars! In all my days, I've never seen so much canvas." It takes five hours to raise it up on two center poles and fix the ropes and side poles, and in that time, I have enough of those firecracker worries go off to start a forest fire. But the headache with this tent has only begun.

"We figure more folks has a mind to come on out when the Skondeen Family's in town." Thing is, I don't see a town, but Sister Watford's not speaking for my benefit.

"You be surprise—praise a Lord!—folks that shows up out of these here woods." Now we're talking. "I've been tellin everbody for weeks, 'See can you be here for the feast that's acomin! Make an effort, now!" Sister Mary Watford stands a little straighter, one nod, "Eyetalian Vangliss—Skondee?—he's on the way and his meetins always satisfy your soul. That man of God can *preach*. And his family's singin? Well, y'all have to be here!" She pats me on the head when she says that about his family. I detest people messing with my hair, but with her hand I feel a blessing. I don't know why.

Then she has to add, "I 'member 'xactly what the Vangeliss said over to the Frisco City meeting, 'How can Jesus Christ come in with His fullness—when you're loaded with y'own nonsense, y'own power? S'full a yerself, thinkin yer s'smart!'" She stands there reflecting, then adds. "Ya don't go forgettin the likes a that!"

I don't know where she gets the *Eyetalian* part. Just trying to make sense of our name, I reckon. Better when folks think they know than to keep guessing, that's what Daddy says.

Seems like the men have new energy even after a long day, just knowing they're working for the Lord. Yelling, laughing, praising Jesus for his help. And protection, I'd say, when a pine tree they're using as a tent pole falls and doesn't hit anybody.

That pole does knock a flying squirrel out of a tree, killing him flat dead. I try to revive him with some water drops but it's no use, so I take two sticks, using them like a stretcher, and cart him off the trail that leads to the outhouse, dig a grave with the sticks, and line it with sweet gum leaves. Jesus says that God sees the sparrow fall, so a flying squirrel should get some consideration, too. His fur—besides the blood and mess—covers him in patchy pieces, not a smooth, brown pelt that he appears to have from a distance.

What I never imagined about this tent that's here before my eyes, though, is how we'll light the inside of it since there's no electricity. Never occurs to me, having no occasion to consider it before now. Here's how it goes: giant gasoline lanterns hung on iron hooks from the two center poles.

Testing them out after they finish setting up the inside of the tent, these lanterns flare like torches in the night. My heart stops dead when I hear the *kawhoosh* of the fire and see the flame leap high. The little fluttery beat inside just quit and left a lump lifeless as that squirrel.

Took a minute to start up again. Never mind those firecrackers, they're nothing.

"We started out here in a tent, men folks comin to help. Women come, too, with food for supper? Ah tell you, Lord's been encouragin us ever step a the way." This pastor, besides being female, registers a difference from all the others we meet. Her dream was to go to Southeastern Bible School and they agreed to let her in even though she was only sixteen. Finally, her Pa had more to say than schooling did. When that first tent materialized, Bible School didn't.

God called Sister Mary into these particular woods when she was eighteen years old. She's been preaching since she was sixteen and she's 26, now. Says Psalm 45 jumped out at her, that's how she knew she had to preach. First, the part early on, ". . . thou art fairer than the children of men: grace is poured into thy lips: therefore God hath blessed thee for ever." Now that's truth to tell.

We're talking around her parent's sturdy pine table over a Saturday supper of fried cheese sandwiches served with a jar of pickled beets her mother put up. "Not a green in sight," is Mama's only plaint on our way back to the trailer. "Cheese gives some protein at least." *Sigh.* Sometimes Mama worries as much about saving folks from their bad food habits here as she does about saving souls. Don't tell her I said that. Not that she doesn't pray about people's eternal damnation, like the rest of us, but she and Daddy do notice white bread, biscuits, cornbread, hog grease, pork and too few vegetables at most tables.

Sister Mary Watford's a tiny woman of God—I like how that sounds, *woman of God*—shorter than Mama. Her hair reminds me of colors in a ripe wheat field, all those shifting hues of gold and brown, fine strands fall into soft waves even though it's pulled into a neat holiness woman bun. Eyes, steady with purpose that look brown as pecan shells but then surprise you with flecks of iridescent green, like a beetle's wing in sunshine. Those eyes land on you with enough weight to go deep.

Her dresses complete a preacher lady—proper, long sleeves and high necks—in soft colors trimmed in lace and flower prints. She lives with Papa and Mama Watford about a mile on from the church house, just off the main road. Her Papa farms with more success than most folks around here. A big wide porch all across the front of their house says right up front, *Y'all come on in* with its swing on one end and four o'clocks, red and yellow, growing wild around the steps.

Inside, the center hall is long and cool, separating four, really, four bedrooms from the living room, dining room and then a big sunny kitchen across the back. "Lord's been real good to us." I can see what they mean. Unpainted wood, like all the houses here, with a sharply slanted tin roof that plays music in the rain. Better than a mansion to me.

When my eyes rest on Sister Mary—the name for Jesus' Mama, but nobody mentions it—her smooth cheeks and perfect nose remind me of the girl in Palmolive soap ads. In *Life* or *Saturday Evening Post* magazines under the soap girl's picture it says, "Keep that schoolgirl complexion." I'd say Sister Mary's managed that right well. Naturally, her Holiness woman hair appears different from the short bob of the girl in the ad, but she's every bit as beautiful. Plus, Jesus lives in her heart and that always shows.

A wee baby here in the Franklin woods crying out to Sister Mary even louder than the Psalm, though, made her notice that this part of Alabama needs care. "Girl child, tiny little ole thing. Her Ma and Pa said her eyes never did open up after she's born." Remembering, she grimaces, "Course they worried. So they carried her on over ta auvr house and my Papa fetched up a healin preacher from Monroeville to pray. And you know! That baby's eyes opened right up. Praise Jesus!"

The baby's whole family was saved, right then and there. But later, with no church house anywhere around, they went back on the Lord. Why, the man even went to plowing on Sunday. Mary Watford recollected that family, though. She told her Papa that people in those parts needed preaching. And he said, "Well, Little Sister, why don't you go." Sister Mary stopped to explain that Little Sister is what her Papa calls her.

With that she got my full attention. Good thing nobody ever up and called me Little Sister even though I am one. I might have had to act ugly like to squash that notion. My name is Pauline Audrey Skondeen. Mama and Daddy figured the Pauline + Skondeen to be a little too rhyming, so my middle name, *Audrey*, works out fine. But *Little Sister*? No thank you.

Psalm 45:7, 10: ". . . God, thy God, hath anointed thee with the oil of gladness . . . Hearken, O daughter, and consider, and incline thine ear; forget also thine own people, and thy father's house. So shall the king greatly desire thy beauty: for he is thy Lord; and worship thou him." And so she went on and did all that. Well, she is still in her father's house, but serving her King is all that matters. That's her call and she's sticking to it for as long as she lives. Her eyes turn on their power and light when she says that.

Sister Mary has shelves of books she studies every morning during her quiet time along with her Bible. And she keeps watch over her speech habits almost as much as my Mama. 'Course she does lop off the ends of words and say *auvr* for *our* and *chirrun*—sometimes with a quick hint of an L—for *children*, but that just keeps time with the soft rhythm of the language in these parts.

While the grown ups talk Jesus, still around the table—Althea considers herself one of them even though she doesn't say a thing—Mama excuses me to find the outhouse. Finding my way, I notice their barn's door, heavy, weather seasoned gray timbers sagging on the hinges, leaning away from the opening far enough for me to slip in to the cool dusty darkness.

Some contented hens cozied in a pile of straw carry on their usual conversations with clucks and murmurs. But what I see as my eyes adjust, strikes me curious: on one wall, shelves high as the loft, displaying the biggest cans ever. On the tops of the ones I can reach, printing tells the contents, *beans, peanut butter*. A barrel nearby, too. Climbing on a wood box next to it and lifting up the lid, I spy more sacks piled inside, containing dry beans, corn meal and powdered milk. You'd think they were fixing to feed the whole army of Israel. Eliza Watford, Mary's Mama, might have something to say about that.

I'm thinking this has to do with the conversation before supper. Acting as if I'm paying no mind to what grown-ups are saying brings in a mess of information. Brother Johnnie Watford—Sister Mary's Papa—says they get worried about being stranded out here and not able to get supplies. He and Daddy were talking about Communism's taking over at the time. Of course Daddy managed to switch to Jesus coming back again being the answer. Could be any day. Any minute. With that thought I figure I better be done with my investigation and quit my sneaking around. Now I really do need to find the outhouse.

Here's one outdoor toilet that demands respect, I have to say. Dug real deep. Cobwebs mostly cleaned out and a basket of fresh looking fluffy corncobs.

And look at this, *three* coverless catalogues stacked alongside the opening: *Sears Roebuck, J.C. Penney*, and *Montgomery Ward*. They stock up in this house. I tear out a page while I'm sitting here—Mama taught me this—wad it up, then rub it real good.

When I complain about rank, dark, falling down toilets, Mama says I can tell my kids about them some day. I don't think so. Folks around these parts would *harumph*, like they do about ghost and goblin stories, which of course we don't believe in 'cept for the *Holy* Ghost, saying, *This here ain no bed time story*. Exactly. Then they'd spit a thick stream of brown tobacco juice out one corner of their mouths, a big, dark exclamation mark.

People talking on telephone party lines speed up both good news and bad, but no phone lines reach through these woods. Here, we have to depend on chatter at mailboxes or folks talking while they ride the mill bus.

Saturday nights, gathered around a neighbor's radio to hear *Grand Ole Opry* doesn't count for spreading news. Then, everybody's taken up with music and laughter.

Our family has a short wave radio that runs on batteries, fortunately. Important for hearing the news and that's all. Daddy's glued to it every day, listening for word about the Berlin blockade. Russia up to mischief again scares him silent.

Of course we never listen to *Opry*. Saturday night belongs to Sunday morning. But I got to thinking one Saturday afternoon about the folks I overheard at the Mercantile in Monroeville that morning planning to walk over to their neighbor's place for the *Opry* that evening. Maybe their laughing, singing and being neighborly gets them ready to praise the Lord on Sunday as much as our praying and Bible reading does. It was just a thought flitting through on account of the feeling I caught from those people. Wouldn't pay to mention it out loud.

This Sunday, Daddy knows that the kind of preaching folks consider exciting gets around and word like that will kick up the talk a notch and pick up the numbers by Monday night. The whole week gets a boost. He aims to fill this tent, I overheard him murmur to Mama. So far, Wednesday, Thursday and Friday nights, there've been crowds down front near the music but that still leaves some of those back benches—made from logs, flattened on one side—empty.

My birthday six lands on this first Sunday of our Scratch Ankle meeting, too. Next Sunday, our last day here, includes dinner on the ground though, and that would be even better. Then there'd be cakes I'd pretend are for me.

Auntie Dorie's box sent from San Francisco for my birthday arrived weeks ago. It was waiting for us when we showed up at the General Delivery window in Franklin the first time. The Post Master—must be, since he's the only one there—grinned his approval for giving him something to talk about. "Ain had no piece a mail in iss here place from at fur way in a US a A!" He goes on to tell us about every letter that came through during the war. The man keeps track.

A Post Office proves the size of the town. Two of the Scratch Ankle PO's could fit inside our trailer. Maybe three.

A piece up the red dirt road from the Post Office—the only other building in Franklin—the Methodist Church stands strong. Fresh white paint with narrow black trim around tall, wide clear glass windows always sparkling in the sunshine. Passing by their green grass and "picky" fence, smiling's natural, thinking God must like His house looking so beautiful. Daddy says Methodists used to have great revivals, not the kind where speaking in tongues proves the Holy Ghost shows up, but still you can say *great* for all the souls being saved and excitement sweeping through towns.

"Course John Wesley preached fire from heaven." Daddy, thinking out loud the day we first saw the church says, "But he stopped short of speaking in tongues and prophesying. Far as I know." Pentecostals figure on new revelations of the Holy Ghost every day if need be.

Anyhow, Aunt Dorie's present is so big the post office man has to hand it to us out the back door. Her packages splash elegance outside and inside. This time, the inside contains a blue coat with a velvet collar.

"Where you goin to wear that!" Daddy claims her gifts are useless. He'd rather she sent money, but Aunt Dorie shops the sales. Mama speculates she probably bought this at Joseph Magnin during their winter sale this spring, or maybe a Leap Year Day sale on February 29th. We know it's *Joseph Magnin* because the box is deep almost red pink and ballet-shoe-pink stripes tied with real satin ballet pink ribbon.

I'll wear it all right. Mama stores it under their bed in front, and every time I help her make their bed, I rub my fingers over the velvet collar.

Daddy says birthdays don't matter besides thanking the Lord you're alive another year to preach the Gospel. We're looking for Jesus to return any day and take us home to Glory and that could be before your next birthday so why should anybody care about the day you were born. Being born again and ready for the rapture is what really counts. When the Sunday School kids sing *Happy Birthday God Bless You Audrey*, yelling the words and giggling in-between, Daddy makes a big fuss about what great singers they are and goes on into the Sunday morning service. He doesn't like to start late. Daddy's not in favor of a lot of foolishness, like I said.

But since it's my birthday, I can arrange for my own gifts so I pretend he's going to preach the 23rd Psalm for me. This message about a farm boy who's special to God surprises everybody. Every time. He's the boy I was supposed to be named for—Billy David—after Daddy and a shepherd who became a King of Israel. A girl showing up instead shocked my Daddy and Mama.

Daddy keeps notes when local preachers visit our meetings—who, what, where—so he'll be sure which text of his preaching they've witnessed. That's how he knows Sister Watford has never heard this sermon.

The Preacher starts out slow, telling the children about little David, just a kid tending sheep, playing on his harp. Could be a mouth harp—harmonica—I'm thinking. Plenty of those around here. This boy has a sling shot, too. Daddy demonstrates, aiming out the window. It's protection David uses against wild beasts that come against the flock and later on, the giant Goliath who threatens Israel's army.

When the Evangelist gives kids his attention and acts as if the grownups are only listening in, it works *right good* as they say in Alabama. Letting adults think they're eavesdropping sneaks them into a bigger picture. They watch his every move. But if he's preaching to them? Some doze off or stare out at the trees.

A picture of Jesus, *The Good Shepherd*, is on the fans from the Monroeville Funeral Home and the Evangelist props one on the rough pine pulpit while he preaches, pacing the sawdust in front of it. Tent flaps are tied up during the day unless nobody's around and let down only after service ends. Without a microphone, the Preacher walks up and around, plotting how to get his voice out there to everyone, telling the story.

> Sheep move with the Shepherd—he knows where to go
> for pools of cool water and green meadows for grazing.
> Helpless!—sheep?—helpless animals without
> a Good Shepherd's care.
> This Shepherd calls them by name. Every one!
> He understands they're weak.

The walking stick in his hand becomes a shepherd's crook, guiding the "animals" right in front of the children all gathered on what must be the oldest piece of canvas in the county, a holey leftover from a long departed tent. Could be from the first tent they pitched here before they had a church house. Now the Preacher's talking for the Shepherd:

> *This lamb tends to wander, have to keep an eye on her . . .*
> *This one runs into brambles, needs healing oil . . .*
> *Poor old Wooly falling into that hole, too lame to walk yesterday . . .*
> See? Shepherd carries a limping lamb like this—
> front legs over one shoulder,
> back legs over the other—a thick, warm shawl,
> til the sheep can walk again on his own.
> Tenderness! . . . his touch, healing,
> and often, in the dark, some places in the rocks
> they pass through are
> so deep the sun is out of sight. Imagine!
> How do *you* feel in the dark . . .

Tommy Miller blurts out, "I'm not scared . . . I even go to the *outhouse* in the dark!" poking his thumbs through his dungaree straps and grinning his bright, toothy, crooked grin. The Preacher bends in front of the burr headed little guy who's got the attention, and says, "Well, let me shake your hand, Tommy, I'll need you later on . . ." and continues.

> Good Shepherd, their Savior, takes
> them—safe!—through the darkest valley.
> Every single sheep present and accounted
> for and not one missing.

Time for shouting. "Thankya, thankya," praising Jesus for finding us, healing us, and keeping us in the fold. Rescued one more time by the Good Shepherd.

> And when enemies of the sheep, the wolf,
> coyote, bear, start sneaking around . . .

I'm glad he didn't mention the lion, I don't want kids to be afraid of the Lion of Judah. He's sweet comfort. As the Preacher's voice reaches a powerful pitch, he whips out the sling shot and again aims it out the window:
    POW! the prowler—that Devil!—slinks away.
Everybody cheers for the Shepherd, adults shout, "Go on, praisa Lord! Go *on*" and, "Oooooee! a Lord sa good," full-on certain how it feels to put satan on the run. Kids jump up and clap and laugh, dancing around. Takes a minute to settle everybody down again.
    "Glory to His Naaaame!"
    "Halluuu!"
    "Thank you Jayzus."
With this momentum the Preacher speeds up:

> *Surely goodness and mercy shall follow me*
> *all the days of my life . . .*
> Tell you what I'm going to do
> I'm going to name you—Tommy—*Goodness.*
> Come on up here, and now,
> who wants to be *Mercy?*

Once Tommy's on the move toward the Preacher, other kids are anxious to get in on the action. Nell's hand is waving as if she's holding a *"pick Me"* flag. She and her sister Grace toss their heads with the most vivid flow of red wavy hair you will ever see. Nell's eight, but she's the same size as Tommy who's six. She has on a brand new feed sack dress, yellow daises scattered all over it, the one I saw at the Mercantile in Elba still full of chicken scratch. No wonder she feels like being up front.

> All right now Goodness and Mercy
> you have to keep up with me, ya hear?
> Don't let me out of your sight!

Calling out his instructions, the Preacher starts moving slowly up the sawdust aisle toward the rolled-up flaps in the back of the tent, *Goodness* up close and *Mercy*, realizing she better move a little faster. Then the Preacher takes off running. The people, startled, laugh and clap as he races around the side, jumps up on the platform and darts around benches where the singers—not really a choir—sit, a stack of accidentally nudged hymnbooks go flying as he jumps off the other side, and heads around to the front again with *Goodness* in hot pursuit and *Mercy* determined to catch up. Everybody's yelling, cheering, "Well, I'll be!" and, "Bless m'soul!"

He skids around sawdust corners and jumps over log benches, on the move. Laughter slips out of the most surprised faces, some that may not have grinned since 1935. Slapping their knees, jumping up to see where the race has taken *Goodness, Mercy*, and the Evangelist.

Slowing as he strides back down the aisle toward the pulpit, the Preacher catches *Goodness* and *Mercy* by their hands, one on either side. They all turn, laughing, to face the congregation on their feet, now, shouting. The Preacher finishes with a hallelujah flourish,

> Praise the Lord?
> *Goodness and Mercy*
> *are right here with you, keepin up!*
> See here?
> Hallelujah!
> *All the days of your life!*

True to the power of the mailbox gatherings and the mill buses on the move up and down these roads, word spreads. Bits of enthusiastic news return to us, too, "I'll be!—a mean a cain stop thinkin bout *Goo'ness* an *Mercy*? On a run! Ever time a sees at pitcher of a Good Shepherd? Ah'm gonna reckleck!" Monday, the tent covers a crowd, all right. Nearly full. That adds fuel to the fire of Daddy's preaching and the Holy Ghost moves in for the rest of the week.

Speaking of "fuel" and "fire" though, those fire lights are never out of my mind. One quick move colliding with a pole, they could explode. By now, I've listened in on folks talking about these gas lanterns, telling stories

I wish I hadn't overheard. Daddy stays clear of the poles, I promise. You have to keep shouting-people away, too. A deacon gently guided Sister Spelman past the pole with the torch at the top when she was dancing with the Holy Ghost while we were singing *I'll Fly Away*.

Mama says not to be concerned, but she can't fool me. One night when I was supposed to be sleeping, she whispered something about those *fire pots* in the tent scaring her to death. Daddy said a few words, but all I heard was *trusting* and *Lord's protection*.

Tuesday's child is full of grace, you ever heard that? I ask Grace who shakes her head, *no*. I study on rhymes that tell a story. They remind me of the book of Proverbs in the Bible, or Ecclesiastes.

> *Monday's child is fair of face,*
> *Tuesday's child is full of grace,*
> *Wednesday's child is full of woe,*
> *Thursday's child has far to go,*
> *Friday's child is loving and giving,*
> *Saturday's child works hard for a living,*
> *But the child who is born on the Sabbath Day*
> *Is bonny and blithe and good and gay.*

I had a suspicion that's how Grace got her name, so I go on and ask was she born on a Tuesday. She returns a real puzzled look for my question.

Nell, quick like jumps in and says her sister's name *come from a grace a God, a course*. She said that last part as if I am too dumb and too little and she has to teach me something even though the Evangelist is my Daddy.

This particular Tuesday of revival week tallies up some strange goings on. Before six o'clock—service doesn't start till seven—folks start trickling in off the road. Some walking the mile or two from their houses and others in pickups with kids loaded in the back bumping in through a cloud of dust, real casual, as if they never thought what time it might be.

Grace and Nell arrive first and knock on our trailer door asking polite as can be, can I come out early for church. Daddy frowns at me and says what he always does, *no running around*, and *no foolishness*, but he does let me go out to see them. He's not so tensed up when the crowds are good.

Their Ma and Pa park the truck way over on the other side of the tent instead of right out front as usual which seems odd. They lower the back tent flaps, too, so I figure they're with the others no doubt planning to pray in the Holy Ghost before the night's meeting starts. They gather at the dinner-on-the-ground tables out back, leaving the inside of the tent free for Mama, Daddy, and Althea to tune up the instruments. A little hard for Althea since we have no electricity—*the vibra harp has no vibe*—as Daddy's been saying. No little bell-ringing sound, but she hits the mallets on the metal keys anyhow, and people are fascinated.

Gracie and Nell wear their matching feed sack dresses from last year, a little small on them now. Tickled to see them so early, I laugh and say they look ready for a party! They pitch me the strangest look.

We stay out front of the tent, the three of us gathered around a stump that has a tree sprouting out of one side of it where the mailbox for Faith Chapel nails on tight. Nell says she's the teacher and we're doing our letters, using the stump as our desk. She's every bit as bossy as my big sister, I'm very sorry to report.

Just before one of us gets a whipping for talking in school, Nell's Ma calls out to come on, *now*. Nell rounds us up and herds us into the tent for a short cut by way of a sawdust trail, zigzagging around log benches, up the aisle and to the left of the altar; out the other side near the rear flaps dropped to protect the instruments.

I'm still wondering what their Ma wants with us at a prayer meeting since we've been quiet and not rowdy or running—what's so important that interrupts our play?—when we round the back of the tent.

Nothing in my life so far prepares, me for what I see. Every person who's been straggling in from all directions gathered around the biggest white coconut cake with six candles blazing on top. Balloons—three red ones—tied from low branches of a pine tree stumble in the breeze, merry and bright, *Happy Birthday dear Audrey, Happy birthday to you Happy birthday, God bless you, Happy birthday to you.*

They laugh and shout *Surprise!* to my shock. Grace explains in a whispered rush of words that they had to wait till Tuesday on account of the *Rolling Store* coming through on Tuesdays.

Right here I have to tell you about the Rolling Store. That's what the old yellow school bus was, the one that lumbered by us the Tuesday we arrived? Today it stopped in front of the mailbox stump out front and went to honking and sure enough, people start showing up out of the woods from directions I've never seen a living soul. All told, there probably weren't more than a dozen, but it sure looked like a crowd. The driver—"Sledge" they call him, at least that's how it sounds—explained to me that anything you can buy in Mobile, you can get a little bit on this here Rolling Store. Even a decent meal, according to Sledge, forty-nine cent ham sandwich on Wonder bread and a moon pie.

Stamps, empty feed sacks for sewing, full feed sacks for livestock, Spam and candy. Hard to believe if it wasn't staring right at you in rows and stacks and loaded shelves. A whole row of government surplus cans, tops gone, filled with marshmallow peanuts, watermelon slices (pressed coconut), plump pink bubble gum twisted in pink paper, peanut butter sticks—called *chicken bones*—in brown paper wraps and lumps of salt water taffy twisted in plain wax paper. A person can dream on that Rolling Store.

Back to the birthday cake, though, 'cause that's a dream come true. White marshmallow—called *seven minute*—icing fluffed with coconut all over, yellow cake on the inside for three layers, and pineapple filling in-between each one. I've never seen another one like it. Somebody made yellow sheet cake, too, with seven minute topping and coconut to be sure there was enough to go around, but it can't match that layer cake for purely royal splendor.

Grace and her sister bought me five lollipops on the Rolling Store and tied them with a yellow ribbon like a bouquet. Mama says I can use the ribbon for my hair.

Daddy, Mama, and Althea show up at the party just as I'm blowing out the candles. Mama's only words, "Well, I'll be!" As soon as I see Daddy my right foot starts tingling and my breath gets shaky. Scared he'll say *Help Us Lord* and shut down the merrymaking. But their surprise works fine. Daddy never would say *sure, go ahead* with a party before revival. *Foolishness!* But nobody asked.

Pickens boys sing the birthday song loudest. They're natural born twins—named Gerold and Herold—whose straw-colored hair sticks out at all angles as if it was just raked up in a field. You can tell them apart by Herold's lazy eye. Their Ma describes them as boys with hair nobody cain't rule over, big ears, 'n at eye at goes off, but it don't matter cause em boys loves Jesus. Praisa Lord. *Em boys lovvves Jayzus.*

She believes that when they sing? That's the proof. Sounds like ten instead of two. She's right about that.

Mama tells me when I ask that I was born on a Friday. Now, Friday's child is loving and giving but this time I'm loved and given to. Doesn't that beat all? Of course Tuesday's full of grace and that's a fact for this Tuesday. The only party for me in my life.

I'm not mentioning any of this Friday/Tuesday stuff to Mama and Daddy, you understand. First off, Mama might wash my mouth out with soap for repeating fortune teller's rhymes, that's what she calls the Monday's

Child poem. I saw it on the wall at a library in Miami last winter and when I told Mama about it, she had a pure fit.

On top of that, feeling proud about a party—I'm pretty sure that's how she'd see it—well, Daddy might whip that right out of me. One good thing about being more grown up now that I'm six is that I'm learning when to keep my mouth shut. That boy I was supposed to be, Billie David, helps me with that. He doesn't talk to anybody about anything.

By Sunday, Daddy's *plum wore out*, he groans to Mama. The edges of his mouth hint at a grin while he's saying it, though. With no electricity he has to use his voice a lot harder, not to mention trying to cover the crowd by walking the aisles more as he preaches.

Sister Mary Watford beams her blessing all over her face that Sunday. And in the last service, itself—after dinner on the grounds and an afternoon Sing—folks pop up all over, telling how they've been "res-cued from sin n shaame! Praisa *Lorrrd*" or "Pulled on up outta at hole a slid into, have mercy! Back slidin fer yers."

Two teen girls, one a little slip of a skinny thing with strawberry hair to her waist, tears flowing over freckles like a flash flood creek washing flat pebbles on the red earth, praises Jesus for saving them. Always together, you don't catch sight of one without the other. Her friend laughs loudly, swinging her blond hair and telling everybody who'll listen that she totes around all the fat left off Suzy, motioning to her tiny buddy.

The mother of one of them—Suzy, I'm guessing—hops up after Suzy's testimony, saying that she's *a-prayin down a Holy Ghost* on them girls. Raising her hands, pale reddish hair pulling free from a haphazard braid, she adds, that they might receive now that they believes. Then she goes to speaking in tongues, twirling in circles while she delivers dizzying words we can't understand.

That's the question after somebody's saved: *Have you received since you believed?* That means seeking for the Holy Ghost to fill them along with speaking in tongues to show it.

Sister Brady rises slowly. She stands out by her stiff, straight posture, square shoulders, always the same dress, gray sturdy fabric shiny with wear. Lace at the throat. Long sleeves. Black hair in a roll at the nape of her neck covered in a net. Her long face bones frame taut pale skin, always slightly lifted as if in prayer, or maybe just not of this world; her dark straight brows join together by furrows of concern above eyes the color of a cloudy sky, pale to brooding. She pulls herself together real tight and keeps every bit in order. Folks whisper that her husband's a drinker, bless her heart.

This is one of those times when there's a lull, a quiet patience. Waiting. Waiting for an interpretation, a message from tongues. Sister Brady's eyes close, her hands extend in front of her, "If thou wilt call on my naaame and seek ma faace thou shalt be saaaved and thou shalt be filled . . . (pause) . . . filled with *power from on high* . . ."

Suzie's Mama starts in crying, a sound of such relief. Sister Watford's right there, her arm around the woman's bony shoulders as if she's holding her together. No doubt Sister Mary was there when Suzie was born, when the midwife sent for her to come pray over this woman giving birth. I heard her telling Mama some bloody stories that made my hair curl up even tighter. What a hard time they have around here living long enough to be born or living through birth itself.

Pentecostal churches aren't common in this part of Alabama. Franklin's carved out close to the county line, and Sister Watford says that over that line there's no Pentecostal message at all. She's talking to Mama and Daddy Saturday afternoon when they're sitting in the church house fixing to pray over Sunday, "Where these good people going to find Truth? Where they going to find Healing?"

"An the young folks . . ." What happens to these young girls as they grow up and marry matters as much to Sister Mary's heart as if they were born in her own house.

"Many of m'folks here—bless their hearts—never had the vantage of education. Appalachia people. Come to these woods searchin for a livin however they can find it."

"30s, after the Depression?" Daddy questions, head shaking. He tells me stories about his own hunger and picking beans to stay alive when his family came to California after drought and crop failure in Canada.

Sister Watford nods, paces a few minutes in front of the altar in the church house, sits back down, "Good-hearted people, but not so sure 'bout themselves. No readin. No writin."

"Lord help them," Mama's always praying out loud, "they need Jesus. No different from the rest of us."

"Don't you know! And with the Lord's hep, folks that come to this here church house take care of each other. See to their chilrun. Pray them through to the Holy Ghost . . . never alone! Hallujah."

Daddy finishes with, ". . . heal us, Lord, heal us. You know we have no friend like you . . . Heal our bodies. Heal our sin sick souls!"

Sometimes it's hard to tell where the praying starts up and the talking leaves off. I like that. *Have a little talk with Jesus, makes things right,* the song says.

When tongues erupt in an evening service, which is when the Holy Ghost gives somebody a message in an odd language the rest of us can't understand like Susie's mom did, a "prophecy" in our own language is supposed to follow. Sister Brady gave Susie's mom's prophecy. Of course, the prophecy is usually the kind of speech that you read in the Bible, with *thees* and *thous* and *comest* sprinkled through it.

Sometimes a group of folks experience the Holy Ghost all at once and they pop up all over the place like kernels of corn when the heat runs high before the lid's in place. Talking over each other, no prophecy can clear things up with a message.

Daddy doesn't like it when tongues break out during his preaching. He says the Lord's given him the message for the moment. If the tongues aren't too loud, he keeps going like he didn't hear it. Being interrupted annoys him. "Gets me off track," he mutters to Mama who only says, "hmmm . . ." or nothing, not wanting to chance insulting the Holy Ghost.

Good thing Daddy remembers to sing Sister Watford's favorite, "Tis So Sweet to Trust in Jesus" this final Sunday. His violin plays along and Sister Mary looks as if she's heading on up in the Rapture:

> *Tis so sweet to trust in Jesus*
> *Just to take him at his word . . .*
> *Jesus, Jesus how I love him . . .*
> *Oh for grace to love him more*

Loving Jesus is Sister Mary Watford's own love story, the genuine romance of her life.

The heat of this Sunday sizzles till a dashing rain squelches it, steam rising off the earth while the Sing is happening this afternoon. Young people sitting on fenders and flatbeds outside, plus folks who seem scared of the insides of a church house—even when it's a tent—rush for cover in their vehicles or under the back flaps of the tent. About that same time, we get to singing *Rescue the Perishing* and can't get stopped:

> *Res-cue the per-ish-ing Care for the dy-ing,*
> *Snatch them in pit-y from sin and the grave;*

Stories in the verses make songs matter to their very end, the next verse telling, *Tho they are slighting Him, still He is waiting.* And the one after that has more to say about sinners, *Down in the human heart, crushed by the tempter, feelings lie buried that Grace can restore.*

See? Singing delivers Gospel, too, including what Holiness people must do for the sinners, *Rescue the perishing, duty demands it!* After that last verse with all the rain-drenched backsliders and sinners no doubt sheltered in the back of the tent, we sing that chorus ten times at least:

Rescue the perishing, Care for the dying;
Je-sus is merciful, Jesus will save.

The hymnals here—tattered and most without covers—are shaped notes, like all the Stamps Baxter Hymnals down here in the South. Shaped notes, not round like the notes in song books in California, show the sounds by their design. But I don't know how much that counts, since like I said, folk only use books to call the page number then sing with no book at all.

When I tried to find out more from Mama, like how's a person supposed to figure out the sound from the shape of the notes, she just said, "It's *Fa Sol La* sounds, the scale? Like when you practice scales on the piano, only these are for singing." And that ends my study.

What I do know is that when folks here sing, they just open up and let the sounds come flying out. Look straight ahead over top everyone sitting in the congregation, like they're aiming for an unseen guest out there in the dark. Maybe Jesus or Moses on his way to the Promised Land.

Take tonight. Our last night here and you know how I dread pulling away from this surprising place. Except, of course, the gasoline lanterns. Tonight, Sister Watford insists on a Love Offering to "help y'all on your way."

She arranges Althea and me standing in back of a Bible open on the altar. People come around to put their offering on the opened pages while the singers stand up on the platform letting loose, *If We Never Meet Again This Side of Heaven.*

Now, I say *letting loose* because that's just how it goes. Full blast, straight ahead, no pretty stuff. "We done it fer Glory n Heav'n," the roundest, rosiest-faced singer of all told Daddy who said, "Well, praise the Lord, we'll all be singing these songs with the angels one day." And that's as good a description as I can come up with for the people of Franklin. Angels. Right here, right now.

My poem about the days of the week? Well, every one of those days describe these angels—fair of face, full of Grace, loving and giving, work hard for a living, full of woe, long way to go, just to get to town, sure enough, and good, with bright spirits—all, shining for Jesus. What else can a person possibly want.

Since that first supper we had with Sister Watford and her folks, I've been mulling over her call to these parts. *Big job for a little person*, I overheard

Daddy comment to Mama. But like the Psalm that spoke to her says, when the King—and that means *God*—calls you, you better listen. I looked up that Psalm myself in Mama's Bible, and here's how it is at the end: *I will make thy name to be remembered in all generations: therefore shall the people praise thee for ever and ever.* (Psalm 45:17) Now I reckon that's supposed to be about God's name, but I think that just might mean Sister Mary, too.

And you know what? A lot of times when I think of Jesus, I think of Sister Mary. I spoke to Jesus about it, saying I mean no disrespect to Him and he says it's fine, he thinks a whole lot of her, too. Comes to me in pictures: Patting the heads of little kids in blessing as she smiles or laughs out loud, holding babies and talking to them like they understand every word, anointing a man who's been feverish for weeks and needs to be out there working for his family. Her arm close around a woman who's weeping.

4

Aberdeen, Mississippi 1948

Living Color

- *The US Supreme Court in unanimous decision orders the state of Oklahoma to admit a Negro to the University of Oklahoma Law School.*
- *In Jackson, Mississippi, 4,000 true white Jeffersonian Democrats meet to oppose President Truman's civil rights program.*
- *Army segregation is ended by President Truman when he signs executive order #9981.*
- *Executive order #9980, also signed by the President, creates a Fair Employment Board to eliminate racial discrimination in federal employment.*
- *African-American leaders end their calls to blacks to stop enlisting in the US Military if armed services remain segregated.[1]*
- *Audrey Skondeen is six years old.*

Now I NEVER TOOK our car—a DeSoto—to be historic in nature until we arrived in Aberdeen, Mississippi. As you can see, I can spell the name of this state, Mama made sure of that. Anyhow, I'm bringing this type of history up because the Deacon from Aberdeen Assembly of God tells us that Hernando DeSoto stopped through this town in 1540. Our Aberdeen Deacon is right proud of this being an historic town. Made me consider our DeSoto with a little more respect.

---

1. Voices of Civil Rights website, created in 2004 by American Association of Retired People (AARP), Leadership Converence on Civil Rights (LCCR), and Library of Congress.

When Daddy introduces his family, the Deacon says, "Two girls, n'ah got me fo-ah boys." Wags his head and purses his lips, "Em boys, they good workers. Haw! Em boys is regler mules, praisa Lawd."

Daddy has to make the joke, then, that he told his wife that if this little one—being me—was a boy, he'd stand on his head. Which prompts the Deacon, praisa Lawd, to say, "Ifn ya learn't ta stan on ya haid? T'wern't cause a no male chile!" He thinks this is funny as can be.

Althea's history lessons mention Hernando DeSoto, and how he discovered the Mississippi River—largest river in the US—which, if you think about it, how could you miss it? Althea says Explorer DeSoto died in Arkansas on the banks of the Mississippi. Brought me up a picture of this Spaniard in those ballet looking tight pantaloons keeling over after a cat fish fry and too many hush puppies like the kind Neely Sasser's Mama makes. That temptation can slip right over you real easy like and cause a person to succumb. Trouble is, DeSoto, being Roman Catholic and all, I don't think we'll see him in heaven to ask any questions and get the specifics.

Daddy keeps calling this Deacon, who met us at the church house to help us get parked and hook up the electricity, "Brother." Probably can't figure out the name "Brother" told him. That happens. The way we say a name differs from the way people here might say it. Take "Miller," it becomes *Mirrer*, leaving the bell sounds out, or Franklin Delano Roosevelt, a big hero in these parts, that comes out as Frankn Denner Roosvet. My ears constantly adjust but sometimes they take a while to catch up.

Deacon *Brother* keeps pouring out facts of Aberdeen like filling cups at a tea party. Not only have famous people *lived* here, somebody named Sykes—near as I can understand, Justice of the Mississippi Supreme Court— but the first Negro Senator *died here*. Personally I don't know if I'd want to be known as a place where a famous person suddenly went to meet his final reward while attending a church conference. Daddy says, "Well praise the Lord, he died serving Jesus, Amen?" Deacon looks a little surprised. Didn't occur to him. Negroes don't seem to factor into people's thinking a whole lot, I notice.

That sure put me in a curious mind about this Senator. I'll find the library—rich looking as this town is, it has to have one—and talk to the library lady about him.

One wide avenue in Aberdeen named Commerce Street, brags out loud with wide lawns and the biggest houses I've seen this side of New Orleans. Although Columbus, about 25 miles away, scatters beautiful houses all around the Mississippi University of Women campus. Very fancy. *A bunch of egg-heads*, Daddy says, whatever that means. Mama didn't say anything, but sometimes her silence is louder than others, this time I think it's for a sadness and maybe a hope that didn't happen. Her family afforded nursing school for her older sister, but there wasn't enough money left for Mama's advanced schooling. She wanted to be a school teacher.

Our Deacon tour guide proves more interested in pointing out the features of the church house than continuing to discuss the town. While he hooks up our electricity and helps Daddy carry in the vibra harp cases, he tells us just how this place came about. Daddy welcomes the extra toting-power.

Of course we can see the church house is red brick, but Deacon Brother's one of the men who put those bricks in place, *we done it to a Glory a God*. A little flame of pride flares up describing how they dug the foundation, set these bricks, put in "em winders." He quick, douses that flame with a *Glory a God* after every detail. And Daddy keeps saying "Amen, Brother," all the way through.

Living right inside a town feels mighty busy. A Piggly Wiggly market looking straight at us from across the street. We're walking distance to the Woolworth Five and Dime.

And indoor plumbing, right here, downstairs in the church! Our trailer cozies into its space near that downstairs door. They cleared a generous corner—slanted—lot for the building, leaving only a few pine trees, but they're enough for our shade. From our trailer, three steps down take you to the basement door in a well like space below the level of the yard.

Mama promises we can spread out into the basement to begin school work since our study supplies arrived last week while we were in Florence, Alabama. Happens in August, just about cotton harvest time when the dark green leaves begin to spot, then dry, and the cotton bolls are fully open for harvest. My thrilled to pieces holiday I've made up for myself—better than the 4th of July—is *The Day My Books Arrive*. That day, I see the slip of paper meaning "package" at the General Delivery window. And the man at the package window—if it's an actual town—hands over a dignified square cardboard box with a child's silhouette and the words *Calvert School* stamped in black at the return address space. My heart pumps hard at the sight of that name.

Here's what happens when we open it: the scent of pencil-wood and new erasers with a trace of glue-sweetness rushes up to please me, while colors of book covers and construction paper urge me to explore. Nothing excites me more than opening that box except, maybe, waking up every morning knowing it's time for school.

Studying in the basement will feel cool all the time. A good thing in late August in Mississippi. But no sunshine or windows presents a problem for me. Sometimes my "studies" call to me from outside; gazing at a red Cardinal or a chickadee with their little white faces and black crowns. Feathered, tiny, but mighty in their flight. Daddy says every one of them preaches a sermon in itself. Unless it gets way too hot before noon, I'll stay at my usual spot, the front seat table of the trailer house. That way, I begin while I'm eating breakfast at seven AM and I don't miss any teachers on the outside as well as on the inside.

You could think Aberdeen runs to uppity just because the church house is built of red brick and there are rich houses close by. But Assemblies of God folks call themselves *true holiness* people, and they stand together as plain, no decorations, no matter where you find them. No steeple and no stained glass. Rumor is, there's a Tiffany window over at the Methodist. Like Daddy says, "We're showing Jesus Christ by how we live, not by how New York our windows are or how pointy our roof is built. Amen?"

As usual, straightbacked benches furnish the upstairs, the meeting room. A well-worn altar runs across the front but sectioned so the center aisle leads up to the platform that has a wood railing—not even hung with a used to be somebody's velvet curtains cut to fit—a sturdy pulpit no doubt the work of Deacon Brother's saw, plane, and sanding. Pine chairs are grouped for singers next to an old upright piano. Never tuned, naturally, so it sounds as if tin cans attach to every key that's struck, rattling through song after song.

"Audrey's the Spark Plug in this outfit," Daddy announces right off on Wednesday night as I bounce up in my good blue dress to lead *I've Got the Joy, Joy, Joy Down in my Heart*. All closed in like this with smaller glass windows—instead of cut-outs and propped-up slats like we're used to in country churches—makes for a big sound, even though the windows are opened wide. No place for the decibels to escape so they keep going round and round, I figure. Forty voices make twice the sound here as in a tent.

You can tell a lot about people by the way they sing. They got to going on *I Must Tell Jesus*, swaying, hands raised. And we told Jesus a whole lot for about the next ten minutes.

> *I must tell Jesus all of my tri-als,*
> *I cannot bear these bur-dens a-lone . . .*

All three verses and the chorus again and again. We stopped right there and gave in to a prayer meeting. Times like this make my chest warm up with love.

Althea tells a story about when I was only four and jumped up on a piano bench to testify, blurting out, "I just don't know what I'd do without the Lord!" She rolls her eyes and says it was obviously something I heard somebody else say. Maybe so. But when this warm feeling rises out of singing and praying, a body has to rise with it.

Mama and Daddy, accordion and violin, roll real easy into a duet toward the end of praying. People aren't so loud at this point, but a sweet spirit still murmurs through the crowd.

The violin picks up the spirit and carries it to a higher level, then puts a tune to it. After they play for a few minutes, other voices still. The duet they sing usually begins with a verse, but tonight they start with the chorus,

Just keep on praying 'till light breaks through,
The Lord will answer, will answer you, God
keeps His promise, His word is true . . .

Preaching a revival's first night helps direct the Evangelist to the kind of folks who fill the church. He'll preach straight to them after this, but tonight he's finding his way. They're not exactly city folks. And yet, there's more information here than in the country, like Deacon Brother likes to point out. Information about the news and how people in the rest of the world live.

Right off, the Preacher tells these people how they encourage him with their singing and praying. Why, he's been a lot of places—you can see that pure and simple, living like turtles, taking our home with us wherever we go—but how often do we hear singing and praying like this? He goes on praising the Lord for all the folks in this Pentecostal church in Aberdeen, praising Jesus for a Pentecostal witness in Monroe County.

Well, I notice he doesn't answer the question and it put me to wondering how often we do hear good singing and I reckon it's pretty near always. People filled with the Holy Ghost have to sing about it. They have to keep praying, too, and tarry at the altar so the Holy Ghost will speak through them.

You know something else? They have to love each other. Or else, as Pastor McGibbons in Florence, Alabama, emphasized last week, they're frauds. At the time, he was telling us about neighbors who showed up in the revival one night. These two men are landowners. Important people in the county. But they'd been fussing over their property line since the survey crew measured off their acreage when electricity arrived. "At propitty done took on a life a hits own," Brother McGibbons said, shaking his head, his broad, always-smiling shiny face topped by a fringe of hair in a halo. "Las night, praise Jay-zus! Both a them ole hateful men was down atta altar,

Preacha!" he told Daddy, "Standin up after folks prayed down a heav'ns on em, one says atta other, 'Ahm callin ya Brotha nah,' tears a streamin down is face. "Ahm callin ya Brotha! Uh loves ya."

After that—by the end of the week—they'd testify to anybody who'd listen, "We s'neighborly, that line don't matta a hill a beans."

I can tell Daddy's heading toward everybody being neighborly here, too, living close like they do. Even being neighbors with people in fine houses.

The Preacher goes on, after thanking them for all that encouragement, saying,

> But why would we do less than our best!
> "He that spared not His own Son—Romans 8:32"
> I ask you, how can I spare *myself*, then?
> You, a child of God, praise His Name! how
> can you old back?
> You, heir to the riches in Christ!

People love to shout about their inheritance as Children of God. One chorus sings it,

> *He owns the cattle on a thousand hills, the wealth in every mine.*
> *He owns the meadows and the rocks and rills,*
> *The sun and the moon that shine.*

"Yasss . . . Alleluuuuu!" Sky blue dress bouncing with joy, the ample bodied woman's pale brown hair shakes loose from its roll across the back of her neck and her pompadour loses its lift at the same time she jumps up and does a victory march down the aisle and back. She sits down, hands high, shaking with the Holy Ghost in pure delight. Her exuberance gives the Evangelist a chance to roll up his sleeves and move down in front of the pulpit.

> Here's the joy, Children of God and heirs to the riches of Christ,
> and you envy those that walk in darkness—How can you envy their
> high livin.
> Beauty—Who's beautiful?
> *I'll tell you, it's the face that's lifted up toward heaven!*
> Soaking up the Sun of Righteousness.

That suits Sister Blue Dress real well and she jumps up, waves her hands, claps, and sits down again as if she just can't contain the hallelujahs.

> Character is like a fence, you can't splash it with white

wash and think you've fooled God.

Some people might say he's quit preachin and gone to meddlin when the Preacher talks about white washing a fence. Too close to mentioning make-up on Holiness women. Most keep pure soap-and-water kind of faces. But I see powder and a little rouge creeping in when we're at churches in town. Daddy and Mama consider that signs of worldliness not to mention pride.

> Flowers grow by constantly turning away from darkness,
> faces always toward the sun.
> Stay clear, then!
> *Nothing* to obstruct between you and
> the Sun of Righteousness.
> Keep yourself in His love!
> "He shall be like a tree
> planted by the water."
> Look at Joseph—snatched from his homeland, thrown in prison,
> yet God's powerful sun come to him through the bars of his cell.
> Look at Daniel—grew in grace even though he landed in a firey furnace.
> Well if God puts you in the furnace,
> you can be sure He'll be there too!
> And if you say your soil's not so good for
> growing beautiful flowers,
> Look at the Hebrew Children—wandering in wilderness—think of it!
> 40 years in the desert! Yet
> they grew on into the beauty of the Promised Land!
> Grow in Grace—HOW—you say?
> First you must be planted in the soil of His wisdom.
> Planted in His Divine Love,
> in the very heart of Divine Love.
> Like Psalm One, planted by the river,
> roots dug way down in the Love of God.
> But now how many times have I pulled up a stick of wheat,
> the seed is Dead—only a husk left—being planted means we have to die with Him!
> Die in Him that we may grow in His Grace, roots watered by Love.

Shouting from happy-in-the-Holy-Ghost folks flits around the inside of the church house like butterflies on flowers. The Preacher closes out, sweat pouring off his face, white shirt damp and wilted, tie loosened, the waves of his hair set loose from the power of Hess's Hair Milk, beginning to tumble across his forehead:

> Come to Jesus
> Come to Jesus tonight—
> Lift your face toward Him!
> Tonight!
> Now is your time to soak up His sunshine!

He motions to me and I go up the two steps to the platform from the first row where I'm sitting next to Mama. While she's shrugging on the accordion, I stand next to the pulpit so I can be seen and sing the first verse of *Where He Leads* with Althea at the vibra harp in back of me and Mama playing beside me. I'll be glad when I'm tall enough to stand in back of pulpits.

> *I can hear my Savior calling . . .*
> *Take thy cross and follow, follow Me.*

The first night's altar call gives a chance for Christians to check in with Jesus. See what they need before they go out and invite sinners to come on in. Altar time hooks people up to power and light, Daddy says, just as sure as when we plug in our trailer. And they're coming to Jesus tonight. I hear prayers for Aberdeen," *Jay—zus, brang us souls fr-m iss ere town . . ."* I hear prayers for wayward children, family members and neighbors.

"Clair . . . Lindaaa. Unca Rog . . . Aint Sulyann . . ."

"Have mer-cy. Mercy. Mercy, Jayzus . . ."

That put me in a mind to sing one of my favorites:

> *Got any rivers you think are uncrossable?*
> *Got any mountains you can't tunnel thru?*
> *God specializes in things tho 't impossible,*
> *And He can do what no other pow'r can do.*

Well I'll tell you right now, the praying goes to singing. And shouting. Then the sky blue dress lady leads everybody in a victory march all around the church. This turns into one of the best first nights of revival I can remember. Daddy says so, too.

Mama informs me while I'm eating breakfast this morning that the song I started into singing last night was written the year I was born, "Must be your song, Audrey." We laugh like it's plastered on my forehead as a cartoon.

But today's my day to begin first grade, too, so it's a natural celebration. Calvert School, Baltimore, has details worked out, even a schedule for every day which I don't need. I make my own. And first grade in Calvert isn't like school anywhere else. They said by now I'd be *ready* to read, but Mama says I'm like Daddy—very curious and no patience—so I zoomed ahead on reading as soon as they started making me "ready." With all the words swimming around, how can I be anything but a hungry fish, slurping up every one that comes my way.

Mama says we can take our walk to the library this afternoon. We never miss our exercise. Where we parked in Augusta overnight on our way up from Miami in March, a golf course was nearby. Mama and I walked that course end to end. Being the Temple of the Holy Ghost means you have to keep in good repair. Strong. And that can be a good time, too.

News at noon blares out of Daddy's radio everyday. Usually I pay little mind to it unless it's about "Commies" as they call Russians, specially in the South. Since Daddy is Russian and not a Commie for sure, I listen close.

But today Fulton Lewis Junior has more information about the "Negro problem." It's a blur of puzzle-words. He has "communist" in there, too, how does that fit? After the news, Daddy turns off the radio, but not before the next program pitches in *Life Gets Teejus, Don't It*.

> The sun comes up and the sun goes down
> The hands on the clock keep goin' 'round
> I jus' git up and it's time to lay down
> Life gits tee-jus don t it?
> Makes me snicker every time I hear it.

Daddy and Mama start talking low after the news, which means they don't think I should listen even though I'm sitting right here. So I look real busy, thumbing through my new science workbook. There's a skeleton on one page, a picture of all my bones. Think of it. How they hang together. What's inside them. I'm distracted all right, but my parent's words are still coming through.

Daddy says that Brother Deacon tells him there are more Negroes in this here town than there are white people. I heard him when he was talking about it, and I can see him now, raising his dark bushy eyebrows nearly reaching to his Brillo-pad hair, thumbs in his overall pockets and elbows stuck out to the side like stubby wings taking flight-messages from his large ears just above. Leans in for emphasis, "They's *everwhere*. Nigras? Don't see'm s'much, course. Workin. Inna big houses." He waits a minute and says, to top it off, "Hits a gooood thang, praisa Lawd, makes hit tol-able, em Nigras knows they place," nodding.

Mama's quiet a spell, then she says, "Guess that's why we don't see so many Colored out in the country, no grand houses for work. Unless there's a cotton farm. See them in the fields, then." She pauses, adds, "In Aberdeen, there's work. That's good. Places to live?"

"Yeah. But like Fulton Lewis says, get a few Commie sympathizers in here stirrin 'em up . . ."

"*Lord.* Have mercy." Mama's gone to praying.

Here I am, still staring at the science pages' skeleton when a thought runs up my mind: Reckon Negro's bones look any different from mine? But I can't ask since I'm not supposed to be listening.

After dinner, walking to the library, Mama exclaims over the houses we're passing left and right, "My lands!" or "I declare." Just about every other place along Commerce parkway has gardens spilling under the fence, over the sidewalk. Flowers idle their days away among trees strewn with curly moss. Shady borders of floppy blossoms colored orange, gold, red and pink, look like giant African violets and remind me of Auntie Dorie in San Francisco. She has rows of African violets in pots along her window sill.

A bright yellow bird with black-tipped wings catches my eye—Goldfinch?—singing a tweedle-dee-dee kind of song as he flits and soars, finally lands among his friends for a full concert. I'm smiling out loud right along with them.

Some of the places have *seen better days*, like Mama says. Still beautiful, but paint peeling, gardens invaded by weeds. Hedges growing wild. Brings up the skeleton again and how we might have the same bits and pieces on the inside but outside we look so different.

The Aberdeen library, built of red brick like the church house, appears small but powerful. The type the three little pigs lived in that couldn't be blown down. And lo and behold, who should greet us when we walk through the door but the blue-sky dress lady from revival. Sitting at her desk in the center of the room looking important, she's surrounded by shelves going every which way filled with books.

"Wallll, praisa Lord! Sista Skondee an 'at Sparky Girl!" That's a new one.

Nobody else is around at this hour of the day. She explains that they're only open a few hours, two until five in the afternoon. And then, stretching out her dumpling hand, "Sister Dottie Lafaver. French grandaddy? Loosana." Louisiana. Right. "They run auvr name all together. Useta be broke in two? La . . ." She pulls her brows together, abruptly changing, "Now,

Skondee . . ." when Mama up and begins to talk a lightening streak about what a wonderful job Sister Lafaver is doing. How her work makes a difference to the whole town! And never, of course, makes a u-turn going back to pick up the Skondee-idea. Whew. Close call.

At last, I'm able to ask about Senator Hiram Roades Revels. Mama twitches a nervous little smile and adds that I'm just starting first grade, see, "And Audrey's Social Studies book mentions plantations, slaves. *You* know." They nod at each other as if there's more to this conversation than the words they're saying. Mama seldom talks so much and usually not this fast. But at this point I still don't know how much Mama can say without making sense. That comes later.

Sister Lafaver shows us to the article about him in the Encyclopedia Britannica, and on the way, notes that his Ma was a white woman. *Yes she was.* "Scottish, Aberdeen's name been import from Scotland, too."

My reading lacks the words for big subjects, so Mama and I sit real quiet in the corner and she reads to me: A Negro woman tutored him first off, then he learns to barber from his brother and before he's a Senator? He's a preacher! *African Methodist Episcopal Church.* Shows what he was doing in that church house when he died, like Daddy said. Serving Jesus just like us. He set up a private school, too. In Baltimore, which is where my Calvert School lives.

But the part that nabs my attention isn't even about Senator Revels. A Negro woman followed after him as Senator, Blanche Brucee. And while he was only in the Senate a year before he dropped dead at the church house, she served for six years, Mama says, 1875 to 1881. She had the same name as Mama's sister, Aunt Blanche, but Mama doesn't exclaim about that. She just says, "Well I never . . ." and that's all.

We walk home a different way, over past some houses that appear more country than town. Funny that out in the woods, places with no paint and rusty, curled-up tin along the edges of the roof look fine, but here they seem a lot more pathetic. Outhouses in back. Like shanties we see along railroad tracks.

Pitiful children, too. Dirty as if they haven't washed for weeks, not just filthy bare feet, but faces—Mama would never let me walk around that way—lounging in doorways and one, kicking a half-deflated ball. Paying no mind at all to a packed-dirt playground in a dry-as-tumbleweed, sand spur vacant lot strewn with tin cans, the giant kind they use for government surplus.

Something's burning in a blackened oil drum in one back yard, the bent-over man tending it pokes a stick in, throwing on trash that sends up a new wave of rank smoke. Smells like motor oil, but maybe that's just from the drum. Mama says, "Bless his heart. Doing his best to clean up." She always figures the best in folks.

A skinny boy, pale hair shaped like a ripe dandelion weed ready to blow apart, no shoes, is the ball-kicker and at the same time hurls insults at what must be his smaller brother, "Dummmb, stuuu-pid, Bubba," who misses the ball and lands on his tiny behind to boot. The older one switches his attention to a can, grabbing a stick. Now he's got noise and motion both.

"Leeeee-roy, whad a tell ya, good fa nothin brat," a woman, worn thin as a flat tire, peers out an open door, mouse hair matted, cigarette dangling from what must be a mouth but no lips. Probably just a few teeth. Her shoes not quite put on, both heels squash down the backs of them as she shuffles on out to the porch. Gazing with blank eyes, she leans against a post looking too spindly to stand even her weight, much less the porch roof it supports. I smile, "Hi there!" But she doesn't answer, just keeps staring.

A couple of doors down three little girls play rag dolls, the railing across the front of their porch, rotted and fallen crosswise to the deck. They don't look up but I call out "Hello," anyhow.

Mama says, soon as we've passed, "Those children need Jesus, Audrey."

"Jesus loves the little children, 'specially thread-bare, dirty and hungry, Mama, you reckon that child Jesus lifts up when he's talking about the Kingdom of God looked like those children? He fed all those people . . . just a few loaves of bread, supper-size fish, why not . . ."

Mama walks so fast I'm nearly running, my words keeping pace. She takes my hand, crossing a street, and says, "Jesus sees hearts, first. All the other needs are set right when hearts are healed." I'll have to do some thinking about her answer.

Daddy's studying this week just like I am. His attitude's a little different when he's preparing a new sermon, like Uncle Mike's hunting dog, Strelka, concentrating on ducks she's hoping to fetch. Intent. He sits on the seat across the back of the trailer house with his Bible and his notebooks around him, reading, silent, then scribbling away. After a while he goes into the meeting room upstairs in the church. Paces. Tries out the words in his mind, or that's how it seems. Later, he might preach it to me. He talks to Jesus, too, while he walks back and forth. Mama's on her knees for praying. Daddy walks.

"Sister Dottie Lafaver—the lady leading the victory March in the blue dress?—she's the library lady, Daddy! She's wearing the same dress but today her hair's in place." I deliver the news, breathless.

"Yeah? She have decent books over there?" The words come out of his mouth, but he's still with his notes.

"Small place, built out of bricks no big bad wolf can blow down! En-cyclopedias and giant books all lined up along one wall . . ." Mama inserts, "*Reference* books."

". . . around the other three walls, the ones you like, biographies and history."

"Don't forget old man Tolstoy, he's so-called *fiction*, true as his sto-ries . . ." Now, I have his attention.

"*Ooops, Tolstoy* . . . in the middle, more shelves stacked around her desk, to the left, the right and lengthwise in back of her—Oh!—And the magazines on racks by some chairs in a corner in back."

Before you know it, he'll be at that library, too. Or, *liberry* as Sister Lafaver says.

Saturday morning, Daddy and I make a dash across the street to see what the Piggly Wiggly Market has to offer. He ran over one morning for milk, but I was already studying that day. We're aiming to get there before all the farmers come in to do their shopping before Sunday. Town turns a corner into *crazy* on a Saturday morning, everything closed tight by noon.

Walking rapidly through the parking lot, we dodge a farmer pulling up in a beater pick up just in front of us, the wood slats he's fixed on the sides for hauling look for all the world like they'll clatter to the ground any minute. Farm hands, a Colored family without their Mama, crowd together in the back of the truck. An older man, two boys about ten and nine, and what must be a girl my age jump down to the asphalt after the farmer parks.

I say *what must be a girl* because she's dressed exactly like the boys, only her patched-up dungarees need another few months before she'll grow into them. The girl-clue is her hair, the cutest bitty braids with yellow, red, blue and green fabric strips tying them at the ends like you would use rib-bons. Set me to wonder if Mama might could get my curls under control like that. The way this girl's face reflects the sun looks close to the color of caramels. And her eyes which, of course, are trained on the ground like most Colored, are velvet brown. I saw her eyes when she was jumping out of the truck. And I promise, no fancy artist ever found a color that dark full of so much light.

I smile real big, but she ducks her head then turns it just a mite side-ways with a giggle-grin but no sound. They head on around back to the Colored entrance while Daddy and I walk through the front door. Just after seven AM, but the Piggly Wiggly's already lining a few folks up at the regis-ter. There's a register for Colored at their entrance.

The white man at the front cash register wears a rough brown work apron with big pockets where a receipt book—looks like—is sticking out, and in the other, a pair of canvas work gloves stiff with wear. He's so short, his hands barely reach the buttons on the register. Wide as he is tall, no neck, but he smiles with his whole head, completely bald so you can see ripples with every guffaw.

Big town grocery stores, the white ones at least—in Miami, Atlanta or Birmingham—generally keep squeaky clean, but small town stores have corners where friendly dirt drifts and never seems to be chased out entirely. Produce brings earth smells into their wooden bins, too. Carrots, potatoes and onions, sometimes still in crates from the farm, wear bits of their home territory. But then there's a warm breeze from ripe peaches wafting through at this time of year and the unmistakeable twang of tomatoes, stems still in and a few furry leaves lending their perfume. Vegetables and fruits, together, play their tunes like a country band. But life's not a bit *tee-jus* for them, growing delicious in the sun and rain. Daddy handles each one with such tenderness, you'd think he grew them in his own back yard.

While Daddy's checking for perfection with the vegetables—Mama's fixing stuffed green peppers for dinner today—I wander down the aisle toward the back, looking for my friend. The door for Colored is straight back, at the end of the produce-bin aisle, and through the door I see her brothers hanging around outside. To the left of their door and cash register, stands the glass case for the meat counter. The two butchers deep into cutting, grinding, and waiting on customers, work between the counter and a giant refrigerator locker, floor to ceiling, where they no doubt keep the sides of beef and hogs hanging, ready to be carved up. Smells a little rank from the cans of scraps being collected as they do their jobs.

But then, just to the left of the meat counter against the far wall, past the canned food shelves, I catch a disturbing glimpse of my friend. She's standing, more like hopping in place, up and down, agitated, in front of the restroom door labeled *Ladies*. Below that in glaring words I never noticed before in my life: *Whites Only*.

My heart stops. Then moves to my throat. Frozen, I watch her agony and feel what she's feeling, her hands clutching around her middle, a look of pure misery on her face, when her older brother dashes in the door and snatches her by the arm. "Zorneely!" or something like that, "get yo sef outta der." He's pulled her through the back door and around out of sight before I can make another move. Daddy, who's moved on to the meat counter for some ground beef, sees the whole episode and says, "Audrey! Come on, we're going."

All the while we're standing in line at the cash register with people whose skin color matches mine, I can only see Zorneely. Tears sting the inside of my eyelids but don't quite squeeze out. Daddy's saying something but I can't hear him for the roar—a Birmingham refinery's furnace—in my head. My face is hot, my hands jammed into my play dress pockets, the yellow rosebud feed sack print. Right now I'm just glad this dress has a way to hide my fists, tight as curled-up doodle bugs.

The old truck with the dangerous siding is still parked out front when we make our way back across the highway. But, peering around for Zorneely, she's nowhere in sight.

Daddy's voice starts making a dent in my hearing, "Audrey! whatsa matter with you." He sounds cross and that voice nearly always gets my full attention, but not this time. All I can hear, all I can see is Zorneely's agony.

Flicking the trailer house screen door open Daddy says, "Don't know what's got into Audrey, she's ornery actin."

Mama's answer is to sit me down as I come through the door carrying a sack of peppers. One hand on each of my shoulders, she plops my bottom down at the end of one of the front seats. Daddy sets the bag of groceries on the counter, reaches for the peppers and puts them in the sink, and they both sit facing me across the table.

When I start to use my voice it purely cracks open. Biting my lip doesn't do a bit of good. "That little girl, Mama, that p-poor little g-girl," sobs hiccup out of me, my fists pounding the seat on either side of me in time to the words.

"What are you so *mad—sad!—over, what in the world*?"

"Jussst," stammering out wet exclamations, "ststanding. No! Hopping. Twist-ing—and . . ."

"What?" Mama gets me a glass of water from the jug on the counter.

"Now calm down! Calm down!" Daddy's scowling. He starts in, "A Negro girl, Doris . . ."

"Colored?"

I nod, taking a raggedy breath. "All she needed was to go to the bathroom, Mama. That's all!" I can feel my face pulled together, lips mashed into each other like as if I ate a wild green persimmon. I attempt another breath.

"What happened?"

"Hateful sign. I never noticed. A sign says Whites Only, Mama. That's what's *ornery*, that sign."

"The child had to go . . ." Daddy tries to fill in, but I'm strong now.

"She was miserable, Mama, holding on to herself. I felt like it was me had to go. I know that feeling."

"And then?"

"Her older brother, standing right outside flashed through the Colored entrance in a hurry, grabbed her by the arm and jerked her outside." My voice increasing, stronger.

Daddy's looking down at the table not saying a thing. Neither is Mama. He raises his eyes, tight furrows between them, "Everybody's got their place, now, uh . . ." but his words sound weak, dumb, and not like him at all.

I can't get loose of Mama and Daddy until I breathe more normal-like and stop screeching. Last thing Mama says, "You can't do anything about those signs, now Audrey. They're there for good reasons." Then she gets up with a this talk's over attitude, and I disappear.

Just when I need woods around, here we are with trucks and cars puttering by, plus a few mules, horses clopping slow as if they're too tired to get where they're going. Only some puny pine trees for hiding. Sometimes a body wants to hide. That's the only place to set your mind right. I finally stash myself on a low stump between the church basement doorway-well and the corner of the building. Cross-legged, chin supported by my fists, staring at nothing.

Mama's words to Sister Dottie Lafaver come drifting back. About my first grade Calvert Social Studies book and *slaves*. I didn't pay any mind to that book, the science skeleton occupying my attention and all. Strikes me curious that folks get talkative when the subject of Negroes comes up but they don't say much of anything worth hearing. Eyes twitching, hands in a whatcha-gonna-do spread, shoulders shrugging. Calling'em *talks* pretty near equals humming a flat line and calling it music.

Meantime, Colored people walk slow, drift around corners or against walls shadow-like, as if they're not even expecting to be real folks. Some towns, they have benches under trees or out back of a store maybe, or the last seats on buses where they get together. Mama did read an historic sign at the Methodist Church in Wetumpka, when we passed through, come to think of it. That church served both white and "slaves" which I take to mean *Negroes*, back in 1854. But that was before everybody on this side of the United States—top to bottom—got in a big fight over the whole thing. What about now?

Few minutes ago at the trailer house table, I said to Mama and Daddy, "If Jesus loves all the children of the world, how come people in Holiness churches don't love all the children of the world?" Mama answers too quick, "Well we *do* love all the children, but there's a separate way . . ." her voice trails off, not making a lick of sense. My motto since I've been six usually works real good—*if you let people talk long enough they'll tell you everything you need to know*—but lately it's not as useful as I could hope.

Most Saturdays, Mama doesn't let me study unless we're traveling the following Monday. Today, it's just as well. When my brain scrambles too many words together they turn into silence. Even Mama's stuffed peppers taste like tin. The only help I can give it—my brain, to keep it still—is singing *Got Any Rivers You Think Are Uncrossable*.

Daddy and Mama never stick to silence when it comes to moodiness, though. Sitting at the dinner table, fixing to ask the blessing, Daddy looks straight at me and says, "We'll have no pouting here."

Sometimes I wear a mask as my own face. Plenty of poking goes on, "Straighten up. Don't slouch," while we're practicing. But at no time do I ever get an urge to repent for my mood or my mask that covers me up to be Pleasant. Somebody has to be strong for Zorneely whether she can be or not.

You can't sleep mad. Mama and Daddy explain words from the Bible, *don't let the sun go down on your wrath*. But it isn't necessary. Mad keeps boiling up misery, anybody knows that. Obvious.

The minute I settle into my top bunk, it comes to me. I didn't even think of Zorneely at first. No, the folks showing up were a big bunch of Holiness people. Good. Loving Jesus like always. A moving picture of them, no words. They're all clumped together tight, busy shouting and in that little bit of space, twirling in circles. Patting each other on the back. Very busy. And here comes The Lion of Judah. He paces across in front of them, then tracks all around their circle, but they're so busy He can't find a way to break into the crowd.

Finally with a sigh, with Him this sounds like a roar, He lays down His big shaggy head on His front paws and looks straight at me. Those eyes—sunbeam brown, I don't know how that happens—just like Zorneely. By now the crowd's completely faded. Zorneely's tiny-braids head is sleeping on one of his paws, so I figure I'll lay my head on the other one.

Sunday morning means, pure and simple, it's time to stick a smile on my face and wake up singing. I've never been sick during a revival, the only indication of *sick* being a high temperature, so there's no chance for any more hiding out.

While Mama's untangling my sleepy curls, getting ready for church, she starts talking real quiet-like. Althea and Daddy are up in the meeting room practicing, but my hair takes a while some days.

"Her name? Zorneely?"

"Something like that."

"We'll go to the library and look up that name, Audrey. This week."

"Library?"

"Mmmhmmm . . . a woman. Kind of famous, she writes books. Maybe Zorneely's Mama and Daddy have high hopes for their girl. Know she's smart . . . like you."

Now Mama never says things like that about me, pride being such a problem for Holiness people. A problem of sin, I should say. Makes me hear how hard she's trying to help. Course this doesn't change anything. But it does make the river seem more crossable.

Sister Dottie Lafaver, the Sunday School Superintendent, organizes the morning classes. Today, her dress beams out sunshine yellow with pink flowers floating up to the neck and down to each wrist. She shines. The under-ten kid's teacher, Sister Bessie Jordan, is as tiny as Sister Lafaver isn't. Gray hair pulled to a tidy knot behind her thin straight nose. A little sparrow wearing a navy blue dress that's her best, witnessed to by the white lace collar. *Sister Bessie* smiles young, pink showing on her high cheeks and blue eyes twinkling through thick lenses in her spectacles. Her flannel board's already prepared. She was born ready.

Flannel boards stand on three legs, covered with beige flannel that can be sand for the Bible's desert or blank for introducing paper characters and landscape details that have a patch of flannel on the backside to make them stick. She's landed a green hill on the beige, along with David before he was King of Israel, a boy holding a shepherd's crook, small harp tucked under one arm. I never forget that before I was born Mama and Daddy called me *Billy David.* That's when Daddy said, "If it's a boy, I'll stand on my head."

I dearly love that name Billy David, for Daddy, first, plus the shepherd boy. That boy always making up songs while he's tending his sheep and playing that harp he drags around with him everywhere he goes. Couldn't be more perfect. But no, my name's Pauline Audrey.

First to arrive at the church house this morning are Leeann, Deetsy, Eddy, Bonniesue and Bobby, with their Ma and Pa, the Sawyers. They make sure everything's ready for Sunday and they're proud of their job. Very busy. Leeann speaks for the other kids, brown braids tied with blue ribbon, her freckles blend together splashing an I'm-an-outdoor girl message on her face that's blessed with dancing green eyes. "Welcome, ya'll!" she says right off to Althea and me, "We s'glad ya'll come fer this here meetin, ain bin ere til t'day, course, but we sure happy y'all's here!" I don't often see so many children with shoes on in the summertime. Every one of them.

When Boyson—can't tell if it's a nickname or a name—Suley, Lomalee, Max and Petie troop in, Sister Bessie arranges our shocks of brown, black, reddish, and yellow hair in a row below the flannel board on a doubled-up

worn-out quilt to serve us a bit of comfort on the cement floor in the absence of chairs. Nodding, warming us with her Jesus-smile that lights this
corner of the basement, she says, "Praisa Lawd! He'sa happy you chirrun
come t'hear about Jay-zus." Sister Bessie settles us down good and proper
and commences telling David's story.

Sunday School rolls into the preaching service, beginning with a tally on
each tote board, one on each side; the left showing the number in attendance and offering last week and on the right showing the numbers for this
week. By the looks of it, Aberdeen Assembly hit their record attendance this
morning, 65! And this being August, not Easter or anything but *Revival.*
Word gets around.

Praising Jesus for all the folks showing up mingles with the scuffling,
people finding their places. Daddy calls me up to rally the children, singing,
I've Got the Joy. I notice usual duties feel like hard work when you're even
a little mad and pretending not to be. I keep wondering if Zorneely gets to
go to church. Maybe to that African Methodist Episcopal church where the
Senator flew off to his final reward.

The Evangelist figures with a crowd like this, he better hit it hard. I can
read his mind, I'm fairly sure. Lots of kids and teenagers are here, too. And
their parents craning to see them, since they're sitting on the back benches.
Some mothers sing on the platform purely for the purpose of keeping an eye
out for their teens.

The Preacher makes good use of Althea and me, too. Mama, Althea
and I sing harmony, *Satisfied with Jesus*:

> *I tried to be, but couldn 't be,*
> *A Christian in my heart,*
> *I struggled night and day,*
> *My moral debts to pay . . .*

Before you know it, we've gone into my singing a solo, *O Come, Angel
Band*, Althea and Mama accompanying me. Daddy's violin even joins in on
the chorus. He calls this *pulling out all the stops.*

> *O come, angel band, come, and around me stand,*
> *O bear me away on your snowy wings*
> *To my immortal home . . .*

I cut it short because Daddy doesn't want to make it too long. Just wants
to get their attention before he starts preaching. And he has it, right down
to the tiniest kid. That's Doody, three years old, sitting on the front bench

next to his pa, Deacon Brother, whose name we hear tell from Pastor Danny Winkler, is "Slocum." Daddy said to Mama that he declares the man said, *Slum* and he knew right well that wasn't it.

Everybody loves an angel band. Boyson's and Lomalee's Ma, Sister Betty Beazley, has arranged her dark curls for Sunday in many-hair-pinned rows caught together like a school of minnows in a net. She looks like one of the angels in her white blouse with flying sleeves and white skirt covering many layers of Sister Betty herself. From the first notes, she's blessed by this song, rising up and swaying, eyes closed and turned heavenward. Before she sits down—folks joining her in praising Jesus for the very thought of heaven—she pulls a white hanky from inside her bosom and shouts, "Ohh-hhhheeeee Jaaaayzus, jess take me on home! *Enny* time!" I don't know how Lomalee and Boyson feel about that but I can tell you certain, I'm more blessed by singing about a whole band full of angels than seeing one of them swoop down and fetch my Mama up to heaven.

> Yes! Hallelujah!
> Ya'll are tuned into the Apostle Paul already,
> Praise His Name!
> Thank you Jesus!

The Evangelist speaks into the microphone while people settle down to listen. Takes a full five minutes.

> Philippians, chapter three . . . rejoice in the Lord!
> Then Paul tells his friends in Philippi all he has to be
> PROUD of! Yeah! Paul has boasting rights galore:
> Circumcised according to the Law!
> Confidence in the flesh—more than anybody else.
> Hebrew of the Hebrews! A big shot Pharisee!
> Zeal so strong, he's persecuted.
> And *perfect* in keeping the Law. *Perfect*!
> "But what things were gain to me those I counted loss for Christ."

The Preacher misses the mood a little, doesn't realize they're going to rise up so easily, shouting, twirling, and I didn't, either. Before you know it, Sister Lafaver is going to be doing another Victory March. He has to run over top some of the praising to keep up his pace.

> Whew! Paul's pride goes out the window
> *"for the excellency of the knowledge of Christ Jesus my Lord:*
> *For whom I have suffered the loss of all things."*
> The fellowship of Christ's suffering surpasses all in its sweetness.

Yes, Lord!
Those who suffer torment in prison camps of Siberia
in the midst of slave labor, freezing temperatures,
desperate hunger—torture—battering! day after day.
Still, able to feel sweetness in Christ's presence.
This sweetness I could've had all my
life—says Paul—it was *hidden* in me.
What Paul's telling us is that only from the depth of prison's misery,
hunger, suffering, much persecution, he's sayin,
only where there are graves is there a resurrection!

Calling out the last sentence, the Preacher jumps off the platform past the two steps, and lands with an exclamation. He holds the Bible opened to Paul's letter with one hand and waves his handkerchief, occasionally used to dab the sweat already pouring off his face at 11:30 on this hot Sunday. He goes on, laying the open Bible on the altar,

Only when you've gone to the depths and lost your
life can you experience that Angel Band!
Everybody wants angels all around,
now don't they Brother Slocum?
But nobody wants ta die!

Laughter and shouts of "Amen, na!" mingle together like cheering at a stadium rally.
"You go-n on an preachin, Brotha!"
"Go 'head ON!"
"Bless'im, Lawdy! Lawd!"

But remember at the start of Paul's letter he already told the people
that he keeps them in his heart! Yes!
Love, humble love, Paul says they're in his heart
because they are "partakers of His Grace!"
We abide in love, that's how
we make it through the suffering to that *Angel Band.*
Humble Love—a fearsome power—the greatest power of all.
Nothing can compare with it.
Wm Frederick Faber, great saint and hymn writer of long ago,
The perfect way is hard for flesh
It is not hard for love
If thou wert sick for want of love
How swiftly you would move!

A hum sounding for all the world like hope begins to rise, a feeling of prayer but low-pitched cheering, too. Babies sleep in their mother's laps, and as the wave of energy rises, they shake off their slumber and they're soon being passed person to person to keep them quiet. Cheering takes over and little kids my age—Bonniesue and Eddy—jump up and clap and Boyson and Lomalee across the aisle raise their own kind of praise, standing and swaying in sync with their Mama.

Wiping sweat from his brow, the Evangelist allows a quiet spell before he comes back to the microphone and says:

> Where we miss that perfect way—
> *we miss it!*—
> shows us men who turn away from God
> turn away from Love and
> turn their world into hell.
> *Homes!* Turn into hell
> when God's left out.
> That's the ingredient that's left out of our
> homes, cities, nations.
> I see young people walking our streets
> no direction, no discipline. *Foolishness!*
> All they learn is mischief.
> No chance to pull themselves up when they're
> pallin' around with the devil.
> *Holiness living.*
> Has to be some Holiness livin at home,
> or children can't see it.
> Listen now—our children can't learn to live Holiness by themselves!

He leans into the microphone and rasps out the words, his voice beginning to tire, yet still, his fervent spirit fresh for the meaning,

> But the wicked never flee from the wrath to come
> til they're fully satisfied there is wrath to come.
> What are we doing to bring them in?
> Bring them into God's House,
> Showin 'em Jesus!
> Nothin's so contrary to God as sin!
> God won't allow Sin to rule His Masterpiece, man.
> Made in His Own Image.

I've probably heard this before but it never impressed my own ears like to-day: *Man . . . Made in His Own Image*. What's that supposed to mean? That Billy David's made in God's image but not me? And how bout Zorneely? I don't have time to think on this right now—I'm going to have to go back up and sing *Angel Band* again, finish the other verse—but this needs attention.

> Men learned to know Sorrow.
> Misery!
> Forsaking knowledge of Christ.
> Men learned Sorrow instead
> and came to love it.

I can hardly hear any more, that refinery-roar coming back and all, but I have to tune in. Somehow or other.

> More have discovered God in Sorrow than in Joy.
> But Jesus shows us the difference and
> leads us to Joy and Peace beyond our own understanding.
> Can you hear me Brothers and Sisters?
> "Papa what are they doing there?"
> A boy saw a coach driver beating his horse
> after the animal stumbled and fell,
> beating him with a frenzied rage.
> "Come on. Let's get out of here," says the boy's father,
> but the child, beside himself with despair
> breaks away from his father as he tries to pull him the other direction
> and with a loud cry, runs through the crowd and
> throws his arms around the blood-spattered head of the horse
> lying on the ground, kissing it again and again.
> Then the boy launches himself at the coach driver and
> with flaying hands and fists,
> attacks the man, forcing him to back away.
> *Except ye repent and become as little children . . .*
> the most spiritual is one who has not lost the heart of a child.
> Where is your heart today?

I'm already at the mic when the Preacher says the last words. Singing:

> *O come, angel band, come, and around me stand,*
> *O bear me away on your snowy wings*
> *To my immortal home, my immortal home.*

In a family living close together as mine does you can't afford to go sour very long. By dinner time—we're going to the Slocum's for our Sunday meal—I'll be straightened out or trouble will be closer than I care to ponder. Singing helps.

But what can a person do with all this love talk. And the Preacher throwing in Jesus' words, *unless you become as little children* this morning as if being a child is God's best prize. What about Bubba and Leroy and the little girls next door to them, I don't see them in the church house being loved on. So who loves them and Zorneely? Maybe her Mama and Daddy. There's Jesus-love—*red and yellow black and white*—even though folks don't pay attention to His kind of love 'cept when they feel like it.

Plus the Preacher's talk that we're made in God *the Father's* image. Makes me wag my head side-to-side, trying to figure which way to go. Where do I fit?

Folks take one look at me and say, "Thet chile's a spit image a 'Vangliss Skondee!" Which I take to mean I look just like him: square-shaped face, wide-set blue eyes, curly hair, his tamed by Hess's Hair Milk into waves instead of curls, of course. But how does it work exactly? Me being a girl. Billy David wouldn't have these problems tying him up.

I can't ask Mama about any of this. She'd get the bar of soap, talking fast, probably saying something about *blaspheme* and *Holy Ghost*. A mouth full of soap, I don't risk. You have to be wary where your words are going to land before you open your mouth and let them fly. Especially when it comes to Father God and His Only Son Jesus who died on the cross to save you from your sins. Falls onto the Serious list.

Put me in a personal mind to consider Hernando DeSoto all over again. Whatever possesses a person to get on a ship that big and go sailing off into a world where he's never been before, I don't know for sure. But me, I reckon he packed up on the day one too many questions beat against his brain. You can only stand so many.

5

Wetumpka, Alabama 1948
Drinking Damnation

- *US Supreme Court ends religious instruction in public schools; Justice Hugo Black says there must be an impenetrable wall between church and state; Justice Jackson contends, however, that nearly everything in our culture . . . is saturated with religious influences.*

- *Pogo, a cartoon drawn by former Walt Disney animator Walt Kelly depicting an Okefenokee Swamp opossum in Georgia, runs its first strip as a comic. Pogo's comment regarding the ecological crisis is, We have met the enemy and he is us.*

- *After taking his dog for a walk in the woods, Swiss engineer George Mestral is inspired by cockleburs to invent Velcro.*

- *The Manchester Mark I computer, invented by Tom Kilborn, 26, executes the first program successfully.*

- *Ray Croc opens his first McDonalds Hamburger stand in California.*

- *Audrey Skondeen is six years old.*

As SOON AS I see the pie tins of broken soda crackers—*the body*—and tiny paper cups of diluted grape juice—*the blood*—I know I have a load of trouble right up ahead. Covered over with a dish towel made out of feed sack cloth, you could ask, "How can you tell what it is?" Believe me, I'd know that arrangement anywhere.

This tray of pie tins holding *the body and blood* are situated on a high, narrow, rough pine stand instead of on a discarded round dining room table too small for a growing family where I experienced this arrangement some time ago. I've never taken account of how much tossed-away furniture people throw in the direction of God's House, but it's plenty. Soiled couches for the fellowship room, chairs with the webbing hanging underneath. Anyhow, these plates for serving the Lord's Supper, pie tins, can be seen above the platform railing which is hung with a rough-weave fabric, pale burlap too stiff to gather very well.

I realize I've reported this church as *Wetumpka*, but that's just the nearest town where you'll find a grocery. We're in Slapout—some call it *Holtville*—about twenty minutes straight across the Tallahassee Highway and up the Holtville Road from Wetumpka, the leafy town with a graceful bridge connecting its residential and business areas across the Coosa River. I was hoping that was where the church was, Mama and Daddy kept saying . . . *next stop, Wetumpka*, but no.

The church house known around here as *Slapout Holiness* where I'm stuck on this bench next to Mama, fills a very small spot on a country road. Folks dispute how the name *Slapout* came to be. There's what you might call a hardware sales, nails and such, out of somebody's garage with the name, too.

Sister Mary Watford in Scratch Ankle reckons the label fits for the expression, *Slap out in the country*, and you can't dispute that notion. But others say it refers to running out of something or other, as in, *Better figger a trip to a groce-ry, bein we slap outta grits*. Going all the way to Wetumpka makes fetching ordinary supplies mighty inconvenient. They have no problem keeping stocked up on Welch's juice and Nabisco Premium crackers at this church, however.

Now that I've been six for a whole month I think I should have a better plan for escaping the uncomfortable damnation situation of receiving the Lord's Supper. So far, I've only been able to come up with the following ideas for escape:

1. Ask to go to the bathroom, but Mama'd never stand for that, "Hold it and next time you'll remember to go right before service."

2. Pretend to have a stomachache, see plan #1.

3. Begin to hiccup loudly so as to need a glass of water, but I don't have the nerve for that one.

Besides, fact is that 1, 2, and 3 are lies and we all know what happens to a person who lies. Flames of hell and damnation. But what's the difference, threats either way. The words that the pastor always says just before you put that cracker—*the body*—in your mouth explain my dilemma. Here they are: 1 Corinthians 11:24–29. Now the passage starts out fine, *And when He had given thanks He brake it, and said, Take, eat: this is my body which is broken for you; this do in remembrance of me.* The *He* who's saying this being Jesus, God's only Son. Of course, this refers to breaking a loaf of bread not soda crackers.

Apostle Paul's writing this letter to the people of Corinth so he's in charge here. This man keeps tight rules and has opinions I don't always agree with, for example:

Women: Paul says to cover up their heads and do without females as much as possible. Indicates again and again that girls are nothing but trouble. Far as we know, he stayed clear of the likes of us for his whole life.

Complaints: "I have a thorn in the flesh," he says. Now that never makes a lick of sense to me. Why not disinfect a needle like my Mama does and get that thorn out? Or if you want to be a he-man, which Billy David would probably be, let it fester then pop it out by way of the puss like Daddy does.

Apostle Paul went on to be with Jesus toting all his problems and ideas with him even while he's telling everybody else to get over theirs. Seems to happen right often.

The Pastor in Slapout I'm going to call "Brother Wilson" since I don't want you to think I'm mad at this certain person just because the words he's harping on turn me upside down and shake me. He's not the only pastor who does it.

This goes on all the time, everywhere in Holiness churches. His voice booms strong on the parts I emphasize:

> But let a man Examine himself and
> so let him eat of *That bread*
> and drink of *That blood.*
> For He That *Eateth and Drinketh Unworthily,*
> *Eateth And Drinketh Damnation to Himself*
> 1 Corinthians 11:28 and 29

See what I mean? Puts a body in a fix. How's a person to know about that unworthy part? So lying, damnation! Or unworthy, damnation! What can I do? Of course he means eating bits of broken soda crackers for *the body* and diluted Welch's grape juice for *the blood.* But still, it's the same problem.

First time I shook like a leaf in a breeze and then shrunk-up over this I was only four. I don't remember which one of the United States we were in but the dirt around the church house was not red, which pretty much rules out Georgia and Alabama, but brownish and full of sand like Florida. I could see the straight-stick pine trees out of the clear glass, rollout windows where my concentration was leading me to work out an escape plan.

When the tins are passed a heat starts rising. My face feels red and the noise inside me so loud that I declare Mama can hear it. Meantime, I have to be mouthing the words of the song, *There Is a Fountain Filled with Blood . . . drawn from Immanuel's veins*, so she won't notice anything is wrong. Putting out my hand to receive *the body and blood* is a whole lot harder than any normal person can understand. All the while I'm figuring what can be done to avoid this. As you can see, I failed. This is a test that won't go away like the ones I send to Calvert School every six weeks or so. Those tests are on *paper* and this one's in *blood and body*. I can see the Lord's Supper coming at me from up ahead over and over again.

This is a week full of meetings you can call a *backslider's revival*. It's not that folks don't invite their unchurched neighbors. They do. Thing is, there aren't that many. I declare, the ground itself around Slapout must be sown with Gospel seeds. Even the mules pulling the plows look like they might be convinced of Jesus and His saving grace. This means few out and out sinners—mostly people who've *grown cold* as we say—but when do they know they've slid into cold is what I can't comprehend. And does it have anything to do with unworthy?

Modest as he is, the pastor here mentions his radio ministry on WAPZ out of Wetumpka. "Jus fifteen min-its a week? But a ma-an can see Jay-zus, no time a-tall. Ama-an?" He nods, bobbing up and down like a woodpecker attacking a tree, except his head's more silver than blond-red like it used to be. He's not any taller than Daddy, but almost equals his height in width and wears overalls and a work shirt except on Sunday. Daddy joins in on his *Amen*, putting his hand on his shoulder in a kindly way as Wilson keeps talking his story.

"Ah bin livin Jay-zus since He call me out fum ahind at donkey in m'pa's cotton patch! Ha! 'Poss-l Paul fell offn is don-key, an me, ahm called fum *ahind* one." He likes this a lot and no doubt tells it often.

But Daddy's not so jolly back in the trailer, saying to Mama, "Pastor springs fifteen minutes on the radio on me two days before I have to go on the air." Preparation plays a loud tune for Daddy.

Mama says, "You have plenty material, Bill, why . . ."

"I know, I know . . . it's the idea of it, Doris."

Mama agrees. "But what about time for music, that cuts it down to no more than a testimony . . ."

"Far as I'm concerned there's time for music—you and the girls—has to be time." My mind immediately goes to what we'll sing, trying out the best for being on the air. I come up with, *I'm Satisfied with Jesus. I'm satisfied with Jesus in my heart today; His grace is full and free, His blood now cleanseth me.* Maybe I just have blood on my mind. They don't choose my idea at all, but *On the Other Side*. Soon as the red light flashes *On the Air*, singing the chorus first, then the verse.

WAPZ's studio is a tiny white-washed cement building about the size of a broom closet; one wall made of a giant window looking toward the announcer/engineer's desk on the other side; a fat microphone the shape of a squarish metal basket hanging from a metal pole swings down on a stand in front of Mama, Althea and me. Daddy's on the other side of the mic, and Brother Wilson stands to Daddy's right. He's going to say a word or two after we sing so people will know it's *Slapout Holiness* on the air.

Those three words—*On The Air*—printed in an arc over the light bulb positioned midway from either side on the wall above the window, always proves to be high excitement. When the light flashes on—red—my heart booms a downbeat and we start singing. That's what I love about being on the radio: the red light bulb flashing into action.

> *On the other side, treasures there have I,*
> *Treasures that this world with all Its wealth can never buy,*
> *When I reach that city And the gates swing open wide,*
> *I'll find my treasures waiting*
> *On the other side*

Of course the Preacher leaves everybody who's listening with something to think about,

> Those who know they have enough are rich!
> Can you hear me?
> We have treasures, you know.
> Waiting on the other side, Hallelujah!

Five minutes more by the clock, a prayer, and time's up. Brother Wilson ends with his pitch for coming to revival for the final three nights.

We're only here one week, Sunday to Sunday, starting on the first day with the celebration of the Lord's Supper, followed by a foot washing in the afternoon. I don't mind the foot washing part. It fits right in for an all day dinner on the ground and singing later on. "Wore out before we get good and started," Daddy's plaint. But you do get acquainted with folks real quick.

The Cox family—which includes Ernestine and Eddie Anderson, the Cox's daughter, her husband and their baby, Lewis—already invited us to dinner this coming Saturday, just after noon. Sister Cox is one of the gentle, shouting people here, more like swaying and waving as we sing songs like, *I'll Meet You in the Morning*:

I will meet you in the morning by the bright river side,
When all sorrow has drifted away . . .

Hearing the Preacher say, "In eternity there are no silver hairs, praise God! No wrinkles! We are beautiful forevermore, Hallelujah!" Sister Cox raises up both her hands and shouts, "Yasss, ohhh Jay-zus!" And that's her kind of holiness happy time. Eternity. No silver hair or wrinkles.

Of course the Preacher knows this is a backslider's revival, too. We've talked about it. He zeroes in on the way folks live that show where a body needs to pay attention. And that goes for the ones in the pews who don't know they've grown cold. See? I knew it was a problem figuring it all out.

Jesus said, "Bring him to me,"
when he heard the cripple call out.
Disciples may fail,
churches may fail
Christians may fail
but He never fails!
It's for this ol' crippled world Jesus came and died.
How do you get up off that pallet,
crippled up with hatred and resentment?
How're you gonna get to Jesus for healing?
First of all real devotion and prayer
isn't something you recite
a few times a day—why the heathen fall to their knees
facin "mecca" five times a day! Prayin to allah—
No, no! that's not enough.
It's devotion radiating from your heart every waking moment.
Paul's whole life was an act of devotion.
Jesus did not come here to teach us how to build beautiful temples in
the midst of wretchedness, hate and strife.

He came to make the human heart a temple.

He came to make *your* heart a temple! Praise God!
Why Brother Wilson, he did not say to
worship in "a beautiful temple for such
pleases the Father." He said
worship Him in Spirit and in truth.

Brother Wilson jumps to his feet and claps his hands in appreciation of the truth the Preacher shouts out.

Roll-out windows in a concrete block church house that's built flat on the ground, no porch or steps up to the front door. Inside, the benches are plain. That's this church. But the details keep picking at my mind. Trying to recall another church house. The one that looks like this one on the outside except for the color of the dirt. Slapout Holiness feels cool inside, painted celery green. But the other church isn't painted at all, inside or out. The cement blocks rise up out of the sand, gray. All gray. And the window glass is not painted there as it is here. They're clear glass panes, I'm sure of that.

These windows crank out sideways for open air—the panes painted a milky white, so teenagers can't sit outside on the backs of pick-ups during the service, looking in. Instead, young people sprawl across the back benches which gives the Mamas who sit as singers on the platform plenty to do: shaking their heads, frowning, giving their young ones *the eye*. Especially during preaching. More than one sermon's going on around here.

Sister Loreta Tuttle's face sends out regular Morse Code messages to her boy Lawrence Tuttle Jr., called *Junior*. He's a couple years past Althea's age but his blond hair and mischievous blue eyes guarantee attention every time he shows up. He and his best friend Buddy Aikens stick to each other close as Tonto and the Lone Ranger. Usually, there are a few girls following, too, like a Sheriff's posse in pursuit. This *Junior* boy steals hearts without a word. I can see it happen. His friend Buddy's Ma, Sister Dolly Aikens, doesn't sit with the singers. When she shows up, she's on the second or third row so she can dance in the Holy Ghost out in the aisle. Keeping an eye on Buddy's not a priority for her. But then he only comes to bask in the glory around Junior, that's my guess.

Overheard somebody say *at boy, Buddy, he needs a maan inna hass.* Hear tell they live with her folks, her Pa ailing real bad and her Ma seldom able to be in church. Daddy and Brother Wilson went out to their place for healing prayer one afternoon.

All of the young people pay Althea some attention, but she's too shy to talk much when they come around before church starts to investigate how the vibra harp works. She looks down, shrugs when Junior asks, "How them rangy-dangs come outta there?" Then with her mallets on the metal keys she'll make a run back and forth—anything to put them off and not have to talk—until somebody comes and rescues her. Usually Mama or Daddy shows up to tune the other instruments.

The sign language between platform singers and the back benches commences during preaching. Sometimes Sister Tuttle manages to quiet Junior and his group. I'm sure curious what goes on at home if she can't. I know what happens to me if I don't pay attention. First, its *Help us Lord* kind of groaned by Daddy, then if I don't snap out of it, and he gets to the third *Help us Lord*, I have the belt to answer to back at the trailer house. It's not pretty.

> Live in a house of hate! Malice! Jealousy?
> And you have a mind *divided*—only shows *one* side.
> And in the house of *ignorance?*—don't have
> no mirrors—you can't see *yourself.*

Wednesday night Eddie Anderson figures out that he's a backslider and he "slid on inta *home*! Praisa Lawd, al-lluuu! Jay-zus he's s'good bringin us back fer a home run when we's gone off astray," in the words of the pastor, rejoicing in Jesus as Eddie heads to the altar. I've just finished singing, *Don't Turn Him Away*:

> *Don't turn Him away, don't turn Him away,*
> *He has come back to your heart again,*
> *Altho you've gone astray . . .*

Eddie's wife Ernestine, willowy in a filmy pink skirt to her ankles and white eyelet blouse, continues to bounce bald, confused-looking baby Lewis on one hip while she walks the side aisle, tears falling over her fine-boned face which she swipes with the back of one hand from time to time. The baby alternates between whimpers and reaching up to clutch at one of his mother's braids and she gently brushes his hand aside with her swiping hand.

You see people so pleased on the outside—like Eddie, all proud of his family—but you never know what Jesus sees on the inside. Some worthy, some not so worthy. Since Jesus died for everybody, isn't the fountain filled with blood for people who aren't so worthy, otherwise how do you get worthy? Once you are, how can you tell? And when you aren't, how do you know that?

Probably wouldn't even think about it if not for the Lord's Supper. That's what gets things so snarled up.

Tonight, a regular Wednesday revival time in September with harvest going on in the fields, three backsliders—Eddie Anderson, Bolivar Dean Smith, the pastor's second cousin once removed, and Patricia Beavis—leave the church house in the midst of shouts for sinners saved by the blood of the lamb.

"Happy day! We harvestin souls fer Jayzus." Homecoming celebrations and harvests work real good together for Jesus people in Slapout.

Extra meetings besides revival every night weighs down real heavy on Daddy. Radio scheduled on Thursday, nine in the morning, and the jailhouse meeting set for Saturday, ten in the morning. "Too many distractions," he grumbles. At least one meal on these days has to be warm, stewed-together bread and milk to keep his stomach happy.

But Brother Wilson's reputation on the radio, he says, sometimes encourages folks to call him up and "ast if a might could call on a boy, ma-an, ya know. Gone bad. Stuck inside a jail-hass?" *Everything works together for good* is the point he's making. So maybe the radio is worthwhile in spite of Daddy's nervous stomach.

In one town where we hold meetings the church house and the jailhouse have a strong relationship, you might say. I'm having a time keeping towns straight lately, was that Sylacauga—where the water tower has those cute scallops around the bottom of it?—or Luverne, where I saw the house with red, purple and white petunias all along the walkway? Not sure. At any rate, the preacher there tells us his "git-tar pickers gits too happy on a Satiddy night?" Too much fun with the Grand Ole Opry, he says, and they start nippin some product they've been making. That's homemade whiskey, sometimes they call it *white lightening*. The git-tar pickers end up raising a ruckus and "at lands'm inna jailhouse." Unless he maintains a real solid friendship with the local sheriff, springing them in time for Sunday morning service "gits kindly diff-cult."

Doesn't seem as if Brother Wilson is quite that close to the Sheriff of Elmore County. Maybe it's because the jailhouse is so far away in Wetumpka. Still, if he ever needs to spring somebody in time for Sunday morning, these Saturday meetings for the prisoners can't hurt.

Daddy only takes me with him, being that the quarters for doing preaching, praying, and singing are limited to a small area along a walkway between cells on either side. A thick bright yellow line stripes the middle of the walkway. You have to stay on that line, the deputy explains, "Cain take no chance some ole boy's gonna feel grabby. Git whatta mean?"

Jailers try to convince Daddy that he shouldn't take a child in where the prisoners live, but he smiles big and says, "She's my Spark Plug. Can't get going without her, can I?" I'll guarantee a jailer wouldn't give it a second thought if I was *Billy David*.

I'm not afraid. Men act more decent with a little kid around. Even pro-
tective. They miss their own children, I hear that all the time. If anybody
acts up or says bad words, the other guys close him down in a hurry.

Sometimes a separate section of the jail operates for women. But here,
they've located Julia S. Tutwiler Prison for females a few miles outside town.
"At Miz Tutwiler," Brother Wilson explains as we head into Wetumpka on
Saturday, "were a crusader fer wimin. Bad wimin, ya might say, she b'lieved
in teachin'm. Givin em jus-tice y'know?" Daddy nods, "Bless her heart,"
which is what Mama always says.

Women I meet in the jail house try to hide their faces, dipping them
sideways so as not to look a person in the eye, or dolling themselves up with
greasepaint, as Daddy calls make-up. Holiness women don't wear make up
on account of being the temples of the Holy Ghost. But deep inside these
poor locked-up souls, Lord only knows what goes on. The eyes they try to
hide look back full of tears or blank as a wall. Nearly always makes me think
about Donny Johnson's Ma. Don't imagine we'll visit the Julia S. Tutwiler
Prison, though.

Men tear up easy when they're behind bars, too. Honest words flood
out of them, words you know they'd never say walking around town. Outside, they swagger and roll a cigarette or take a pinch of snuff as if that shows
them to be something instead of nothing. But as Daddy points out, anybody
can roll a cigarette and stuff tobacco in their lip. No talent required and very
little practice necessary. Daddy's big on practicing.

As we come across the Coosa River toward town, Brother Wilson
points out the first jailhouse here on the banks of the river. Called the Callaboose, a one-room whitewashed building, thick adobe-looking walls with
the bars still in place. The Bibb Graves Bridge built of long sloping arches
separates houses and churches on one side of the river from most of the
businesses, movie theater, court house, and jail on the other.

As usual, Daddy gives his sales talk about the *Spark Plug* to this Sheriff
as he starts unlocking the double doors, beginning at the first guard station.
Daddy adds, as the big man in the chestnut brown uniform tight-fitted with
a wide leather belt hung with holsters on either side casts a skeptic's eye over
me, "She's seen the inside of many a jailhouse. *Singing*, of course." Then he
flashes his lightening smile at our guide. With that, the first heavy metal
doors swing open.

From a cleaning fluid metallic odor tinged with tobacco underlined
by that damp cement scent at the guard station, the smell begins to change
when bars come into view. A toilet with no lid adorns one corner in the
larger cells. The whole area—one long barred room on either side of the line

where we stand, plus smaller cells on both sides of the walkway up where we can be heard but not seen—twangs with a rank stench.

You get used to it, the odor? Not a lot of fresh air wafting through here. I've seen giant rolling waste cans with rags for cleaning draped over the top, but the job's never complete. Or ever done well.

One man sits close to the bars on the end of his bunk bed in the big cell facing us. Hair flopped forward over his bent head, hands blackened by motor oil, seems like, clasped in front of him as he rests his blue-jail-uniformed elbows on his knees. He stays like that through all the speaking and pitiful hymn singing.

I try to get them enthused about *Amazing Grace*, good to sing in the jail on account of that *wretch like me* line as well as the Preacher's few words of convincing the men of sin. I'd say no convincing is necessary here. They look ragged in soul and body, too, the dozen men flopped in various positions around the cells on both sides of the line. After the singing come the remarks by the Preacher:

> God said *let us make man in our image,*
> but man says *let us make* God *in* our *image* and that's
> where you get in trouble!
> Tryin to take God's place, makin yourself
> the one to answer to; makin yourself the boss
> with no thought of God takes you
> on the path to sin,
> lands you in a place you don't want to be.
> You can't fool God! Don't you know that?
>
> But you can come to the cross,
> let the blood of Jesus
> free you from your burden of sin and shame.

Brother Wilson's praying takes a good five minutes, and by then it's time for me to sing by myself.

> *Almost persuaded now to believe*
> *Almost persuaded, Christ to receive . . .*
> *O wand'rer come!*

Just a few words are out when the floppy dark hair raises up slowly and to my surprise, deep blue pools of misery look straight at me—I'd have guessed dark brown eyes—his mouth a shadow, surrounded by at least a week's worth of black bristles. His mouth quivers like a little kid with hurt feelings.

Time for the Preacher to pray now, closing out. While we're fixing to leave, I step over to the bars and extend my hand to the man. He full on breaks down, shoulders shaking, at the same time grasping my fingers, choking out words.

"Y'you . . . like . . . m'Bettyann . . ."

But the jailer, not the Sheriff but a Deputy guard, sees I've gone off the yellow line which I confess I didn't even think about and quick as a wink jumps in-between me and the bars, shuttling me back to Daddy's side. Scared me—the guard, not the man.

This same Deputy marches us out through the first set of locked doors with a *somebody's-gotta-be-in-charge* attitude, clanging the barriers back in place again extra hard. Muttering under his breath. Then another set, *clang! Clang!* at the guard's station.

The Sheriff's leaning up against the blank cement wall, one side of his big belly lopping over the top of his gun talking to the man on duty, saying, "We got us some catawba worms? Fat ole thangs . . ." and the guard responding, "Yeah! They the best off them tobaccy leaves, em fish gobbles . . ." When our Deputy, before opening the last two doors for us, interrupts the conversation. The Sheriff lifts himself away from the wall deliberately. Our Deputy, his thick blond hair clipped close with a matching mustache, muscular, and considerably taller than the Sheriff, bends to the older man's ear and whispers a long secret behind his hand. Real conspicuous like.

The Sheriff takes charge from here on out after shuffling a loud set of keys on a heavy round metal ring big enough to be a handcuff, fitting the final locks and turning them slow, very slow. Slamming them with a sound opposite of resurrection, saying as it resounds, "Na we don allow no contac with these here priz-ners." Puffing his body into a rooster ready to crow, he continues, "Ah heah a jailhouse Rules bin broke." Lets the gravity of this register, frowning, wide inky brows meeting on his nearly bald head underlining his every word. "At air *ma-anl* Name's Leroy. He's brought in lass night, ain got a full story? But they's a man bin kilt. Leroy, na, *LEroy*, could be he's a killer. Oughta be in sol-tary, ya git what ahm sayin?"

His message like to paralyzed my heart on account of Bettyann. I declare it stops the beating for a minute or two. What can a girl do when her daddy's in that kind of fix? She goes on the list for talks with Jesus right now, along with Zorneely. Not many Negroes in this town, I notice, but with troubles like Bettyann has, there's no shortage on worries.

Brother Wilson's the first person to speak when we pile ourselves back into his 1939 green Ford pickup, three of us in the front seat with me in the middle. He just sits there quiet, not starting the engine though he puts the key in the ignition. The knot in my throat, moved up from my tightened heart, causes a continued clanging in my head—those metal doors—echo-ing. Fright for Bettyann plus disturbance from the Deputy and the Sheriff just add to the loud noises rolling around inside me while I'm still as a cat waiting for a mouse to move.

Quietly, Brother Wilson begins speaking, "When you was reachin out t' at Leroy, Chile? You's pure-ly bein Jayzus. *Lil chile shall lead'm* ats a truth." Shaking his head slowly in a sort of wondering way as a witness to the scene, "Don't matta none wut at Sherff has ta say? Ya done what Jay-zus woulda did." He nods decisively, then cranks up the motor and we set off in silence back across the Coosa toward Slapout.

That's the thing about this pastor. Those damnation words come out of his mouth only because he has to say them. It's how he's come up, raised in a church house where every preacher yells Apostle Paul's words so as to be sure everybody hears them real good. Or, in my case hears them real bad. The Evangelist doesn't have charge of the Lord's Supper, that's for the local preacher. Sometimes an evangelist might read the scripture, but if that's ever happened I don't recall hearing it from Daddy. Certainly isn't a big memory marked *Do Not Open* like these screaming episodes turn out to be.

At the trailer house, a visitor's relaxing on a canvas chair just outside our door. Mama's sitting on the edge of a folding metal chair, with her sweetest smile plastered on her face. Nodding, polite, eyes no doubt darting in the direction of the road, waiting for us to return. We have dinner scheduled today and Mama's trying to figure out how to detach Dolly Aikens from her chair.

Mama stands as we arrive and Brother Wilson calls, "Hey, Sista Dolly!"

"Hey, na, Preacha Wi-son." she says without much welcome. Fixing her gaze on Daddy, "Vangliss Skondee! A came a callin on y'all!"

Daddy already decoded Mama's distressed face and body-message, and says briskly, "Hello there, Sister Aikins." With hardly any pause, "When are we due to be in Wetumpka, Doris?" And he flicks the trailer's folding screen door with a move of his wrist, steps in past the visitor and goes about the business of getting ready to go.

It matters that Daddy made this trailer. He tells me he designed it to be more *aerodynamic* than the commercial ones he tested. I mull that word *aerodynamic* over when I see our little trailer—painted dark green on the bottom and a lighter ivory kind of green on the top to match our car—trailing along behind us. That screen door? He designed it to fold in-ward down a central set of hinges. As you approach it from the outside, part of the door's wooden outline set in the middle slides back so you can touch the edge in order to open or close it. Or flick it like Daddy just did. Very clever, really. I love that little door.

There's no hint strong enough for Dolly Aikins. She stands, too, like Mama, but peers in after Daddy, "Y'all's lil ol traila hass! Ats a pityful lookin thang, shor is," she shakes her head. Sister Dolly's hair is still wearing its faded nighttime red bandana wrapped around her pin curls, tied so one tail lops onto her wide, pale forehead.

"Whyyy, this here lil box'll fit on auvr front porch!" She continues to edge against the closed door.

Daddy's answer is, "Well, Sister Aikens, we're looking to our home in Glory. Amen?" She responds with a small voice, "Ama-an, Brotha Skondee."

"Bless your heart," Mama continues in her campaign to get the mes-sage across, "all you must have to do with a growing boy, but taking time out coming by to see us." Being polite is the only way to talk to rude people, that's what Mama always tells me. "Audrey, are you ready? Althea! We're leaving," Mama calls as she starts for the car. Daddy's out of the trailer hav-ing retrieved his wallet—he takes nothing to the jail except identification papers in his shirt pocket—and we're all getting in the car.

Alhea and I, stashed in the back seat, smile and wave. Sister Dolly Aik-ens' wrap dress of daisy patterned feed sack fabric flaps around well-padded ankles that suddenly appear to me as tops of upside down milk bottles, feet poured out into generous once-fuzzy blue slippers. She musters a wan, "Ya'll keep on keepin-on," as we pull out of earshot down the road, dust kicking up behind us.

Just barely out of harm's way at the jailhouse and then have to spring ourselves from the Dolly-trap. But when Jesus walks along with you, you can rest quiet, sure that every discomfort finds a comfort. That truth shows up as pure fact over and over again. Well, most of the time.

We set off for dinner at the home of Brother and Sister Cox in We-tumpka. That fine dinner with the Cox family speaks peace to my heart, even while I keep wondering where Bettyann might be.

"We's ast all a time, whyn't we go ta church right heah n town? Why travel s'fur! A tell ya." Sister Lou Cox—some folks refer to her as *Loula*—shakes her head side to side, blue eyes turning misty as she speaks, "Hits a reckleckshun ever time we drives up at air Holtvl Road. Lawdy, lawdy! M' Gran-Pa n' Ma—their ole hass pert neah back to dust, na—but pre-cious mem-ries!" While she talks, pausing from time to time to stare out the win-dow, north, in the direction of the Holtville Road, Sister Lou continues her tasks of occasionally stirring the gravy and mashing potatoes in a huge tin pot. The aroma of roasting beef fills the air of her sunny kitchen.

This house, itself, is sunshine for me. Pale yellow like February sun, highlighted by white-framed windows and a porch that wraps around two sides. Daisies waving you up the walk to the four broad steps leading to the solid oak and glass front door. A comfy dwelling on the living-side of the Bibb Graves Bridge over the Coosa.

Mama, Althea and I sit on chairs at the round table in the middle of the cooking preparations, sipping glasses of sweet tea, which means *iced tea*. They're fortunate at this location to be right in back of the Wetumpka Ice House which is only one block over, across the street from the L & N train depot. The tea's tasty and Mama's experienced in letting somebody else talk while she agrees.

An oval wooden bowl big enough for a trough holds self-rising flour cut with lard, a clean feed sack dish towel covering it on the tin-topped counter of the pie cupboard. Of course it makes me think of the other feed sack dish towel covering the body and blood I saw up front a few days ago, but I push that back down in the *Do Not Open* box.

"M'Gran Mama give me iss here pie keeper," Sister Lou says as she begins to stir buttermilk into a portion of the ever-ready flour; flopping it out onto the counter, patting it into biscuit cutting shape. Her daughter Ernestine, fluttery, thin, gets the pans ready for the biscuits. Tall and narrow except for large breasts—which Sister Loula smiles about, knowingly, whispering "Ernstine's still feedin lil Lew's"—with hair exactly like her Ma, she's handed baby Lewis off to her husband Eddie Anderson while she helps or *heps* as she says it.

Eddie looks mighty happy. Being born again-again this past Wednesday night seems to be agreeing with him and the whole family by the looks of things.

I'm more restless than Althea, so I tend to drift back and forth, kitchen to living room. "W'tumpka? Hits a Creek In-jun na-ame," Brother Cox holds forth from an easy chair of shiny pink, yellow, and green flowered fabric. He's telling Daddy about the history of the town's name, "means rumblin waters." The river's partially blasted out by a meteor, he says, from thousands of years ago. I'll be. Plus, the South part of the river flows out from this bridge and all the way down to the Gulf of Mexico.

Tall maple trees pull me outside while the biscuits are baking and the men start talking Jesus and Heaven. Every maple leaf overhead takes seriously the job of sheltering this blessed house. They've been caring for each other for over 70 years, now, I gather, that's how long Brother Cox says the house has been here. Yep, this tree watches over the street, shades people and gives the breeze a boost. But some houses on Tuskeena Street are over 100 years old, so this one's just a kid you might say.

Cardinals feed on the high ledge Brother "Bubba" Cox built for birds on the east-facing porch near the railing. Odd sort of bird feeder, filled from the top with holes letting seed dribble out along the bottom where the ledge is built. The father of the cardinals, a loud red male, prepares the way for the quiet-colored female, fussing the rest of the birds aside so she can do her personal pecking. When Sister Cox pointed out the feeder to me as we came in earlier, she said they've seen seven families of this pair of cardinals come and go.

Sister Loula Cox calls out to me good and loud, "We escapin a blazin kitchen, ooeee!" when she comes to fetch me around back to dinner laid out on a long plank table covered with forest green checked oil cloth in the yard under a magnolia tree. Tall pink glasses full of ice and sweet tea mark the places set with silver knives, forks and spoons—all matching—carved with tiny roses at the top of every handle. The dishes are ivory colored with pink roses, dark green leaves, large and loopy in their design, welcoming us with their loveliness.

"M'aint Ola give'm t'me. Na, Aint Ola lives in Mont-gom-ry? Rich, ya could say. Rich in propitty. Her n' Unca Donal dint produce no cud-ns for Erns-tine. Ahm the onliest livin rel-tive." Sister Loula nods, telling the story of the fine setting as we find our places. "Praisa Lawd! Ah use'm everwhar. Indoors er out! They's a gift a Gawd ya know."

Ernestine's lanky smiling Eddie, his rust-colored hair trying to make a comeback after a pomade ordeal, gives baby Lewis back to her as he finds his place somewhere in the middle of the chairs all lined up on both sides. She disappears into the house to "feed a baby." Brother Bubba and his wife Sister Loula are book-ends for the table.

Daddy says the blessing, "Thank you Lord Jesus for this great banquet and the hands that prepare and provide it! We praise you today, hallelujah! Looking forward to that NEW day when we will be at the banquet table in Glory with You. Amen!" Closing shouts echo from all around the table, including from born-again-again Eddie.

Besides roast beef slices dripping with juice on an oval white platter and mashed potatoes cradling a small pond of butter on top piled high in a loopy-pink-rose bowl, and gravy in a boat matching the bowl, there's succotash—fresh lima beans and corn pulled together with a little cream—tomatoes so sweet you can taste sunshine, and biscuits that float onto my plate and slurp up home-churned butter with strawberry preserves. I hate to disappoint Daddy, but I don't think Glory's banquet is going to beat this one.

And all the dishes matching? This is an astonishing sight.

"Praisa Lawd, Brotha," booms out Bubba Cox, "We took us off a fine dinna time, t'day. Eddie 'n me? Our son-by-mar-age, he sells with us, too. Doin fine. Yas at young'un's doin fine. Praisa Lawd. Course we close on a Satiddy affer-noon." Brother Cox is responsible for the insurance office in town. Eddie and Ernestine live here, upstairs. They seem like a thankful bunch of people, I can say that.

After dinner—"needs to make room fer at lemon pie!"—we walk through the neighborhood and across the many giant iron scallops of the Bibb Graves Bridge, "hits name fer Gov-ner? Back air n 19 n 37."

Arches appear to move in majesty, flanked by tall single-globed light standards along the wide walking path on both sides. At the center, we paused and looked up the river, small rapids swirling in counter currents around rock outcroppings along the shore. Made me want to stay there, watching, being very still and letting the water carry worries away. At my back, cars passed, horses clopped, but their noise grew faint. I stared out over the rippling water, a wide thoroughfare of birds, dragonflies and un-identified flying things—silvery seed parachutes?—lifting in the airwaves. A breeze straight out of Glory.

Althea's tugging at my sleeve brought me to again. I didn't care about walking around much, wanting to stay with the river. But my sister scolds me as if she's Mama, saying everybody's already over on the other side. We catch up with them at the Callaboose, the pioneer jail. Daddy picks me up to let me see through the bars. At least prisoners could look out over the water and dream of floating away to freedom.

There's something about loitering on the walkway of the bridge and walking the lush green grass on either side that feels like royalty. Wetump-ka's friendly again in spite of the jail house fright this morning. Mostly that was about Bettyann, anyhow. When I see children playing in yards we pass, I look for her. Course I don't have a clue how she looks. Maybe dark hair, curly.

Crossing back over the bridge—no stopping this time much as I want to—I experience everlasting arms the Bible talks about in the branches of a magnolia. This magnificent tree is twice the size of the one shading our dinner table and grows on the residential side of Wetumpka on the banks of the Coosa River. I was so anxious to get to the bridge's walkway, I didn't even look up when we passed it before. But descending to the green from the balustrade this time, the magnolia is right in the path.

I know *everlasting arms* are supposed to be God in Eternity or some-thing like that? But in the presence of this tree, you feel that Presence, not just hear the words and work up your imagination. A lower branch offers a dinner-plate sized creamy white flower to bury my face, inhaling a scent soft as summer night air. A fragrance that stamps out any leftover jail house stench. As I look into limbs climbing high above, I see other slender flower cylinders shedding their brown husks and beginning to unfurl.

Even the Kudzu vines cooperate in Magnolia's beauty as they trip from lesser trees over to her shiny green patten-leather-like leaves backed in bronze suede waving toward the river. Frills of giant Kudzu swing in the air, catching the edges of her branches, making no attempt to smother as that vine usually does. Here, Kudzu plays. The new growth—tiny and pale—bursts with good humor from the center of its leaves.

Back on Tuskeena Street, Sister Cox trots ahead of us to her neighbor's yard in the block beyond the sunshine-house address, excited over seeing something—what, a bush?—"hit's still abloomin!" Loula Cox cradles a spire of red blossoms in her hand tenderly and once we catch up, she whispers, ". . . name's a *Blood a Christ*, yass Lawd, a *Blood. Christ.*" And after a few seconds, adds, "Some calls it a *Tears a Christ* but I say it's a *blood*."

Her reverence and awe fit each heart-shaped blossom, the part that dips at the top creates a tiny pleat where it attaches to the stem. Must be fifty blossoms on each eight to ten-inch spire ranging from the largest blooms at the top near the double-crescent strong dark green leaves, to its far end where tiny red ovals await their opening. All the branches on this bush—taller then I am—radiate outward pointing toward the sky. Some, blooming red spires, and some, leafy green.

At first I stand, staring. Then I move closer, closer, and closer still, petals breathing soft on my lips. Father cardinal's feathers aren't near the glowing depths of this red. Even fully bloomed out, these satin flowers soak deep into the color.

All the way back to Slapout the wealth we've been given on this day runs through my attention, vivid and alive. The river, Magnolia, red blossoms, and the sunshine house on Tuskeena Street.

Everyone finds their own place for an afternoon rest soon as we arrive in Slapout. Mama and Althea recline on the two seats, each side of the trailer's table. Daddy's in the backseat of the car, studying.

I go into the church house and sit on that bench where I was stuck with my Mama last Sunday. This time more comfortable, even though the air smells of cement and old wood. No breeze breathing through. Windows closed, painted panes a ghostly white. Words disappeared. Then, slowly, those windows take me to another church house, all in pictures.

I began to see what choked me so bad on Sunday. Besides being worried about *unworthy* and damnation and all, which, Lord knows, are enough. Seeing everything in pictures. I closed my eyes and let them tell me what I need to know:

The round table in the church that's twin to this one but far away with different dirt around it? Lord's Supper was on a Sunday in that church house, too, but the day before—Saturday—my Mama, sister and I are standing there singing, *Dear Jesus, Abide with Me* followed by a chorus of *Abide with Me*:

> *Sometimes my way seems rough and long,*
> *But the road to Heaven is the way to Home;*
> *My trials here will soon be o're,*
> *I see Jesus on the other shore.*
>
> *Abide with me, fast falls the even tide,*
> *The darkness deepens, Lord, with me abide!*
> *When other helpers fail, and comforts flee,*
> *Help of the helpless, oh, abide with me.*

We're singing on the platform next to the pulpit and on the church house floor in the middle—an altar on either side—rests a tiny white casket atop a funeral parlor's midnight blue velvet covered stand. No bigger than my pillow, that casket. The lid, open, and on a cloud of white satin forever sleeps a tiny baby girl, three weeks old when she took her last breath.

Her mama sits on the front row, thin hair pulled back in a rubber band, body bent to her lap, face dropped in her hands; sobs wracking her boney frame. The baby's Daddy—must be—his fawn color hair looking like it hasn't been combed for a week hanging in greasy clumps over his broad forehead, round blue eyes staring straight ahead, has a hand on one of her arms with his other arm over her back, holding on to her as well as he can. Their boy—my age, about four years old at the time—a shock of hair matching his daddy's, freckles over his nose and worried, red-rimmed blue eyes, clutches his Mama's black skirt with one hand. Neither the daddy nor his boy can reach the mother sunk to the bottom of her well of tears.

Comes to me that Pastor told us they lost another baby girl, too, "Las one dint live outta bein born." But Mary Ellis Wagner seemed fine "til croup gotta holt a her. Taken'r life right out."

I was really little, only four, but I remember that baby and I knew something wasn't right. Something *besides* the baby girl taking her last breath. I couldn't figure things out then like I can now. Well, mostly. Daddy insists on thinking situations through besides asking questions. *Think! Audrey, think!* But now, the questions he won't like, I don't ask. And sometimes puzzle-words still don't fit even if there seems to be an answer.

"That baby . . . Lawd Jay-zus, jus taken er on home, praise His name," the pastor had to say. Reckon he had to, otherwise why would he.

What does Jesus need with babies in heaven is what I want to know. If I was that mama wouldn't I be upset with Jesus? When preachers talk that way—blaming croup and everything on Jesus—it makes me wonder all over again about *unworthy*. But I couldn't bring those words up then. My mind just went quiet and stopped. I'm still not sure where *unworthy* fits in, or even if it does. Maybe it's the words, the words some preachers say at times like this are purely worthless for comfort and don't make a lick of sense.

Mary Ellis never had to choose between cracker or no cracker. Body or no body, blood or no blood and drinking to her damnation. Yet look at what happened to her. Are babies born worthy? When do they get to be *un*worthy?

The pictures keep moving. Only now can I describe them.

At the graveyard standing over the hole in the dirt where the casket's being lowered, the pastor drones on again, "God A-mighty Fath-r n heav-n took iss here chile cause 'e love her so . . ." And then Mama, Althea and I singing *Angel Band*. I was too young to sing alone like I do now.

The day after that funeral, Sunday, the whole scene of sitting in that cement block church house feeling how the gray walls smell, returns. I can't hear the preacher—no words sound out—but I can see him pounding the pulpit with one hand and the other holding an open, well-worn King James Bible. Glass windows rolled out, showing the straight stick pines and sandy out of doors where I long to be. Tins of *body* and tiny thimbles of *blood* being passed and that same preacher's words from the grave site rise up and drown me all over again even though I can't hear them. Plus now he's yelling out the Apostle Paul's words about damnation, turning red faced as he does.

Reaching out for a crumb of body appears to be way beyond my capacity but I do it on account of Mama being at my elbow. Swallowing the body, out of the question.

Probably, then, I took a deep breath. Closed my eyes. Made my voice strong as I could for when we sing *Nothing but the Blood* at the end. That's what I did last Sunday—take a deep breath—too. But first I drained all the trouble words from my mind so it became a deep white sink with black letters swirling out of sight. Then I chose the tiniest cracker, put it on my tongue and let it fall inside. No swallowing. No chewing.

Sitting here now, letting the Lord's Supper situations mix up and jump around with me mouthing the words to *There Is a Fountain Filled with Blood* or trying hard to sing *Nothing But the Blood*—besides Mary Ellis Wagner in the casket hidden by shadows—purely chills me to the bone and makes my face get hot all at the same time. Words crash into each other, a traffic jam gnarls inside, horns honking and voices yelling.

Careful, I lie down flat on my back on the bench. Smoothing my good pink play dress with daisies printed on it over my knees, then putting my hands over my ears. Eyes closed while the traffic jam fades.

I don't know how long I've been lying here when I feel a faint rumble of the bench . The Lion's purr. Opening my eyes a little bit, I can see a big velvet paw lopped over the edge of the bench just above my head. Don't know how He manages to arrive so silent like but He always makes me smile. Quiet visits the space around the purring and the slight vibration of the wooden bench beneath me soothes all my senses.

Spirals of red blossoms return.

6

Minot, North Dakota 1949

Marketing Revival

- *The Great Plains states (Nebraska, Wyoming, North and South Dakota) beset by the worst winter on record; Red Cross, Army Corps of Engineers, Air Force, National Guard and Civil Air Patrol, all brought in for rescue of people and animals.*

- *President Truman declares in a speech that the Soviet Union will either destroy itself or abandon aggression.*

- *The Vatican issues a decree threatening to excommunicate Catholics who defend Communism or are members of the Communist Party.*

- *Saskatoon, Canada, was, until 1900, covered by mountains, oceans and great fern forests. For most of the last million years it was a land of glaciers which began their retreat 20,000 years ago, forming the South Saskatchewan River. Human habitation began about 12,000 years into the glacier's retreat, habitation by Ojebwa and Cree speaking groups from the eastern woodlands.*

- *The Dominion Lands Act passed by the Canadian government in 1872 set up a square township system of survey for new territories, offering free homestead lands to prospective settlers. When Serge and Elena Schondiene came to Western Canada from the Ukraine for religious freedom in 1907, Serge secured property for a wheat farm by waiting in line for three days at the Battleford Land Office.*

- *William Skondeen—Serge and Elena's youngest son—now travels north with his family to visit his elder sister Lucia and her husband Michael on just such a farm.*

- *Audrey Skondeen is seven years old.*

FROM THE OUTSIDE, YOU may not be able to tell how much a camp meeting tabernacle resembles a grocery store, but on the inside it's clear as can be. Think on it just a minute. Everybody gathers at the tabernacle during camp meeting. Now I realize camp meeting happens once a year and a grocery market happens every week or every day if you're not all that organized. It's about the purpose. Both of them aim toward a welcome table. Finally sitting down with loved ones either here or up yonder. Heaven.

At camp you gather goodness ingredients—songs, preachers, singers, youth meeting ideas, Bible studies and friendships—for holiness meetings twelve months of the year to come. At the grocery you gather goodness ingredients for your family for the whole week long. Both feed us, one on food for the soul and one on food for the body.

We sing a song, a spiritual, about that Welcome Table. When Althea and I go to squabbling, I sing in my heart since no one in the car ever sides with me:

> I'm going to sit at the Welcome Table
> I'm going to sit at the Welcome Table one of these days . . .

Then the next verse is the one where I turn up the volume real loud for myself. Sometimes I hum it just for the sake of annoyance.

> I'm gonna tell God how you treat me
> I'm gonna tell God how you treat me one of these days
> When we sit at the welcome table one of these days . . .

I set to thinking about this after we ran up on a clean, full of freshness grocery in Tupelo, Mississippi, on our way north to Kansas Camp Meeting. This is no ordinary bunch of travel days. After Kansas Camp, *Lord willing* as Mama says, we'll travel on north to visit Uncle Mike and Aunt Lucia in Canada. With so many miles in the back seat there's plenty of time to consider matters a girl might ordinarily not have time to consider.

Tupelo's where we spend our first night, leaving Gadsden, Alabama, and traveling to the west on Highway 278. That market in Tupelo sticks straight up as a beautiful landmark. Anticipation of freshness in the produce and cleanliness in the surroundings—no corners harboring greasy dirt build up—completely rewarded. A crisp scent greets you at the door. Folks working there, friendly, everybody happy to help. No grumps and no fakes grinning empty headed looks and saying *How you, Honey?*

Such details are obvious to a person who finds grocery shopping a pleasure like I do. You can say it's a trip by myself with Daddy and that's the reason, partly true. Or maybe that we often take what's given us in "grocery showers"—when folks bring canned goods for the Preacher—and we sort through them, using what we can and donating the rest to the pastor in the next town so as not to insult anyone in this town who brought us a tub of lard, say, and that's why choosing our own goods feels thrilling. That's partly true, too. But over all, hunting for good food that will make up a meal at our family table fills in pieces of a puzzle picture that include good aroma, familiar faces, and being nourished, besides. There is nothing better than that.

Singing gospel songs anticipating Gloryland where we'll gather to feast with loved ones puts one of those puzzle pieces in place, too. Reminds me of the Longfellow poem Mama and I learned last week, *O gift of God! O perfect day* . . . then something about no work but play and finally, *it is enough for me, not to be doing, but to be.*

At the grocery store? We're on a treasure hunt discovering what's *going to be.* We're doing a chore too, but it's play for me. Those words *it is enough for me, not to be doing, but to be* start going over in my mind while we're in the Tupelo grocery.

Folks show up for camp with a lot of expectations for what they'll find. The one we have, besides Daddy's #1 hope that he'll hear good preaching from the camp speaker, is that we'll be in the display counter like the best peaches or potatoes or green beans at a market. At camp we're the fixings some pastors hope to take back home to their congregations for singing, playing and soul saving.

Pastors shop for evangelists at camp meeting you might say. When they hear us sing and hear Daddy say a short word to introduce us which of course serves as a tiny sample sermon, they experience a glimpse of being together for a holiness revival at their own church house.

We sing favorites at camp:

How beautiful heaven must be,
Sweet home of the happy and free;
Fair haven of rest for the weary,
How beautiful heaven must be.

People join right in. The friendliness and at home feeling warms you in a hurry. Daddy doesn't know people at Kansas camp though some may have heard of him. Revival news travels by letter and phone. It's the good news of the county for plenty of people and they spread the word to family and friends like the best gossip they ever heard.

Highway 287 took us out of Alabama, then Highway 78 into Mississippi. We pulled out by 6:30 this morning, Althea helping me fasten my bunk bed to the ceiling across the back of the trailer as soon as I was up at six. When Daddy built this trailer, he made sure there wasn't an inch wasted.

The front of our little traveling house is fitted with two small seats facing each other, each about half the length of the one at the rear. At night the front seats pull together to make a double bed for Mama and Daddy. Every morning—except travel days like today—the bedding is stowed in drawers underneath and they're pushed back up into facing seats. Then a table lets down in-between them from the ceiling where it's hooked. A plexiglass window looks out across the front, over the table.

A man named Coleman in Pensacola who has a big fishing boat says our trailer's a lot like the inside of his boat. We park by his house for the night when we're on our way through their town. Mama and Daddy are his friends *fer yars n yars*, to hear him tell it.

Coleman calls ours a *galley kitchen* opposite the door, just a sink, two burner hot plate, cupboards overhead, and one cupboard for pans and a tiny ice box underneath. "Yup, it's perty much the boat." And Daddy says, naturally, "Well, Brother, that's what we're doing. *Fishing!*" He's talking Jesus when he says that, Jesus saying to His disciples, *Follow me and I will make you fishers of men.*

Left of the door as you enter is a set of drawers as tall as I am—that's about four feet—and over it is a round mirror fixed to the side of our one closet. The other side of the closet displays a larger square mirror anchored in the wood, and a two-and-a-half-foot-high set of drawers that make a dressing table in front of our bunk beds/rear couch. Arranging the inside of only 18' demands compact planning. Daddy has sketch books filled with his designs.

So this morning preparing for the road, every cupboard door hooks closed with everything in the cupboards nudged together. No bouncing around. After double-checking drawers, cupboards, and the front bed and table for security, Daddy brings in the vibra harp cases. The flat metal keys, sound-pipes and frame of the harp have been disassembled into two flat black boxes that fit on the floor. That's the last thing we do. Daddy's violin case is braced between pillows on the front bed. Mama's accordion moves in, up against the outside of the back bunk next to the chest of drawers and then the vibra harp cases on the floor wedge tight under my parent's bed. There's no room for anything to wiggle, that's for sure.

Today, the blue speckled enamel pot used for our toilet at night—a trek to an outhouse in the woods after dark sure isn't practical—stows away under the front bed, held in place by a box of our schoolbooks and Daddy's study books. The bed rests in its down position and the table hooks to the ceiling for travel.

Mama insisted on writing the Willits who live in Tupelo last week, telling them *Lord willing* we plan to park in their yard tonight. Daddy would just as soon show up with no warning but that mortifies Mama, to use her exact word.

I don't know the Willits, Herb and Gloria, but Mama and Daddy met them long ago in Birmingham before I existed. Usually I can only imagine not being here at all—unborn, that is—when I'm mad. But then, when I've just had a spanking for instance, I imagine the other end of life. *Dead.* And since I'm not here any more, having been tragically hit by a truck, Mama and Daddy get real low in their sorriness about how I've been treated in this life but it's too late. A kind of judgment day without God getting involved.

I say Good for Mama! writing ahead like she did. Gloria's ready with a roast chicken for supper. "That's the trouble," Daddy grumbles, "don't wanta be no trouble, Doris." And Herb's fishing boat has been moved to make room for us next to their little white cottage. Green shutters adorn each window and happy yellow daisies dance along the front walk to the street. We back our home into the driveway right next to theirs.

Even though Mama doesn't talk back to Daddy, later she says quietly so Althea and I can hear, "Being no trouble means people don't have to be surprised and scurry around at the last minute." She knows what the last word is, whether she says it out loud or not.

Gloria makes biscuits, too, mainly for the Tupelo honey they're proud to serve. Tupelo trees have a tiny fruit and bloom that bees love to buzz. "They likes Florida the best a heared. Appalachicola? But the leave us some at air sweet stuff, too," according to Herb.

Gloria's bright as a new penny, her hair close to that color is tied back with a pink scarf, left free to wisp and wave down her back. And her husband's smart enough to notice. They don't have children so they dote on each other. My Daddy doesn't hug Mama like Herb does Gloria, coming up and putting his arm around her shoulders when he talks about her. Giving her a peck on the cheek. Daddy acts kind of embarrassed about hugging as if it's *foolishness.*

Early morning we're back on the road. We've crossed a corner of Tennessee into Arkansas before morning traffic has a chance to slow our progress. This trip, we'll travel across five states for a stop in Kansas Camp Meeting; then four more states before we leave our trailer in Minot, North Dakota. That's where we head into Canada.

Last time we visited our Russian relatives was four years ago. No matter how long it takes for the trip, though, Daddy stays connected to his roots. The rest of the time he has to keep those roots in a cellar, out of sight. Like when we're in revival meetings—you know—the *born in Russia* secret.

Daddy says his sister Lucia mothered him and his brothers and sister while she was still a little girl herself, only eight years old. His mama died of pneumonia when he was my age. I don't want to imagine such a thing. Think of it: dead because of washing clothes. They were frozen hard in a Canadian winter. She chilled while gathering them off the line.

Daddy tells the story again and again of his sister Lucy, as he calls her, trudging over to visit their mother's grave holding on to her littlest sister and two younger brothers. The four of them sitting on the mound of dirt, weeping. You can understand why my Daddy devotes himself to going to see his sister like he does.

Out here in fields of tall golden-looking grass far as your eye will carry you, travelers see *Burma Shave* words pop up on four successive sign posts in a farmer's field.

> A Chin Where
> Barbed Wire Bristles Stand
> Is Bound To Be A No Ma'ams Land
> *Burma Shave*

This shaving cream has everybody's attention. Althea's and my eyes hunt Burma Shave signs. Otherwise, the most you can hope for in the way of a view is a farmer on a tractor. A farm house. A barn and tall silos. Rhymes pull us along the road like our DeSoto pulls our trailer house.

> Don't Lose Your Head
> To Gain A Minute
> You Need Your Head
> Your Brains Are In It
> Burma Shave

We wind up somewhere in Missouri for another night, this time parked next to a gas station. Sleeping near a home felt better, not so lonely.

Kansas meets us the next day with what seems like endless wheat fields close to harvest. Suddenly, a flurry of long, dark, majestic feathers rise in the midst of the mass of slender stems. Two? Yes, two pheasants flashing gold, orange and green highlights in the sun. An airy swirl starts from my chest and whirls up with them in their surprising rise, "Mama, look!" I'm yelling; Althea and I bounce in place. Daddy's scolding us for distracting him, *don't you know I'm driving?* But the drama takes us. We peer back through the side windows trying to catch another glimpse of the magic moment so quickly passed.

"What a sight!" Mama's high point for excitement, "Settle yourselves girls. Can't be too long, now."

The sign we anticipate is larger than *Burma Shave* ads. This one's a message on one wooden plank with the date hooked below it on a separate board:

Welcome to the Assembly of God
Camp Meeting
Held Annually
August 7 to 17

It's a tradition for families to get together at camp decade after decade. Whatever else happens during the year, cousins, aunts and uncles, parents and grandparents can count on gathering between two dates of these weeks in August, three miles outside Woodston, six miles west of Alton, on US 40N. Where you bunk doesn't matter much. You can rent tents and cots for the week or bring your own trailer like we do. Some families even build cabins on the site. However you plan for it, one thing you can count on is a *hallelujah* party along the creek.

We arrive on Thursday and find a space along a shady lane in sight of the creek, lined up with other trailers, tents, and camper-rigged pick-up trucks. Shower rooms, men's on one side and women's on the other, demand a short walk from us but we can't lose sight of them considering the acid green they've painted the cinder blocks. Inside, the smell's of moldy soap, old cracked floors sloping to a center-of-the-room drain. Raggy-looking curtains hanging over bare pipes double for curtain rods across the stalls. But who cares. They're a luxury for us however pitiful they may be.

Meetings here were held in a barn first, then a *tent cathedral* and finally, next year or the year after—Lord willing—there's a plan to build a tabernacle. Excitement, expectation, anticipation swirl in the air like tiny tornadoes of rising hope and pure pleasure. Small things happen at camp meeting that have a chance to grow large in meaning through all your lifelong. Kids sing and find new friends, teenagers make eyes at each other—I saw two of them kissing out in back of the tent just after we pulled in—and adults are satisfied by a place to stow their worries for a while.

You best not underestimate a meet-up at a camp meeting. Folks who gather here can make a difference to your life now and later.

This year, Charles Blair is the preacher; he's why we're here. Besides the fact that we're headed for Canada and this camp is on the way. Daddy says Blair's "a man of few years but blessed with Holy-Ghost filled words. No nonsense." And you know how important *no nonsense* is to my Daddy.

The sweet news so far is that I can hear creek water slithering through rocks and falling into deep pools when I'm going to sleep at night. That's music that lulls me like the Lion's purr.

The Skondeen Family Evangelistic Team sings Friday night minus the vibra harp. Too much trouble to unpack for a couple of songs. Cases are stowed away as usual, flat on the floor underneath Mama's and Daddy's bed which we leave made up for sleeping. Their bed being down also means that we don't have our own table in place so we eat outside on a picnic table. Still, it's hard to maneuver around the cases with all of us inside the trailer. Daddy, of course, will mention that the vibra harp is missing, a form of advertisement, when he introduces our song. Dropping in a bit of curiosity works wonders.

We spend most of our camp time at gatherings that are meant to give you something new to take home. Prayer, Bible study, children's story time full of heroes like David, Samson, Moses and Daniel. The book of Revelation shows up as a favorite in the Bible studies of every camp I've ever visited. Nobody feels prophetic enough to teach it at home but they can say, "Now Brother So n So said . . . atta camp meetin'?" with confidence even if it doesn't make a lick of sense. Most of the things I've heard about Revelation fit the Confusion category even when the lesson is accompanied by elaborate wall charts.

I figure the teenage choir for kids old enough to belong to Christ's Ambassadors proves to be a hot-spot for meeting somebody to kiss. But the evening service in the tent cathedral? Now that's the exclamation of every day. Like I said we're singing tonight, Friday.

Daddy and Mother begin with,

> *Will there be any stars, any stars in my crown*
> *When at evening the sun goeth down?*

Plus, all the verses about Glory and receiving a crown for work well done in Heaven. Folks love this one. After the shouting begins to subside, I stand on a chair and lead the children in singing *Sunlight, Sunlight in My Soul Today*. All, together—Brother Blair says, thanking us, when he gets up to preach—sets a mind right to listen for the Word of the Lord. Daddy fairly glows as he hears Blair's complement.

Saturday morning's hazy, overcast sky feels more like smothering than awaking. By noon the air's cooling, filled with a feeling of thunder just out of earshot. Daddy hurries back from the morning Bible teacher's gathering in the tabernacle full of worries and warnings from folks who know this place well.

"Doris, get ready to move."

"Move? What on earth . . ."

"If there's heavy rain and the creek rises we won't be able to get out of here." Mama doesn't need any more information to flash into action.

We hitch up the trailer in minutes and drive into Woodston, the air in the front seat full of tension, words usually traveling easily between Mama and Daddy, suddenly still. At a one-pump gas station, the man agrees that we can park for the night close in to the back of his garage and hook up to the electricity for a few dollars.

A hovering sky lowers overhead. Storm clouds stumble over each other in a rush to gather, surging dark shadows churn; random lightning and thunder tucked into mysterious silence. The feeling of a tumultuous quiet I can't place.

Mama clears up after supper of macaroni and cheese while Daddy keeps a vigil for the wind'a increase as it reaches out and shakes nearby trees. They quiver and bow to the raging weather.

At last the kettle of black clouds can't be contained and boils over, spattering water with the driving beat of loud tympani all over the trailer. Like Goliath sized drum majors gone crazy using our little house as their instrument. No particular direction, that's what's so scary-strange. Noise comes from everywhere and flashes of light that don't seem at all like lightening appear in the early dark.

"I don't like the looks of this," Daddy murmurs.

"What can we do, Bill?" Mama's voice is muffled, tight.

"I'm going to bed with my boots on."

My bunk is let down from the ceiling and my sister's bed below me—a seat across the back between sets of drawers during the day—is cleared. We settle in and turn off the lights but it's an uneasy night time. The wind hurls sticks and the sky continues to cook more fury. My eyes close as I curl into the soft strength of the Lion. His whole body, a curved furry shield. I'm feeling his warmth, singing to myself, *Sunshine, sunshine in my soul today*.

But my reverie lurches. The float into sleep jolts—*hard*—with a gust of wind, then another more forceful than the last. Quick as a shot we're picked up, our container thrown high by the angry air, swooped into a current, and dropped with a reverberating shudder and a deadening thud: *Pow*.

Dropped *hard* on the side of the door. Time stops inside a roaring silence.

The Lion's loud, *deafening* loud purr is all I can hear.

Then Daddy's voice comes from far away. Sounds as if he's at the end of a long tunnel.

"Althea, you all right?"

"Uh-huh."

"Audrey, you?" When I try to answer I can't make my mouth work at first. Something's all wrong and I don't know what. I'm not even sure where I am. Muffled words manage to get out: "I'm down . . . here. Under all this stuff."

Cupboards from over the sink coming loose from their travel-hooks emptied their contents all over me as I tumbled with the motion, clinging to my pillow; finally landing at the foot of the wedged in vibra harp cases.

Dry substance I can't name covers my face, some falls in my mouth. Oatmeal. My eyes are shrouded in a dish towel and a box full of oatmeal dumped on top of that so when I open my mouth, it's filled with dry oats. I feel around in the roaring dark and come up with slices of bread, tea bags, dish towels and towels. The vibra harp cases, fit tightly under Mama's and Daddy's bed except for about twelve inches or so out in the walk way—that's what we've been stumbling over during camp—are tipped as far as they can go up against the secured bottom of the front bed.

Daddy growls, "This means fire, Doris . . . twisted wires." Using the heavy flashlight he's kept locked in his grip, accompanied by sounds of human or storm like fury—who knows—he makes a way for us to escape by crashing through the front window. Daddy becomes *storm* to get us out of there.

The rest of this is blank. A blank piece of stark white paper. Not a word on it.

Did Daddy stand outside and take my hand? Help me step out through the broken window? All the while I'm struggling with a cotton blanket wrapped around my flimsy rosebud sprinkled nighty, me with my oatmeal hair now gathering twigs and leaves from the storm's blowing through us. I have no idea. Did I go first? Last? I don't know.

What I remember is the closed in warmth of the DeSoto sheltering us. The dusty warm comfort of mohair seats. And all I can think is that I don't want the trailer to catch fire because my doll Peggy's still in there. Somewhere.

We huddle in the back seat while Daddy drives through littered streets. "Gotta find a truck with gin poles." I'm too numb to ask what he's talking about. Mama asks. Daddy explains, "Wrecker. Somebody with a wrecker. He can pick up the trailer. Less damage." Mama only says *Lord have mercy* to that.

My Daddy has a way about him when he goes in search of specific kind of help. Some might say he has Help from on high. Me, I say it's just Daddy going straight to what he needs.

"You folks been prayin?" It's midnight by the time the man with the farm-implement business and a wrecking company on the side sees our trailer.

Those words *Lord willing* hold new meaning. Can't tell you what that meaning might be, though, come to think of it. When everything goes hazy like it did during the storm, I hold real still inside. Going to sleep again that night? No problem at all, I return to the silence where the Lion lives.

If somebody saw me tumble from my bed when the storm fetched our trailer to the sky, they'd probably think I was holding on to my pillow. But no, that wasn't a pillow. It was the Lion of Judah. Fits just right wherever He needs to be.

Sweeping up and throwing out sums up the day after the storm before driving to the next stop on our trail north, Grand Island, Nebraska. Daddy's determined. We're still headed to Aunt Lucy's and Uncle Mike's farm. You might say the trailer's trailing along behind constitutes a regular miracle. Mama and Daddy recite a constant stream, *Help us Jesus, Mercy, Lord.*

Dead animals scatter along the road, probably drowned, caught in a flash flood Daddy reckons. Some drowned and run over both, just too sad to see. Solemn, bedraggled work crews pick them up. Scooping squirrels, two possums, a cat, some sizable rats into a black metal drum.

But Peggy's with me and sitting in my lap, secure, watching with me. We're all right.

This in the air ordeal set me to thinking about that *meeting in the air* we sing about, *in the sweet, sweet by and by.* And I best not leave out the part . . . *in that home beyond the sky.* Now this very minute I have to say that describing *in the air* as *sweet* whacks a person fresh out of a storm straight into a cell at Chattahoochee. We visited that asylum—Sister Bailey, a fine holiness attendant there sees her work as a mission—and being out of this world like a lot of those folks seem to be feels more like a terrible storm than a rapture.

By the worries falling around us and the repairs tugging at Daddy to keep us on the road I'd say the rapture needs another plan. And as for this kind of thinking, I better keep it to myself.

Mama and Daddy put the inside of our home back together again while we're in the trailer park where we stay the night. As well as they can on short notice, at least. Fixing hooks straightened out by the storm's sudden force and replacing crushed cupboard fasteners. But the black eye of the bashed-out window—plywood hammered over it—spells trouble anybody can see.

The storm is over. But the tune the truck driver whistled as he worked in the dark of midnight, that's still with me:

Zip a dee doo dah
Zip a dee a
My oh my what a wonderful day.

Our North Dakota destination, a holiness church sturdy as a red brick barn outside the city of Minot, looks small and hazy against what Daddy calls the Black Hills. We park in close to the church house preparing to leave our home behind the next day, and finish hooking electricity up just as Wednesday prayer meeting begins.

About fifteen or twenty folks gather. Their sun-browned faces and farm clothes bear witness to a long day of work.

Preacher's asked to say a few words, his best smile shining through the tired miles we've traveled, "Praise the Lord, the storm took a few groceries and our front window but not a hair on our heads! He still has us covered by His insurance!" Since this is not a shouting kind of church, there are only a few saying *Amen*. But I can tell they mean those *Amens* with all their heart.

As the Preacher talks it occurs to me that nobody can imagine exactly what being subjected to a storm's bad mood is like until you've had the experience. The people in this room know storms. By the collection of lines on their faces—eyes full of dark wisdom—I reckon as well that a heart full of Jesus may be what keeps them on the sunshine side of life. Otherwise, they wouldn't be here on a Wednesday night.

Minot, North Dakota, is a big town in a barren state. Oh, it grows crops, but mostly one crop, wheat. And it's all you see until the land meets the sky. That, and some hills moving up over the landscape that look as if they could use some company. Daddy knows this pastor, Brother Goodwin, from when they attended Fellowship meetings together in Nebraska. Parking the trailer here works out well since it's directly on the way to Saskatchewan. We part ways with our pitiful-looking trailer house and travel toward the farm in the morning.

But tonight, the coyotes Daddy loves to hear in the Black Hills are ready for their sundown serenade. When the lights are out, quiet in our sleeping places far from Kansas storms, Daddy's voice comes through the dark, a loud whisper, "Listen now, girls, you can hear the coyotes. Singing. Far away in their mountain hideouts."

Through the rolled up vent I see pale blue moonlight and silver stars. Silence. Then the coyotes. If Daddy didn't say it was music I might have mistaken it for a lonesome howl, but the longer the singers croon, the closer I feel to their songs. A lullaby.

Our DeSoto aims in the direction of the Canadian border soon after daybreak. We're uncommon—lightweight!—with no trailer behind. As if we can go twice as fast, but of course we don't.

Mama says, "It's just an ordinary US/Canada border crossing, Audrey," glancing at my worry-wrinkled face as men in their Canadian uniforms look into our car. Makes me feel like I'm hiding something. Very suspicious. She turns around again, staring straight ahead, ignoring me and saying to anybody who wants to listen, "We're all right." This ordeal ranks in uneasiness right up there with a gas gage needle bouncing on E.

All day along both sides of the highway, combines raking in the harvest roll across vast expanses of wheat. Silos stand against late summer's sky awaiting their fill. We seem more silent today, Althea and I not even scrapping over who gets the most room in the back seat. Maybe it's an air of expectation. Maybe it's relief at being past the storm and leaving our broken home behind for a rest.

Then we see Saskatoon city limits. Where we'll sleep for tonight is the question. Too far to the farm.

"Probably make it, Doris . . . mighty lonesome roads 'course. Out that way."

"Don't push it, Bill. Wouldn't do to be stranded."

After some talk, Daddy decides to look up the Bible School he remembers here, Prairy Institute.

A few dead end streets and asking directions a time or two before he pulls up in front of an old stucco building that's a combination apartment house and run down hotel. He and Mama discussed a college but this sure doesn't look impressive. When he's headed for what appears to be a main entrance, I ask, "Mama, what is . . ."

She anticipates my question, answering, "Dormitory. Where young people live when they're in school here?"

"But . . ."

"There's no school during summer. Probably not til September. Daddy's going to see if they have beds where we can sleep tonight." Seems a little spooky to me, looking up at the windows. All dark.

He comes out, jerks open the poor DeSoto's door and plops himself into the driver's seat, *"King George Hotel.* All they have to say. *King George Hotel."* He's muttering, disgusted, while he's starting the car. "They think poor preachers are made of money?"

I declare, as Mama would say but she's silent as can be. Vapors seem to be rising off the top of Daddy's head, "They say dorm's closed. Nobody here til September. All the more reason we should be able to stay." Mama makes her dirty shame sound and keeps still while he continues to fume.

"And when I say I have two girls, the woman looks stuck up. Haughty!"

Mama fills in, "No children allowed?"

Daddy stops at the intersection with a change of the light to red. He's slamming down his words, "I tell her, *Don't bother, I'll go drown my babies in the bathtub, maybe then you can find room for us."* Daddy sure enough had a proper fit in there.

As we sit at the intersection, sidewalk lamps flicker on in the growing darkness. Across the street we see some folks gathering around two young people, singing. One plays a guitar. As we drive over there and coast to a stop at the curb, we hear familiar strains of ". . . *waiting for the harvest, and the time of reaping, We shall come rejoicing, bringing in the sheaves."*

A street meeting. "C'monkids," Daddy says, "Let's go." We're in! It's Mama who looks a little worried now.

The boy plunking his guitar strains his voice with, "re*joic*ing . . . ," black hair slicked behind his ears forming a wet helmet in the lamp light. All elbows, skinny long fingers animatedly playing, wrists stuck out of a wrinkled white shirt that fit him several summers ago. He finishes with a flourish and smiles at the wispy blond girl by his side.

Welcoming designated sinners—people spilling out of a nearby office building, lunch pails or briefcases swinging—the young singers call out with their songs, "Here! find Jesus right here!" So far no one seems to see them as they rush headlong toward home. A dimly lighted bus putters to a noisy stop midway up the street and the people who've rushed by the singing jostle each other in semi-polite confusion, finding their way up the steps toward the driver and back along the aisle. Standing room only.

A preacher looking leader—I can tell by the earnest look on his face and the Bible braced under his arm—wearing a suit so worn to a shine it has a life of its own, keeps glancing at the few Christians by his side as if he's nervous they'll run catch the bus, too. He takes the worn Bible from its place, the slight movement causing what remains of his sparse, mousy hair to fall across a V-shaped face stretched around a mostly painful smile. He's trying hard to be enthusiastic but it's a big effort. Opening the Good Book and forcing a high crackly voice out of hiding, he shouts, "This is the accepted time. Today! Is the *day of salvation*." The man's doing his best for Jesus.

We're singing *Love Lifted Me*, when a few stragglers pause, slightly interested. Encouraged, the suit shined by time asks if any one has a word for *our friend*, Jesus.

Daddy hops right on the opportunity to testify, blue suit jacket pulled around him, shirt and tie in place as always. You never know when you'll have to look like an Evangelist. "A traveling preacher without a trailer is like a turtle without his shell," he begins. The ripple of chuckles rewards him and he moves on, saying, "But when we get to heaven, these troubles and trials won't matter now, will they brother," addressing the suit, assuming he's a preacher, "because we'll see Christ!"

An instant revival on the boulevard, busy with people going all directions. Some of them—like the woman in the brown plaid coat, head wrapped in a yellow flowered scarf, arms heavy with bulky parcels and a face full of trouble—look like they need some cheer.

Our voices make a big difference in the street meeting tonight. We double the volume on the singing. By the time we've concluded, Daddy has a new friend in Brother Carl Jensen. And Brother Jensen and his wife have guests for overnight.

Mama clasps and unclasps her hands as we follow the Jensens ten blocks to a house next door to Good Shepherd Baptist Church. Tightlipped in the car, she spends the next hour in the modest wooden parsonage surrounded by a rickety porch, apologizing to the gracious Sister Lynn Jensen for their sudden hospitality. Not ever mentioning Sister Lynn's quietly—no fuss at all, like it's ok and normal—adding potatoes to the pot of soup we share for supper.

Everybody says good night to the young singers after we eat together. Hugs from the Jensens and waves from us. *Just married*, Sister Lynn confides to Mama with a little smile as the couple disappear into the shadows toward the married-student housing at the Bible College. Later Mama murmurs to Daddy, "My lands, Bill, those kids don't look old enough to be outside in the dark, much less married."

The Jensens nudge the ten-year-old twin boys out of their own beds, though the boys seem happy at the prospect, and onto the opened out living room couch. Althea and I prepare to share a bed roll on the floor of Mama's and Daddy's room where they're now sleeping in the twin's twin beds.

I'll remember this night.

"Atomic bomb! Atomic bomb!" Aunt Lucia greets me when I rumble through their old wooden gate crowded by uncontrolled scarlet roses reaching out from the archway. I'm first to rush out of the car and up the walk onto the grand porch of the farm house. A *domesticated barn*, that's what Mama calls it, with a smile and a twinkle that say *good to be home*.

Aunt Lucia doesn't use many English words and that makes her first words to me even more surprising. When I was three and we had heard the radio broadcast reports of Hiroshima, I heralded the news, yelling those words—*Atomic bomb! Atomic bomb!*—as I ran into our house in Falls City, Nebraska. Last time we were here it was only a year after Hiroshima happened. She remembers.

That's the sweetness of family. Remembering. Even when most of the conversations around here are in a language only Daddy can speak and understand. But laughter? Yeah, laughter always speaks the same language.

I'm caught up against Aunt Lucia's pillowy breasts in warm soft arms, an embrace nobody else can imitate. A person can depend on her warmth. She's the best reward for all these miles in the back seat.

This farm, measured by *squares*—which means *square miles*—defies imagination. It includes twelve lakes. For Uncle Mike and his boys that translates to twelve choices for fishing or hunting ducks. Daddy always extols the virtues of wide open spaces but until you arrive in Western Canada his descriptions might as well be in Mandarin.

Farm days begin at four AM for the Shakatko family and two hired hands. Best clues of a new morning come from Aunt Lucia's kitchen, of course. Uncle Mike's strong coffee he douses with cream, and bread, warm and fragrant from the oven, together, shout *welcome-to the table* through the house.

This wake up, understand, begins even for our family by six AM. The entire household quiets and sleeps by eight in the evening. Come morning, we join them after their chores in the not-quite-dark—this far north it's light most of the time—about six thirty AM.

Welcome to the breakfast table, which means meat and potatoes plus pancakes bathed in freshly churned butter with additional options of sour cream or thick sweet cream and strawberry preserves. Maple syrup isn't a custom in this household. Instead, fruit of every description—peaches, berries, figs and apples—summer's bounty lives in this kitchen all year round in one form or another.

My teen-aged cousins Leon and Walter shovel in the energy before they head back out into the field's early light. Fall and winter, the five children—aged fifteen, twins Leon and Raisa, Esther sixteen, Walter seventeen, and Vera eighteen, must be ready for the school bus by six.

It is the aromas, not kitchen noises, that awaken us, though sounds of pots and pans like clappers in awkward bells rise up the wide stairs to the bedroom floor, too. The big beckoning comes from the smell of ham, bacon, pork chops, that's my guess. Where else in creation can you experience morning like this? Not anywhere I live, especially the ham, bacon, and pork chops part.

In my opinion, Mama and Daddy own a prejudice toward pigs. Daddy eats kosher when it comes to pork anywhere else we roam. But here, not a quiver of indecision. He forks into it with pleasure, bragging about his sister Lucy as he savors every morsel. *Lucy* as Daddy calls her, and *Lucia* are interchangeable, but I stick with *Aunt Lucia*.

Six bedrooms occupy the second floor of the house. Our room is kind of two rooms, one with a big feather bed where Mama and Daddy sleep and a smaller sunroom with two daybeds along adjoining walls. I love the daytime when sun streams through the thick-framed windows just above the wainscoting. Nighttime, the room is darkened by pulling down dark shades. Mama explains that this is like Alaska, something about *northern lights*.

Awaking with a dream come true of an oval table laid with sturdy crockery—some blue, some gold—and good food is the first thing we can count on. Then Althea and I go into the upstairs bathroom with Mama.

This bathroom up here is so big at least three cows plus a calf or two could take a nap in it. Mama hustles both of us girls in there at the same time. One can be brushing teeth, another washing face and combing hair, so we won't tie it up for too long.

The rest of the family is already gathered at the table. We're the last to arrive.

Two hired hands, eyes steadily trained on the floor unless they're eating, live out in the little cabin-like place attached to the barn. It's hard to see their faces, one tall and gangly, his mop of rusty curls streaked with sunshine flopped over his forehead. The other, slight in his build, all muscle and bone, dark hair sticking out in spite of all his efforts to tame it. Their names, I can't understand. Serge? The curly one. A lot of Russian men are named Serge—that's Daddy's middle name—I think of them as Ser and Chee. They don't speak English. Uncle Mike and his boys speak Russian to them, and they duck their heads for sure if Raisa, Esther or Vera are in the area.

When Aunt Lucia is finally able to sit for her own breakfast, she commands "No, no, *nyet!*" motioning with the flat of her hand, turning back the platter stacked with old fashioned donuts, their fragrant, crisp edges wafting past trailing a faint air of vanilla and nutmeg. She pats her derriere as reason enough for refusal. Then her laugh rolls out of her as if she's just invented the egg and she immediately calls for sour cream to bless her buckwheat pancakes. She's pouring melted butter through the hotcakes right after her donut-refusal. Finally, she slathers it all in strawberry preserves.

But she's not having a donut, please note. Aunt Lucia's the best.

I recognize a lot of the Russian conversation and stories even though I don't understand the language. Watching faces doles out more information than words through eyes, eyebrows, mouths shaped a certain way. And shifts of bodies tell me some things, too. Shoulders say a lot. Hands. Aunt Lucia's hands caressing my cheek or the quick motion of patting my hair. Her hands *fly* making pelmeny—tiny meatballs for soup—or nalesniki, thin pancakes rolled, bathed in butter, served with peach or raspberry preserves and sour cream. And talking? She's all flying hands in speaking Russian, too, naturally. "My girls, school! Me? No school!" she apologizes for her lack of English.

Out in the hammock one afternoon, Raisa speaks quietly about her mother's shame from being a kind of slave girl growing up. That's what being mother to her brothers and sisters was like, especially after her father, my grandpa Deede, married a woman he brought over from Russia. An eighteen-year-old.

The new wife used Lucia harder than ever. No school possible. "I grit my teeth . . . such meanness . . . every time I think of it," Raisa's sharp words slice through a fierce whisper. An unperturbed blue sky contrasted with my beautiful dark eyed cousin's rage sets off a siren through the sweet peace of the afternoon.

She paints *Stepmother*—as everyone calls her if they speak of her at all—by mixing frozen dirt and melting mud from that first wheat farm through the woman's complexion. My imagination hears it this way, at least. That was before Daddy's family had to abandon that arid farm on account of drought, heading south to California.

Stepmother left her older husband when they hit the bright lights of San Francisco. I've heard those words shuffled aside like dirty secrets before, but I've never known much about the actual woman.

Raisa's version grinds bits of farm with crushed misery into ugly for the woman no one will ever talk about. She appears much the same as I imagine Queen Jezebel when Daddy preaches about her, the hateful wife of King Ahab putting sordid trials in the path of the prophet Elijah.

'Course Elijah won. God being on his side and all. So did Aunt Lucia.

A female the likes of Jezebel never trots out any good news for a household. Somebody failed to warn my grandfather. Or he didn't listen. He still suffers from what I understand. A broken heart, Daddy says. Sounds to me from Raisa's telling that more than that was broken but I can't say what.

Raisa points out Stepmother as one who has babies, lolls about, and orders little Lucy to fetch and carry for her. That's the Canadian story. The California story ended soon enough. All I can think is no wonder Daddy honors his big sister Lucia. She's his hero and he never lets her forget it.

The rush of every day excites the whole household including the grand orange cat who holds forth at the top of the porch steps. He's the house guard, ignoring the barking dogs and greeting every family member on his own terms, keeping dignity about the place. But mornings, he's scouting the perimeter of the kitchen with an occasional browwww, rubbing against Aunt Lucia's sturdy legs set in black, lace up, thick rubber soled shoes. Hardly ever see her when she's not on her feet.

The girls cook—Raisa, Esther and Vera—with their mother. They feed animals a little later after the cleaning is done and I scurry along beside them, carrying empty buckets, scattering feed. Keeping track with the family's morning as it moves along proves to me that a farm tolerates no idleness.

After breakfast while the girls clean the kitchen, Aunt Lucia motions me out the door, headed for the barn. All sign language. The cream separator turns out to be our mystery destination. Who knew—not me!—that a machine exists to turn out a steady stream of thick, golden cream. Just waiting for a spoon. Mine. *Dis!* her only word of instruction, thrusting a deep round bowled soup spoon into my hand after taking the first exaggerated slurp, eyes twin blue sparklers and cheeks peach perfect, murmuring, "Mmmm, mmmmmmm!"

She doesn't have to convince me. Our family's signature curls tumble her cherry brown hair about, flashing a strand or two of silver. All of it supposedly caught in a holiness-lady's bun in back but misbehaving, escaping the confining pins and clips. My kind of hair. And she's not even as tall as Daddy, though they say he's the runt of the litter at only 5'7".

Raisa's the daughter that has the glow of Aunt Lucia inside her. I can feel it when she takes my hand and whispers *Let's go*. Whatever we do is magic. I'd never tell Mama or Daddy I'm using that word—magic—but it's the only one that fits. Even going out to feed the chickens, she shows me how to toss the mixed grains with a flair that reaches the limits of the yard but wastes not even a kernel. Her twin, Leon, and she have the loveliest mellow brown eyes with long, dark fringy lashes. Like a calf I saw leaning against it's mother in the barnyard.

Leon glances fast all about, checking, measuring, figuring. But Raisa studies any area slowly and when her eyes rest on me, I feel warm and royal. As if I'm the princess—there is one that goes to my school, Calvert, only she's in India—living in halls of gold and ivory.

Raisa's hands extend into graceful fingers fit for a piano. I can hear pieces of a symphony like Daddy sometimes listens to on the radio as Raisa passes dishes at the table or kneads the dough making piroshki. Her hands move in smooth, deliberate gestures.

And when Raisa walks, her slender, taller-than-her-mom figure doesn't move as others do, slightly out of step with the music. She glides. Even though I feel like a midget beside her long legs, she pays attention and considers my shortness, allowing me to keep up. Raisa will definitely have great pillows like Aunt Lucia for hugging close, too, but now her shape simply complements whatever she wears including a white blouse, gathered skirt of undetermined color, and an old green, stained checkered apron. Her hair, dark as midnight shadows, falls in waves to her shoulders framing an oval face that is all morning light.

Raisa's telling me a story of when she was my age as we cozy in the canvas of the hammock which is stretched across one end of the front porch. Her voice resonates through me and in a vague sort of reverie, I wonder how many summer seasons it takes to soften the thick woven threads of the hammock's fabric, stripes faded to a faint recollection of blue, red, yellow and orange, colors of a summer rainbow you see far up ahead.

Here, the Canadian plains are emptied of skylines or city limits. Saskatoon is miles away and from this perch, not even farm buildings intrude on our view. A field along the road leading to the gate and walkway of the house, left fallow, Daddy calls it—no wheat planted there this year—manages, instead, to produce a bumper crop of accidental tiger lilies. Our eyes fill with the sight of them. Slender stems arch, flaring into orange trumpets, masses of them blur into intensely deepened gold and then, immediately above, the endless cerulean sky. Raisa teaches me that word—*cerulean*—she says it's all about sky color as we gaze out of our sheltered hammock-home into wide reaches of all the world. I've never felt so safe.

Anybody can understand why my Daddy's voice changes here. It's not because he speaks another language full of rocky mountains with thundering passages. No, that's not it. Even in the rough of the Russian language, his tone is completely altered. It took some puzzling—concentration—to figure out, but here's what seems to be different: It's the comfort of family he can count on everywhere he goes all day long, out to the milking shed nudging the grumbling cows or into the eerie light of dawn, equipped with a well-oiled shot gun. That's why he sounds like a boy who's playing kickball in the street instead of a man worried about the gas indicator bouncing on e for empty. Why, he could see storm clouds racing across the prairie and not worry at all like he does when our family travels with only the road under our wheels to depend upon.

Uncle Mike declares a holiday in Daddy's honor and all the boys clean their shot guns on Thursday night, ready to hunt ducks before dawn. Daddy's face looks the same as the teen-agers, Leon and Walter, bent to the task of disassembling the *shooting sticks*, as Leon calls them. Walter uses the correct terminology for the type, the gage. To my ears, speaking Russian and talking guns are the same. Foreign.

Strelka their favorite black and white longhaired shepherd kind of a dog zeroes in on what needs attention like her name—Daddy explains—tells you, arrow. She goes on the alert in the presence of gun cleaning. Still patient but tense. I've never loved a dog before, just Strelka. Burying my face in her warm fur, her cool nose nuzzling my cheek feels like a smaller version of the Lion.

Cooking stove, utensils, bed rolls, food and water are ready on site for the season in a tent set up near the duck blind. Daddy wears rubber boots up to his bottom in the makeshift leanto in the water. I watch them from the shelter of the open tent flaps, wrapped with a wool blanket, cross-legged in a canvas chair. Mystic morning floats around me, unexplored scents of earth and water.

Pop pow of the shotguns sound across the prairie. Birds fall from the sky and Strelka splashes out to retrieve them. My heart plummets with the feathered creatures. Diving for a pillow and holding it fast around my ears on the pallet inside the tent quiets the pounding and I'm still. Waiting. Waiting for the string of ducks to weigh heavy enough for a feast.

Strelka returns with her fur wet and rancid-smelling from lake water. She shivers—a twitch-flicker—from her head to the tip of her tail, still watching a duck in flight even after she's back from the water's edge. Imagining feathers riding lightly in her mouth and bringing the prize to Leon. As Strelka's being praised by the boys or Uncle Mike, her head raises just a little with pride, nose straight ahead but eyes viewing a horizon the rest of us can't quite see.

Tea hot enough to *burn the hair off your tongue* as Daddy insists it must do, with cherry preserves stirred in for sweetening, banishes the hunters' chill before they take a little more shooting practice in the adjacent wheat field. This time, popping off prairie dogs who peer up out of their holes in the ground. In my eyes the wee things appear innocent and sweet but Walter assures me they're deadly to the crops. And with his pronouncement, there's one shot after another. I still can't look.

Strelka's twitch is contagious. I feel it during the ride home with the wild prairie whipping through me. Across golden fields, the flame of tiger lilies crowding unplowed patches of earth and witnessing the pure love between them and a dazzling blue sky. Russian language rolling around me in the cab of the truck, I'm perfectly alone in good company.

Black bread's baking, the yeasty aroma curling up the stairs, when we awaken this Saturday morning. Tonight the bread will be spread with sweet butter, served alongside ruby red borscht. Beets never had it so good. Of course Aunt Lucia adds thick cream, called "sour" elsewhere but not like any ever tasted this side of heaven. Duck roasted crisp—golden—filled with oranges, herbs, onions, maybe. I don't know her secrets. Dishes happen in such rapid succession all day long it's hard to keep up.

Raisa and Esther put me to work sorting knives and forks and spoons to be set on the extended table covered with a cut-work cloth from Uncle Mike's family. Mostly-matching chinaware, pale flowers disappearing into scrolled edges, their gold returned to years of service on the many tables of Shakotko ancestors.

Why so many places at the table? I wonder out loud. I've counted, and the usual grand board that groans with our daily bread displays three more places.

Ahh, the girls respond to my curiosity, the Levechenkos and his brother. He's here, the brother, from the *Motherland*. That means the *Ukraine*. Then Esther whispers, *escaped*.

What a word. Seeps in then explodes with more words like how? Where? When? *Why*, in this house, is unnecessary: Red Army. Communism. Questions emptied of words but full of shadows and images of nighttime woods loom. Whispered commands spat into the night follow a searching light. Sudden bumps and shudders in the human storm.

Esther rushes to follow the word escaped with *it's ok, it's all right*! He's fine. *Now*. It must have been my face.

The sunroom just off the dining room, a wintertime porch that catches the light but not the frigid cold, crowds dishes of every shape and description awaiting the feast. Ready for the oven or their time on the table.

Althea reads *Treasure Island* in one corner of the sunroom, watching dishes arrive on the side board. Mama fills in when she can, but we are well aware this is not a time to interfere with the Master. Aunt Lucia knows what she's doing.

She prepares two types of *vareniki*, one to go with the borscht for a first course—deep fried—the yeast pastry rolled, cut in small circles and filled with mashed potatoes mixed into crisp bacon bits and onions cooked in the bacon leavings. For dessert *vareniki*, she puts white cheese and pitted cherries in the rounds of dough; plops each one into boiling water to cook before being sloshed into a well-buttered baking dish, warmed and sprinkled with powdered sugar for serving. Alongside sour cream or sweet cream, your choice.

Nalesniki's my favorite dessert: thin pancakes—blini—rolled around a slightly sweetened smooth white cheese, fit into a glass casserole and flooded with melted butter. Served warm, topped with whole strawberry preserves and cool, thick sour cream.

But if you think food serves up the only pleasures of this evening, you'd be wrong. Food welcomes people. And this food no grocery market on earth holds, but the result of assembling the dishes still provides the same end. A table where people gather with great thanksgiving, giving thanks just for being together first of all. Gratitude's alive in the room. This feast is a living pleasure for every single person to take away and treasure, and that's the part that purely glows my heart.

Uncle Mike asks Daddy to bless the food as we're all standing in back of our chairs fixing to sit down around this welcoming table. Standing in respect, I'd say, respect for this house, these people, the hands that grow and tend and the family that befriends every one who approaches. You can tell a friendly house by the welcome-power that lights the inside and illumines the doorway. No electricity needed.

As my Daddy begins to raise his voice in prayer, I hear a tiny wave in the sound, like Coosa River water softly lapping bridge pylons in Wetumpka. Squinting with one eye, I watch his face crumple in slow motion. Settled back into prayerful solitude, my Grandfather Deede appears. The tall gray man I've only seen as sad, misplaced, even though friends have found a little house in the middle of alfalfa fields for him as caretaker of a Russian Baptist church in Kerman, California.

Deede's stories come from the hardest of times: chopping wood during their first winter in Battleford to keep coarse, black bread on the table, sleeping in line for days at the land office to be assigned a square of barren wild countryside. The long trudge out to that wasteland called their farm, pushing a wagon loaded with the boards of a barn he traded work to acquire. The beginnings of home. This same man—my grandfather—praying with Russian neighbors for the *Motherland* and loved ones left behind, prostrating himself on the sod floor of their one-room dirt floored house in a grief Billy's—my Daddy's—young mind couldn't comprehend. And Lucia.

Always, always, sister Lucy. Our father tells those sacred stories over and over again just as regularly as he tells Bible stories. Here, the grief and goodness all wash through him as he begins the blessing.

Names are raised in the prayer, dim, familiar patterns shrouded in a fog of Russian words. But foreign as the language may be to my ear, I can hear my Daddy's heart spilling praise and gratitude in faithful trust from an underground river always flowing inside him.

7

Jasper, Alabama 1949
Learning Curve

- *A year on the verge of a new decade.*
- *President Truman assures newsmen that the nation is not going to hell despite a wave of anti-Communism hysteria sweeping the country in the wake of spy trials and loyalty inquiries.*
- *Jackie Robinson, voted Most Valuable Player by the National League, refutes Paul Robeson by saying that Negroes will fight Communism.*
- *Louis Armstrong and his jazz trumpet is roundly welcomed in Paris.*
- *Harvard Law School begins admitting women.*
- *Mississippi/Jefferson Military College receives $50 million gift on condition it teach white supremacy.*
- *South Africa: race riots kill 100, injure 1,000 in Durban.*
- *New York: on April 30th, 117,000 March in Loyalty Day parade to protest world Communism.*
- *Pope Pius protests Eleanor Roosevelt's support of a bill in Congress which would provide $300 million in federal aid to public schools. He calls her attitude unworthy of an American mother, since other private schools and Catholic schools are excluded. She responds with a statement of her strong conviction that church and state must remain separate.*
- *Audrey Skondeen is seven years old.*

SHE STANDS THERE GATHERING every bit of her importance up around her full height, but I can tell it's not going to be enough. I'm watching from the trailer window next to the front door. The knock from a stranger alerts a body to *unusual*. And in the middle of my school time, too. She's taller than Mama and Daddy even though she stoops a little, her shoulders cupped around her chest, ribs on guard duty. "Miss Clara Ainsley," introduces herself, "Officer for the Board of Walker County."

The ground outside our trailer house door is uneven, parked on a rocky grade as it is; she can't seem to find her place. Shifting her feet, Miss Ainsley's thin ankles appear unsteady, protruding from shoes that remind me of Grandma Honey's—Mama's Mother—when she's on nursing duty at the hospital, only these are brown instead of white. The Officer's eyes are brown, too, more the color of a lizard's back blending into an earthy rock just before it darts away.

Miss Ainsley's fidgity-looking, wishing she could be gone. Suddenly. But that's fleeting. Now, she stands a little straighter, as if assuring herself of her mission, and begins to address us.

Strange situation, I can tell you that. But first I better say how we got here with her knocking on our trailer house door smack dab in the middle of Reading. I'm impatient to get to the assignment and even more anxious to dip into the book my sister is beginning, *A Child's Shakespeare*. Mama promises she'll let me listen when they read together.

Evangelist Skondeen has a reputation for pulling people together, and not just during revival meetings. He doesn't care much for squabbling, period. 'Course that can drive Mama nearly to distraction if he won't answer a simple question she asks, preferring to leave on out the door than talk. But when church folks start picking at each other or at their pastor, "Doris, I tell you . . . that House of God might's well be a chicken coop. Sharp beaks! Can't tell no difference between their corn feed scattered in the dirt and the other fella's hide."

Daddy continues to reason through his chicken-coop thinking, point by point. "Resentment gets planted . . ." shaking his head in discouragement, his voice begins to rise, and Mama keeps a steady hum of, "Lord help them" and "Ummm-hmmm," nodding to keep up with his summary. "You let that bitter weed Resentment start growin' in the middle of the henhouse feed and sooner than you can count ten, you've got a whole bunch of roosters takin over." He likes this idea. "Preening. One crowin louder than the next, tryin' to convince everbody to follow their bad advice." He considers this for a minute, then he adds, "Holy Ghost wants no part of it and neither do I."

This talk was going on in the front seat while we were on the road, traveling south on Highway 287, returning from Canada. I could read maps even before I started Calvert School kindergarten. After we've been to a town, ever after I can see it when I look at the lines, dots and dashes on Daddy's maps. Helps me locate myself.

An ordinary Monday, but always a satisfying kind of day when Peggy travels by my side. She's been waiting for me in Minot. Aunt Dorie sent her to me this last Christmas. "Another useless piece of junk to carry around," is how Daddy sees her, of course. But just to look at her—bright blue opening, shutting eyes and shiny dark hair I can comb—nestles a quiet smile around your heart. I named her Peggy. I don't know why. She has a blue dress to match her eyes plus patten leather shoes just like me.

While Daddy keeps his attention on Highway 287, grumbling as he goes, Mama agrees with everything he's saying. However, since they're only talking about *maybe* going to supply pastor in Jasper, she's careful not to say too much. He might switch the argument to why we ought to say yes to the request—right now he's not interested in the least—and she needs to be ready to change with him.

"Bill, are you thinking that's how their preacher all of a sudden up and leaves?"

"Sounds like it to me. By what people *aren't* saying."

Mama nods. "How long do they want . . ." her question hanging in the air between them.

Daddy's considering options, not talking, just as a logging truck turns onto the road in front of him. When a heap of trouble pulls into sight, it's time to concentrate. This rattle trap of a truck blowing black smoke out the tail pipe as it chugs up the incline ahead of us is as haphazard as most. Looks as if he backed up to a grove of trees, cut them off at the roots and let them all fall onto the truck bed. No order to them, and so loose they appear to be ready to bolt any minute and torpedo through our front windshield. As the driver signals with his arm that he's choosing to go toward Beulah at the crossroads, I can hear Daddy exhale.

"I already told the folks in Jasper *no more than six weeks*. Told them we've been up to Kansas Camp and Canada. Mid-September. Can't go til then."

"Mmm-hmm. That's right around the comer. You want to delay Miami?" Our usual routine is heading South with the geese near Thanksgiving.

He shakes his head, "Don't think so, Doris. You know the pitiful offerings in these parts."

Mama sighs, "What was it in Elba? Fifteen dollars, forty-two cents. Lord bless their hearts . . . *dear Jesus meet their needs.*"

"At least we pay for new tires, upholstering in Miami. *Fountain Bleu* always has a job waiting for me."

If Daddy's right and there's a split in the Jasper Assembly of God Church, he'll have the two sides talking to each other before you know it. Then he'll probably leave like he always does even though people beg him to stay. "Being a pastor's the hardest job in the world. No thank you!"

The next news I hear, September nineteenth, we're on our way to Jasper, Alabama. We just closed our meeting in Bessemer, a town attached to Birmingham. Daddy repaired our trailer window—bashed out because of the storm in Kansas—while we were there, too. More little things needed fixing than meets the eye.

The storm and our trip to Canada make me think of Raisa. Feeding chickens, swinging in the hammock, staring at the true blue dream of a sky. I sure miss the Saskatchewan farm. Only a month ago, but it's so far away my heart hurts a little when I remember.

Driving north from Bessemer, Highway 269, the rocks become massive, the pine trees more straggly. You can tell these hills are full of rocks underneath, too. Black rocks. *Coal.*

Curving green hills, some spoiled by gashes slashed across them to extract the bounty—called *strip-mining*—introduce us to Jasper, Alabama. Strip mining blasts the coal out of the earth from the top, giant cranes scooping it up. In other places, miners go in underneath and whack it out with picks. These hills give up their coal every kind of way.

"Look at that mountain, Doris, God's creation . . ."

"Ruined. Lord, Lord . . . left in bits and pieces."

All I can do—Althea, too—is stare out the window. Men surge through work yards, hard hats in place, operating equipment I've never in my life seen. Some contraptions heading up to the open air buildings full of looping, chugging wild goings-on. Machines that sort, sending dark rocks up a long chain-rigged chute to the top of a huge hill of earthy substance, spewing them out ready to be trucked to refineries. Dump trucks return empty, backing up for another load.

As huge vehicles leave the area, they bounce fragments of gravel over the roadway and our car if we're in reach. A dark cloud of dust rides along with them, but believe you me, that doesn't compare to Birmingham, where coal refinery fires burn day and night in tin-roofed buildings grand enough for trains to pass through them.

At least this town doesn't breathe black soot. Coal dust or something like it blows over every square inch of Bessemer and Sayreton. We hold a meeting in one or the other every year, both towns stuck to the west side of Birmingham. The outside of every building—Sayreton, worse than Bessemer—looks like the inside of a fireplace.

When we're finally in the Jasper city limits my head turns, quick, as we roll past a majestic building made of cream-colored bricks, "Mama, look at that church . . ." I begin.

Daddy can't look, he's concentrating on the road. The formal jewel-toned window brings out my words in a gasp. Mama's quick, too, "That's no church, Audrey. See the Star of David in the stained glass? That's a syna-gogue. For Jews."

Imagine. In a little town like this. We don't ever see or hear tell of many Jews in the places where we go in the South. Daddy guesses they came over from his part of the world—Ukraine, Russia, maybe Poland or Hungary—as merchants, dealing in dry goods and tools for the miners. "But to be honest, you're better off being known as a Jew here-abouts than a Russian." Then Daddy tells Mama in that quiet-don't-listen-girls voice, that either one is *dangerous*.

"Difference is, after Hitler and his dirty work, maybe Jews have a little sympathy."

Mama answers, "Maybe . . ." as if there's something else she's thinking but doesn't say.

Brother Walter Wiggins putters around the outside of the Assemblies Church looking up from chopping weeds at the front steps when we pull into the parking lot. Even though he straightens and starts toward us, his posture is like a bear's walking on its hind legs. A skinny bear, maybe just coming out of hibernation. Or one whose nap's been interrupted. The joy of the Lord is no where in sight on this man, his face long-settled into frown lines that draw his small eyes to the ground. Mouth looks as if it's been damaged by chewing on a live electric cord, no chance of a near-smile, even. Most of his hair, bristles of dirty gray stubble like a teddy bear's, as if it's been rubbed off, but not from being loved on. Just a guess.

This church house makes me think of a white clapboard family home on a hill, front porch and all. I sure do like it. Five steps up through green shrubs Brother Wiggins clipped into shape already, leaving the scraps helter skelter with a scent of freshly cut greenery in the air.

When we ride through towns, I pick out houses like this—I especially approve of red, white and purple petunias crowding the walkway like one I saw in Waycross, Georgia, with a porch swing and rocking chairs—where I imagine living with a doll like Peggy and a little dog named Biscuit who has floppy brown ears and follows me everywhere. I don't mention this to anybody, though. I'd get a lecture about working for Jesus.

While we jump out and stretch—even though it's only been a couple hours on the road when you add in filling the gas tank and checking tires— Brother Walter helps Daddy situate the trailer just to the left side of the shrubs. Dragging cords to connect our electricity through a slightly opened basement window.

"Don't pay a be care-less. Iss 'ere church house ain in-sherd. Heah what a say?" Right, no insurance. Try not to burn the place down.

"Some folk done leff . . . follern a fuss . . ." he starts, explaining why they're so poor.

"They find a new church home?" Daddy wants to know.

"Naw. Jus gone off mad fer as a know." He considers that a minute, "Mebbe thet ain correck. They's a Penny-cossal church house yonder, bout twenny mile?"

"Well, praise the Lord, Brother," Daddy says with his hand on Brother Wiggins' boney shoulder, "we'll all be together again in heaven." That's Daddy's first commercial for peace on this patch of earth. Our grumpy helper looks at him, startled at the prospect, but doesn't say a word.

The parchment letter with a Calvert heading—a child's silhouette inbetween *Calvert* and *School*—including a graph for reporting my grades, and space for my teacher's comments, is waiting for me at the Jasper Post Office.

> Calvert School
> Home Instruction Department
>
> *My dear Audrey,*
> *Your second set of tests was excellent. If all of your marks had been "1" you would have earned a gold seal. I hope the red seal for excellent preparation will console you.*
> *Next time, try to earn a gold seal.*
>
> *Sincerely,*
> Susan B. Kellerman
> (Mrs. Lawrence R. Kellerman)

Art, Science, Social Studies, Reading and Composition are all "1," same as an A in other schools I hear tell. It's Mathematics where I only have a 1–. She's right about my being disappointed. So is Daddy. Mama points out the excellent preparation remark, though, always looking for the best. That's her way.

It says "Home Instruction Department" at the top because they are a real school in Baltimore, Maryland, too. A private school. Last year, we visited.

Third grade keeps time for me and puts me in my place—at the table for studying—every morning. I'm up by seven since my books arrived in August. First, I help Mama make their bed by folding their blankets, pushing the two halves apart from the middle into seats, stowing the bedding in the deep drawers underneath those seats and then letting our table down from where it's hooked to the ceiling.

Calvert sends a *suggested daily schedule* but I'm ahead of them by two hours. They start at nine thirty but I begin at seven thirty. They have three and a half hours with a twenty-minute recess and a half hour lunch. I use their order—Mathematics, Reading (then Recess, which for me is about five minutes of running around outside) Spelling, and Composition—every day. For all five days, after Composition, I take turns with Art, Science, Poetry, Science again, and *Picture Study*. That last one uses photographs of famous paintings by Rousseau, Gainsborough, Van Gogh, Manet, Gaugin, and others. I keep an art notebook where I put my favorites. They have a course of study for music, too, and that adds to what we already do on the road with singing, harmony and *instrumental coordination*. That last one, of course, is the way they say *violin, accordion and vibra harp, played together.*

There are 160 numbered lessons and Mama won't let me do more than one a day now that we've passed Kindergarten. After every twentieth lesson, there's a series of detailed Progress Sheets. They're tests, but they use softer words to say it. *Test* coming at you short and hard might be a dread. *Progress Sheets* are so much more pleasant to receive.

When the Progress Sheets are filled out and sent to my teacher in Baltimore, a letter like the one I received here in Jasper is the result. She writes back within a week, so I'm careful to give her the General Delivery address that will fit the timing.

Wednesday night prayer meeting, our helper Bro. Wiggins directs the service for the dozen or so people who straggle in around seven, introducing Daddy as "Vangliss Skondee, he only a fill-in Preacha."

Not one face in this sad bunch seems glad to see us. Rather be feeding the chickens or mowing the weeds. Anything but in the church house fixing to pray. But no matter how they look, Daddy delivers that smile of his right on time. Mama, Althea and I sing *Sometimes I Get Discouraged* before the Preacher says a word. *Sometimes I get discouraged and think my work's in vain I'm tempted then to murmur and complain . . .*

As Mama shrugs off her accordion, Althea and I go to sit on the front bench. The Preacher begins his giant task of sweetening this sour-looking group of what must be Holiness Christians, being we're in a Holiness church house, but there's no telling it by the folks around us. Feels like we're surrounded by hearts as hard as the coal they're stripping out of these hills. Preacher can see the mood here and figures we'll soften them up a little bit first.

> Here we are again, my Friends—
> and the Skondeen Family is glad to be with you
> good folks in Jasper, Alabama—
> *Praise the Lord!*
> Yes, here we are again—as I was sayin—prayer meetin!
> But do we take time to pray every day?
> How does this past seven days, since last Wednesday,
> look to you?
> Think it over, now.

> How about Thursday? And Friday?
> Where were you on Saturday, and
> even Sunday—were you too busy with church-goin to pray?
> Monday, Tuesday . . . ?
> The Bible says, *Pray without ceasing.*
> Never quit!
> You mean to tell me we're s'posed to be a-prayin
> on the job?
> At the grocery?
> Plowin the field?
> Walkin to the post office?
> Well, folks, if prayer is a way of life when
> we walk and talk with our Jesus
> it might just show on our faces.
> *Amen?*

Hardly a sound from the people in the pews. Well, a sort of whimper. One woman sighs, "Ummmhmmm, Jay-zus come on n hep us." She must have a resurrection in mind for this valley of dry bones. Preacher keeps up his pace, anyhow, so he won't get bored himself, never mind trying to stir the hearts of the people in the pews.

> In Jude we find, *For He is able*
> *to keep you from falling and*
> *to present you faultless before the presence of his Glory*
> *with exceeding joy!*
> If we intend to be like Jesus *someday*, why not *today*?
> Why not today, while you're still able to help somebody else?

> Why talk about the wonderful promises,
> then live, buried in our own faults and
> pointing out everybody else's faults?
> So busy! Wallowing in the mud of self-righteousness
> Lord, have mercy

The Preacher chuckles, here, as if this is something so far away it's nearly unrecognizable. Not a problem in this church! He's discussing it as the opposite of Christ-like people. Christ-like people such as we are, of course. Has to do with praying through.

> All right then, here's what *pray without ceasing*
> demands: *Never* be out of touch with our Savior!
> That's how we guard against the ambition of excelling
> over one another in show-off prayers, too:
> "Ahhhh" says so and so, "that was a beautiful prayer!!"
> Listen, the most spiritual prayer in God's sight is
> *a groan* which cannot be uttered, Romans 8:28,
> or cry *Abba Father*, Galatians 4:6.
> Hannah wouldn't have taken the prize for the most beautiful
> prayer—priest thought she was drunk on wine!
> We are so cruel when we judge one another's public prayers.

He's laying the foundation for a building that's as they say "not made with hands." On a mission for the Holy Ghost to convict these people of their sins of back-biting meanness. The same Holy Ghost, I heard the Preacher tell Mama, "wants no part of what's going on around here. Good people, falling in hard-hearted ruts."

> Yes my friends,
> Jesus keeps us from falling into that kinda mud.
> Keeps us from being mad at our brothers,
> fussin with our sisters, and
> pickin at the preacher, *Amen*?
> Keeps us holy, sanctified, and filled with the Holy Ghost.
> We sing "Oh to Be Like Him" but
> do we mean it?
> That's how we want to live. *Like Him.*
> What have I done this last week worth remembering?
> And yet some day we must give account for these seven days.

The Evangelist calls Mama to play her accordion and sing "Have Thine Own Way, Lord," while people get themselves down to the altar. And by the way, nobody said "Amen" when he encouraged them back there. Just to give you an idea of how quick this group can be, a woman bent over her cane—her silvery holiness bun nearly undone—manages to be ahead of everybody else in arriving at the altar. It's hard to watch her move, one painful step at a time.

> *Have Thine own way, Lord!*
> *Have Thine own way!*
> *Thou are the Potter; I am the clay.*
> *Mould me and make me After Thy will,*
> *While I am waiting Yielded and still.*

First time I go to the library—only two blocks away, the best yet—Mama walks me over and the library lady isn't a bit friendly. Felt like we were back in Wednesday night prayer meeting. When Mama asks her for the history of Walker County and Jasper, too, she sweetens up, but the tiny curve to her lips still doesn't go so far as to show her teeth. "We like to get acquainted with a place," Mama explains real pleasant like, adding, "we're going to be here over a month." No comment.

Funny how this woman with burnt brown sugar-colored hair chopped off at the ears can look so much like a man even when she's wearing a skirt. Her hands are larger than Daddy's and her length unfolds out of her chair in an awkward way, as if moving away from the desk requires instructions. Standing, pushing the chair aside as she walks back to *Reference* to show us a stash of Jasper history pamphlets, she puts one flat black shoe in front of the other very carefully. Her legs attach at the hips, naturally, but don't seem connected to her body.

"Here they are," making *here* and *are* sound like they have more than one syllable. I learned about syllables in Reading.

What we found in those little booklets confirms what Daddy said when he saw the synagogue: Jews arrived in Jasper as peddlers about the time Daddy was born (1907) as well as a few years before that. They carried packs on their backs selling their wares to coal miners. Kind of like we pull our trailer around to bring salvation. When they got enough money together—I picture them stashing dollars in a sock under their beds like Daddy does—they opened a dry goods store in Jasper. Sol Green and Ike

Engel related by marriage, Mama reads, were two of the most important and they came from Polish Russia.[1] Yep. Daddy figured it out.

After Mama takes me to the library, I go by myself. This time, the Stiff Lady is more friendly. She even comes to talk to me when I'm at the children's round table in the back corner beginning to look through the *Wizard of Oz*. Mama would have a fit if she saw me reading a book with *Wizard* in the title so of course I'm on alert, feeling a little jumpy. The Stiff Lady near scared me to death.

She smiles when she realizes she surprised me—her teeth look like a picket fence gone wrong—and she actually sits in one of the little chairs. Can't imagine how poorly her body took the news that she was going to double down into that bitty chair.

I'm always happy to talk about Calvert School. Turned out to be her big interest.

"A school in the mail? Well ah swan, nevah heard a such a thing."

"It's true. Why, I have classmates far away as India, a Princess! She takes Calvert, too. My teacher told me."

"Ya teachah?"

"Sure, she writes me letters every time I send in my Progress Reports. Her name is Mrs. Lawrence R. Kellerman? I met her last year when we visited the school."

"Visit . . . ?"

"Balitmore, Maryland."

"But ya don't go to school heah in Jaspah. Bein in a school room with a real teachah? Ats very important, ya know."

For some reason she makes me feel as if I'm a little kid. A not very smart little kid. Reminds me of being 6 with missing teeth. I'd catch sight of myself as I was walking past a store window and be real surprised at my look with two teeth out on the top, two on the bottom—snaggly looking—but what can a body do? Talk about a picky-fence gone wrong. My looks must be off today for the way she's acting though I didn't notice anything particular.

"This building represents *higher* learning, like a mansion on the hill top," Mama said in a whispery voice as we walked toward the glass door yesterday. Afterwards, back home, she told Daddy that it's kind of an uppity place and the librarian matches. Maybe that's the reason she let me come by myself today. She doesn't take a fancy to the place.

---

1. Goldring/Woldenberg Institute of Southern Jewish Life, *Encyclopedia of Southern Jewish Communities*, http://www.isjl.org/encyclopedia-of-southern-jewish-communities.html.

While I was walking on back to the trailer house the Stiff Lady librarian's talk set me to recollecting my school on Tuscany Road in Baltimore. Althea and I have a picture of us standing under the wooden sign that swings from a post by the front walk—*Calvert School*—right in front of the curved driveway.

We waited to meet our teachers seated on leather chairs deep green as a midnight forest. And so soft, I wanted to pet them. *Two* of me could fit in one, just inside the entryway next to the receptionist. The warm dark wood of the prim young woman's desk, polished to a glow, and a faint aroma of lemons and leather in the air. Double doors and windows on each side of the entry soar toward the ceiling in a sweeping arch.

I sat very tall and I was glad to be wearing my new patten leather shoes. Aunt Dorie sent the money for them at Easter time. She was very specific, knowing Daddy like she does. "No rummage sales or Salvation Army shoes now, Bill. New!" Mama kind of smiled when Daddy began to grumble under his breath as she read the letter aloud. Sometimes I wonder if that's really what Aunt Dorie writes or if Mama just *reads between the lines*, as she says, and inserts the words while she's at it.

We watched children arriving for their day at Calvert School in long black Cadillacs while we waited in the grand entry. I know my cars and I've never seen any like these. Even though fins came in last year, we've only passed a few on the roads we travel. But they're an epidemic in this neighborhood. Some have a man in a black suit wearing a hat that looks like an army officer—Mama calls them *chauffeurs*—who come around and open the door for the children to step out. He hands them their books and papers before they start up the walkway.

And the students wore matching clothes! Plaid skirts or jumpers for the girls and navy blue or white shirts; the boys wearing navy blue or tan pants and white shirts. I asked Mama could I have a Calvert uniform but she says they're probably too expensive. Maybe Aunt Dorie would like them. I'll have to think about that.

Then she appears. My teacher. Mrs. Kellerman's blond bob, blue-sky eyes, and smiling, perfect red mouth startle me. The white collar of her shirt standing high, grazed by gold loop earrings. Her smooth pale skin has a sheen I'm not familiar with and as she extends her hands, my fluttery chest makes me think I'm meeting a *star of the silver screen* as they say. Then she bends toward me, taking both my hands in hers, welcoming me, and that settles all my butterflies sure enough.

But then a whiff of something like a magnolia blossom, the kind that's so huge you can bury your face in it for a deep breath? Well, when that swept over me, the butterflies almost fluttered up all over again.

Althea's teacher, Miss Anders, was ill the day we visited. But maybe it wasn't as much a disappointment as you'd think. Althea doesn't feel about school the way I do. Daddy says it's because she started first grade in a Nebraska public school and hasn't quite gotten the idea of Calvert. *Big difference*, he always adds.

Whenever I see Mrs. Kellerman's name signed, now, I also see her standing there in red wedgie shoes, slim navy skirt and crisp shirt and I'll admit a proud breeze ruffles the edges of my mind. Fortunately, only I know about it. And of course, my Mama is the best teacher you can find anywhere. Teaching Calvert gives her the chance to be what she always wanted to go to school to learn. I think I heard somebody call that *on the job training*.

Our adventure on Tuscany Road comes back to me in little details as I start my study day, too. Sometimes I see my classmates in those grand rooms doing the same lessons I'm doing. Or the Princess, the Maharajah's daughter, in her palace.

But today, Miss Stiff didn't much want to be impressed by Calvert. After her first questions, in fact, *she* was trying to impress *me*. John H. Bankhead II, US Senator, lives here, she tells me. President Roosevelt even came to see him about ten—or was it nine?—years ago. And you know who his daughter is! I must have looked stupid. She displayed disappointment at the blank look on my face.

"Tallulah Bankhead? A *famous* actress!" Even with her drawl, her words still come out almost like a California person's would.

"Oh, I think I heard Gabriel Heatter talk about her on the news . . ." were all the words I could pull together.

". . . in a theatah . . ." she adds as if that'll help. Not for me. Sin is sin, theater or moving pictures makes no difference. I just smile politely. Mama says all you can do is pray for people who don't know any better.

Fall weather—in Florida we call it *hurricane season*—settles in this week. Sister Nita Beasely comes over on a rainy Saturday, carrying a box with a pressure cooker in it holding a few good helpings of beef stew. That's the most neighborly Jasper folks have been so far. She even brought us a loaf of homemade bread, golden brown and fragrant.

"Y'all mights well have auvr leff-overs—las night's?—this weather n all feelin wintry and what a wind! Course a bread ain leff-overs, hits bran new," she laughs at the end of running all her information through in one breath. Made me want to say, "Lord bless her heart!" like Mama always does. Leftovers can be delicious.

Sister Nita brought half a chocolate cake, too, "Don't need no more pounds and Eddy don't need none 'sides everbody else aroun us has di-bedees? An ya know a cain be addin no worries to a bidness s'bad fer ya like at, can a?"

We each had one bite of cake so we could tell her a kind thank you but I'm not used to something so sweet. And, as usual, the rest went to the waste can. "Better in the waste than on the waist," Daddy always says, "If we ate all the pies and cakes folks carry over to us—Lord have mercy!—we'd be too heavy even for the DeSoto to pull us around."

Sunday, the Preacher continues his campaign for peace, preaching to the twenty-six people, only four kids, who sit themselves as far from each other as they can, seems like. Here I thought since we'd be around Jasper six weeks, maybe I'd find a playmate.

Sister Beasley's children, a girl of ten—Betty—and Roger, eight, are quiet and backward. Neither of them interested in playing house, I can tell. The other two children born to the Jackson family and they're only eighteen months apart, two and four.

"Pert near kilt me, em two a'squallin day'n night." Sister Biddy Jackson opines.

Mama answers, "Lord does make a way, now," followed by, "Lord bless your heart."

The Preacher does his best warming up the crowd—if you can call it that—singing *Joy Unspeakable* and *I've Got the Joy* but nothing cracks their watery eyes open to actual tears or laughter. Those two, tears and laughter, aren't far from each other.

This stoney collection of faces maybe needs to be strip-mined for smiles. A blast or two. I don't mean any harm but thinking about some kind of possibility is the only thing that brightens. Outside, there's no sunshine anywhere, either.

That knock on our trailer house door at nine Monday morning changes everything about my Calvert schedule for the day and my opinion of Jasper in general. When Mama opens it, there stands Miss Louise Ainsley.

As our visitor gathers her courage around her, determined to make good on this call, her voice changes from sounding like it's in a hallway far away to closer in. She clears her throat, ". . . an officer of the Board of Walker County. Truant Officer." Mama wipes her hands on her apron and stares at her, perplexed. The Officer tries to make it more clear, "It has come to my at-ten-tion that your child is *not* in school."

Daddy, who's been reading—studying—in back where the bunk beds are, comes into the doorway next to Mama and says, "Child? You mean Audrey?" I don't know why Althea isn't automatically considered a child, too. Puts me off to feeling peevish-like.

Miss Ainsley nods, "I believe . . ." with very little Southern sound in her voice. She's trying hard to be official, for one thing. Daddy chuckles, as if the joke's on her, "Oh. We have *two* children. *Not* going to Jasper schools . . ." That's better.

Then, I declare! Mama comes on strong. She finishes his sentence, ". . . but they're in school all right. Would you like to come in and see?"

Miss Ainsley's the one to be surprised now. She stoops slightly to step through the trailer door, clutching a saddle brown leather satchel like a life-line. Mama suggests I scoot in so our guest can sit next to me. As the Official perches on the outside of the seat at the table, placing her fat, worn case at her feet, I cram in toward the front wall. Upclose I see that her walnut shell colored hair has unnatural curliness. People are always asking me, *natural curls*? Here's the difference I can see in the fried remains of an old perm lingering in the ends.

Mama says those permanent waves can nearly kill your hair. When we were in Wildwood, Florida, she watched Pauline Brown give her neighbor a perm: "Just get a whiff of that solution they roll into it. Why, you can smell a paper mill in that one little bowl." That's all you have to say.

The woman at the door—Louise Ainsley—doesn't have an old looking face. Not like ladies with powder settling into creases. Then again it isn't young, either. Not rosy or bright. Her face has the look of the paper my letter from Mrs. Kellerman comes on: thin, crisp, and already wrinkled so you can't do it accidentally. Her work does force a serious attitude, going to people's houses and asking them why their children aren't in school. Some might take offense. She never knows when it's all right to smile, I can tell.

We show her my art history notebook, putting a ruler over the name and artist while I say what each painting is, *'Blue Boy' by Gainsborough*, or *'Starry Night' by Van Gogh*. She reads a two page composition on *My Friend Dobbs*, about a squirrel I met in Luveme, Alabama. Miss Ainsley looks through my science workbook, too, while I explain the different systems of the human body which was my lesson for last week. Then I tell her how knowing about—for example—our skeletal system, helps us live more safely. Helps us stay healthy.

Mama does manage to get in the story of how Calvert began. First off, she's being quiet, letting my school work, including Mrs. Kellerman's letter, speak for itself. But when there's a crack in Miss Ainsley's attention, Mama shines some more light in about Calvert history. Besides the fact that their Headmaster wrote *A Child's History of the World*, very impressive, and Althea studies that now.

Beginning slowly, Mama says, "Calvert School's *Headmaster*" pausing, letting a tiny message sink in, "a Mr. Virgil Hillyer, young as he was, only twenty-four. Imagine!" she inserts, easy as can be, "Harvard educated. Cambridge, Massachusetts?" Even I didn't realize she knew this much about my school. Mama smiles real sweet, "Mr. Hillyer convinced a bookstore in Baltimore, I believe that was in 1905, to sell materials for Kindergarten so parents who couldn't afford private school like Calvert could still have the very best for their children. The *very best* education," she nods, making her point.

"Well, I'll be. How much was . . . ?" Miss Ainsley starts to ask.

"Five dollars—my lands! Just five dollars—don't you know it's a lot more than that now. But Lord willing we'll continue to make the sacrifice til Jesus comes again if need be. The Lord does provide." She still has her sweet smile situated on her face. Mama can be mighty angelic especially toward people who scare her or make her mad which she never shows out front. "So the Calvert *Home Instruction Department* began and before you know it, word spread. Mr. Hillyer put an ad in *National Geographic* magazine."

I pipe up at this point, saying, "That's how come we have classmates all over the world. You can see that ad—has a silhouette of a child's head?—in every *National Geographic*."

Mama adds, "Of course, Audrey and Althea have classmates at the private school in Baltimore, too."

Althea reads to Louise Ainsley from this book I love so much, Charles and Mary Lamb's—they're brother and sister—*A Child's Shakespeare*. By this time our personal Truant Officer looks very tired.

After over an hour of saying, "Oh my," and "Well I never!" Miss Ainsley is ready to leave. I'm not as occupied by the surprise of seeing her, now, so I notice her clothes more as she goes out the door. Colorless—gray brownish bluish or just faded black—dark skirt that comes a few inches from her shoe tops, a white, long sleeved blouse sprinkled with faint blue daisy looking flowers with a black grosgrain ribbon tied at the neck. Very neat and clean. Her eyes in parting are still Careful, not too happy but holding back from telling you *Don't worry*. Keeping the serious look steady as if it's too soon to be friendly. They're the color of leaves, her eyes, between late summer green and fall beige, but I can see kindness in them even through the double thick lenses of her dark rimmed glasses.

Turning toward us once she's out the door, her words wipe Careful away. "Don't ever put these children in public school!"

With that, my eyes almost overflow from a full cup of Happy. A bouquet of red and yellow four o'clocks slowly unfold their itty bitty parasols in my chest, and a flag unfurls whose letters spell, "I Love Calvert."

As if to hide her own embarrassment at losing her Careful with us watching, she straightens and is on her way, her old bulging satchel clutched in her right hand. Miss Louise chooses her steps to avoid rocks, tire ruts and mud puddles after the cool September rains. I'm pretty sure there hides no hint of daring in her feet, no urge toward adventure. Miss Louise Ainsley's not that kind of person.

In a fast picture show running in my mind I try to imagine her as a little girl. Some people still have the little kid they were at my age with a grin like the one I saw on my face when I was six, teeth missing and all. When the last tooth was ready to leave, Daddy threatened to tie a string on it with the other end tied to the open door of a Sunday School room, then slam the door, if I didn't pull it out myself. "Get it over with, Audrey!" he said, "stop that wiggling and messing around with it." So I did. But Miss Louise Ainsley? Nope. Nothing like that ever happened to her.

Maybe I'll write a composition about our morning with *The Truant Officer of Walker County*. Or even a letter just for Susan Kellerman. We learn to write in cursive in the Calvert method. There's no printing, ever. Mrs. Kellerman will be pleased. Just think of that beautiful cherry red mouth spreading slowly into a smile as she reads. She won't have any trouble at all feeling proud, I'm sure of it.

> *Ready to go, ready to stay,*
> *Ready my place to fill;*
> *Ready for service,*
> *Lowly or great,*
> *Ready to do His will.*

We sang all four verses of this hymn on Wednesday night. After the prayer meeting droned to a close, Daddy said to Mama back at the trailer, "I sure don't feel no leading to tarry on here in this church. Thank the Lord we only give them six weeks."

"That's enough all right."

"How d'you suppose folks let themselves kill a church like this, Doris?" Mama's silent for a minute, "I don't know. Can it be they fall into habits? You know. First, a little restless. Then discontent . . ."

"Start talkin foolishness. That tongue! Apostle Paul names it. A *viper* . . ."

"They don't mean to be troubled like this. Oh, Lord. Have mercy. Always hope in the Lord, Bill," that's about as much correction as Mama comes up with for Daddy.

"But Doris, Bible says *touch not mine anointed*. How can you slander a preacher who's doin his best? Now that's just imitatin the Devil . . ." Daddy has the last word. Of course Mama does add, "Lord help them. Help them, dear Jesus."

Saturday afternoon once a month or so, Mama reaches up into the cubby hole in the top of our closet for the big square dish towel wrapped around sharp nosed scissors, hair clippers, and a fine-toothed comb. Daddy fetches a chair from a Sunday School room or gets out the folding wooden-framed, red, yellow and green striped canvas chair we carry with us, and sits himself on it backward. The whole procedure happens outside so that clipped hair goes away in the breeze. While they talk—they're still analyzing Jasper— Mama tucks the towel between his collar and his neck, holding it with a snappy kind of wooden clothespin in front.

Mama's skilled with clipping, combing, squeezing the handles of the clippers, guiding them to clean up the hairline on Daddy's neck. He never looks as if he's just had a haircut, either. She could be a barber besides being my teacher.

Tomorrow, Daddy's preaching his last sermon in Jasper without reaching his aim of getting everybody back together again. That's why he's going around in these worry circles.

One man who left for the "Pennycossal church house up a road," as Brother Wiggins describes it, has stopped by several times during the weeks we've been here. *Brother Gordon* is what we call him. He works at the hardware store just across the "rayroad" tracks in town, as he tells it, and we're on his way home from the job.

This good man, *brother in Christ* according to church house relations, seems to have a permanent worry crease between his eyes even though there's plenty of plumpness to keep the dent from going deep. He certainly isn't old. 'Course I have a mark like that, too, young as I am, a scar left from falling on the faucet in the bathtub when I was only fourteen months old. I hear tell we had a real bathroom of our own when we lived in Nebraska and Daddy was a pastor instead of an evangelist. The Good Brother Gordon's mark strikes me as a natural result of worry, though. That whole idea of *take your burdens to the Lord and leave them there* doesn't seem to be working, at least not for him. Daddy, too, for that matter.

He tells Daddy it's the few who like to shout and dance in the Spirit who pulled away. We can tell. The former pastor was holding on with all his might but it just wasn't enough. "Twern't is fault . . . fine fella, jus run up on a buncha folks hard ta handle. All in one lil ole chuch hass." He shakes his floppy straight mop of red-hen looking hair, mournful pale blue eyes reflecting his sadness under bushy blond brows.

Today, he unfolds the other canvas chair and sits while Mama clips Daddy's hair. Jasper stores close at noon on Saturday, so he's come to bid farewell.

"Y'all get on in iss here town?" he begins, "OK fer everbody?"

"Well, yes," Daddy responds, then with that twinkle in his eye, he adds, "although, the Walker County Truant Officer did pay us a visit, tried to throw my girls in jail for not bein in Jasper schools."

Brother Gordon, caught off guard, begins "Ya talkin bout Miz Ainzey? Miz *Louise* Ainzey? Ah neva know'd kids could . . ." then he breaks into a guffaw, his hefty hands slapping the thighs of his bib overalls. "Preacha, ya done got me on at'n!"

Daddy laughs with him, then continues, "Lord was with us. Kept the girls here, right Audrey?" He glances his eyes in the direction—can't turn his head and interrupt Mama's job—where I'm perched, sitting cross-legged in the trailer doorway, my elbows on my knees, chin in hands. Here's my chance. I sit up, now.

"Brother Gordon, you can tell everybody you know that we love this town," I tell him.

"Ya dooooooo?" he asks, making a croon out of "do."

"I surely do. That Truant Lady? She loves my school Calvert just about like I do. When she left out of here after seeing what we study, she said, *Don't ever put these girls in public school!* Can you beat that?" I finish with a flourish and a little nod of satisfaction.

Brother Gordon shakes his head in amazement and says, "Well ah'll be switched!" He shifts his body a little, clears his throat, "Ya gotta a interstin womon, at Miz Ainzee . . . yep. Shor nuff."

"How's that?" Daddy says to the rhythm of Mama's *snip snip* before she combs one side smooth.

"Y'all bin atta liberry?"

"We sure have," I say, wanting to add how much I like being only two blocks away on account of I can walk there by myself? But he rushes past me in his turtle way of talking.

"She shares a house w' Miz Gentry atta liberry? Her Ma n Pa—na they's Jews, Miz Gen-try's Ma n Pa—they leff er at house," he says by way of explanation, "Ole house? Them wimin's fixin fools, a tellya! Like a coupla lumba jacks!" He laughs, "Ain seen a likes a em two nowheres."

Mama pipes up, "Strong women! Like Dorcas—in Acts of the Apostles?—taking care of a big household and giving to the poor." She smiles, that angel smile is getting a workout in Jasper, and says, "We find both of those ladies to be very helpful, don't we Audrey? It follows they'd be helping each other, too." Just a breath, then, "Hard to find good help, I hear."

Good Brother gives Mama his full attention, "Shor nuff!"

Personally, I'm glad to know Miss Ainsley has a friend. Miss Gentry, too. Neither one of them seem all that neighborly. Fact is, one night I talked to Jesus about her having a friend, Miss Ainsley. I admit I didn't think of it for Miss Gentry. It was just before going off to sleep with my purring Lion. I'm too old for imaginary friends, now, being that everybody in my family used to tease me about them when my friends and I played mud pies together. I do still have Jesus, though. We all know we have a friend in Jesus. When I can't find anybody to play dolls, He fills in. But I'm not sure if Miss Ainsley knows about Jesus or not.

First thing I see on our last Sunday in Jasper is blue sky. Not through my trusty spy square in the ceiling—the vent—rain kept that from being rolled up for days. All week, clouds, dribbles and stormy weather, except for that little break when Mama cut Daddy's hair yesterday. Even some showers after dark last night.

During Postum and porridge time, I'm glad to see the sun, "You know what all this shinyness puts me to recollect?"

Mama, at the sink, murmurs, "... *shining causes me to remember* might be a better way to say that, dear."

Daddy, across from me at the table—Althea's still making her bed— lets out a "hmmmm" in the shape of a question.

"World's first day!"

"How's that?" Daddy wrinkles his brow, taking a loud slurpe of hot Postum.

"Sparkly! All sparkly!"

"You there? At the *world's first day*?"

I make a frowny face at him and go on to the real point that anybody should know, "Well, if the Holy Ghost is in the waters like it says in Genesis?"

"Spirit of God . . . on the face of the waters . . ."

"And God calls light to come and then trees and everything! That's today after rain when all the trees and grass are wet . . . like as if the Holy Ghost came in overnight . . ."

Daddy smiles, "Well, that's quite a sight, now, isn't it," he chuckles between small slow bites of his oatmeal. His digestion works better when he's happy. Heading for Miami tomorrow morning perks him up today.

And in the very first words from the Preacher this morning:

> We've got us a beautiful Sunday morning
> in Jasper, Alabama!
> Like the first morning the Bible tells us about in Genesis when
> God wanted Order out of Chaos,
> *Praise God*!
> He called on the Holy Spirit to bring *order* and *beauty*;
> when God wanted to decorate the Milky Way,
> He called on the Holy Spirit!
> Now we're going to be leaving here tomorrow morning.
> The Skondeen Family's pulling out.
> But I believe the good folks in Jasper
> can depend on this same Spirit
> to put things in order around here! *Amen?*

Lo and behold! There are at least three Amens that ratchet around the meeting room. I'm next to Mama, Althea sits on the other side of her on the front row, so I can't twist around and see who said them. That wouldn't be seemly. But hearing *Amens* encourages my heart.

Daddy and Mama pull out all the stops for the music, *Lift Me Up Above the Shadows* for the first singing of the day. That was after the Spark Plug opened the singing with *He Owns the Cattle on a Thousand Hills*, about how God is in charge of everything—all the wealth of the world plus the sun, moon and stars—and as His Children, we own that, too. Reminding us who's in charge.

After that it's *More about Jesus: More about Jesus I would know, More of His grace to others show.* You can see Daddy's setting up a message of how to behave. Not that he doesn't always have Jesus and Grace in mind, but here, now, it matters more than usual is what I'm saying.

Mama sings her favorite solo, on the verses it's a solo at least. Daddy joins in on the last chorus and the rest of the time he plays a violin obligato for harmony, *Give Me the Roses While I Live.* Several people requested it. Maybe they're thinking more about how to treat each other.

Right off, the Preacher makes the most of second chances, that's the way I hear it. He's talking a lot about the Holy Spirit in every possible way. Every possible place the Spirit works, then he says:

> The Holy Spirit's not given so you're fit to go to Heaven
> it's to help us win others and bring them *with us* into heaven,
> Amen?
> *But Lord, I've failed!*

Preacher wails this out like somebody who's been tossed in the Lost box and isn't Found yet.

> *I've faillled!*
> Well boo-hoo.
> Who in this old world hasn't failed!
> Spirit's prodding us—beggin us!—to stop our bellyachin
> and go to prayin!
> Samson prayed! *I know,*
> *Yes, Lord, I know I've failed, but please,*
> *One More Time!*
> *One More Time let me feel like I did*
> *when I was surrounded by those enemies*
> *and won the victory.*
> *Let me feel again like I did when I took hold of that lion.*
> *Just one more time, Lord.*
> Of course we have failed. We've been playing with this world
> until we lost all our Joy! Lost our Power!
> Our churches are cold—lifeless—nothing to be desired.
> Our young people have gone to the world to look for satisfaction.

He's been creating a feeling of despair. A feeling this group of people must be familiar with, and the silence around his words seems very loud to me. Then he hits the nail on the head:

> Jesus!—*Just one more time*—please have mercy and
> give us a Revival!
> Revive Us Again!
> You might have to tarry for Revival
> but remember this—You
> aren't waiting on God,
> God's waiting on you!
> We could have the greatest Revival if

we could *buy* Revival.
Why Brother Wiggins, we'd
all be willing to give a week's salary.
But that won't do it,
we havta *Pray*.

The invitation to the altar song I'm singing is *Almost Persuaded* even though there aren't any sinners here, unless you count everybody in on that. That could be. Daddy didn't explain his reasoning so I'm not sure.

"Al-most per-suad-ed" harvest is past;
"A l-most per-suad-ed" doom comes at last;
"Al-most" can-not a-vail; "Al-most" is but to fail.
Sad, sad that bitter wail, "Al-most, but lost."

As for me, I mean exactly what I said about Jasper to Brother Gordon on Saturday afternoon. Pulling away from here, I see hope. Some movement in the folks who've heard the Preacher these weeks. Walter Wiggins even smiled a little when he patted Daddy on the back and gave him the final offering. $21.48. Not bad.

"Lord, Lord, fer a man a fine out what's ail'nim. Wrecked, cain go on no more. Like at Samson? Gotta fine a way, na don he. Yep." I reckon the tiny smile I detect means Brother Wiggins may be finding his way.

Leaving town, Mama made a final call at the General Delivery window and that brought me the answer to my latest Progress Sheets. They were quick in coming around again this time on account of Mama letting me work on Saturdays. Besides, there were no travel days. I'm saving my letter from Mrs. Kellerman to read when we stop for dinner. That's real hard for me, waiting. But maybe there's a gold star inside and I'm going to have plenty of back seat time to think about that till then. I should say Peggy and I have time to think about it.

Headmaster Hillyer says, "The whole realm of knowledge is the true field of study." That word realm comes up in hymns all the time about Heaven, so it fits right in here. He finished his thought with . . . *school is not the preparation for life, it is life.*

8

Miami, Florida 1950
News Junky

- *Clashes between communism and capitalism dominate the decade.*
- *Senator Kefauver resolves to fight organized crime.*
- *Alger Hiss—former top State Department official—is sentenced to 5 years for perjury; passing documents to Whittaker Chambers.*
- *President Truman orders the hydrogen bomb built, 100 to 1,000 times more powerful than the atomic bomb that destroyed Hiroshima.*
- *Senator Joe McCarthy tells a Republican Women's Club that Communists have infiltrated the US State Department.*
- *RCA announces a three-color TV picture tube, a new threshold in television.*
- *Tennis admits the first Negro, Althea Gibson.*
- *Congress votes to override President Truman's veto for an anti-communist bill: Mundt Bill becomes the law of the land, requiring all Communist organizations to register officers and state how money is being spent.*
- *President Truman judges certain aspects of the Mundt Bill to be unconstitutional, advancing communism, not hindering it: ". . . like trying to get thieves to register with the sheriff."*
- *Roman Catholic Bishops protest sex education in public schools.*
- Crackers *connotes a backwoodsman, rustic, countrified person; a poor White person. 1836 Knickerbocker 7.453, It is the killing of the cattle of*

the "crackers"—as the southern backwoodsmen are called—that is most fruitful source of disputes.[1]

- *Audrey Skondeen is eight years old.*

MAMA SAYS LORD HELP us under her breath when Daddy sits close up to the brown wooden radio box for his dose of world news. Daily events weigh on him as if he's Atlas, carrying the earth on his shoulders.

Even the lush thick green of a Miami trailer park's grass framing our slab #31 and the Poinciana tree's splayed branches over our patio frosting our space with drifting flame-like flowers don't distract Daddy one bit when Fulton Lewis Jr., or Lowell Thomas is on the radio. Gabriel Heatter does say, "There's good news tonight, Ladies and Gentlemen," whether there is or not. And you can't forget Walter Winchell on the Mutual Broadcasting Company.

We're in Miami, as usual, for upholstering opportunities while churches take time out from revivals for the holiday season. Practicing for Christmas plays. Then tarrying at Watch Night services around December 31st, hoping Jesus will return before we have to start a new year.

If you ask me, Miami colors in winter are bent on Happy, no matter what world conditions might be. But not for Daddy. Communism in the State Department, Communists walking out, invading, capturing, overtaking, all happens to him as a personal assault. No smiles included. He cannot say with Brother Wilson in Slapout, *A thank God fer everthang.*

However, encountering a Genuine Florida Original will cheer Daddy considerably. Somebody like Arden Gilley, who wears a wide smile under his thick salt and pepper mustache until he sees a license plate from New York. Or Pennsylvania. "M'fam'ly bin heah nigh unta hunnert yar," nodding, "not jus since Janyary!" Proud to be a *Florida Cracker*. Course, nobody else better call him that. Lives near Goulds, Florida—Daddy built our trailer there—and doesn't think highly of *Snowbirds* flying south every year, crowding highways and complicating the real estate in general.

Yep, Gilley's my Daddy's kind of Floridian. Not that Daddy disrespects anybody at all but truth is, when he meets a genuine backwoods Floridian he has a smile inside his face as well as on the surface. Always happy to hear news told in the tales of the Glades, Key West or life along the Suwannee River.

There are some newsmen Daddy does not listen to on any day. The ones who choose to report certain events and speak of them with a slant Daddy disapproves, he labels *pinkos.* I'm not sure what that means but

---

1. *Dictionary of American Regional English*, s.v. "cracker."

rather than be lectured about it after I ask, I thought about it and figure it has something to do with being too close to *Red*, which is *Communism*. Voices such as Edward R. Murrow and Eric Sevareid—just the sound of them—cause Daddy's face to turn down the light, set up a raft of thunder and consider a hurricane right on the spot.

My Daddy takes the news as seriously as the Second Coming when Jesus returns to earth again. The word *rapture* speaks to the moment when Christians meet together in the sky with our Savior and Coming King.

That never used to entertain my imagination much. When I was a little girl I depended on pictures in the King James Bible of Jesus riding high on clouds with arms outstretched in welcome. As far as I was concerned, that's how the Second Coming would happen. But since that Kansas tornado when our trailer tried to meet Jesus in the air ahead of schedule my mind does not light up with those glory pictures. Meeting Jesus in the air in the sweet, sweet by and by no longer strikes me as a sunny situation. Clouds are dark, full of mudslinging sticks that sting my face and lodge in my hair.

Sometimes I ask the Lion if He knows how this rapture thing works. So far, He only purrs loudly in response. And the more I ask questions I know I can't ask Mama and Daddy, the less the Lion seems to come around. You'd think a Lion could stand up to tricky subjects.

So far an event such as even the possibility of Rapture hasn't made the news, though Daddy does say after reports like the trial of Alger Hiss and Senator McCarthy's latest quote on Commies here, there, and everywhere, *Doris, how long will Jesus tarry, the world in this Mess?* And she replies, *Lord knows*, followed by the dirty shame sound. So news of the day and Jesus returning to earth to fetch us up to heaven do touch in to each other. Seem to be close neighbors inside Daddy's head.

Now I realize that most advertisements for vacations, cruises, and winter holidays show Miami crowded by palm trees and dripping with crystal blue ocean water along white sand beaches. That's all true. But I see bananas when I imagine Miami.

Not because they grow here, though big friendly fan like leaves on thick green stalks clump together in a lot of back yards. No. Thing is, Daddy makes sure he has time in his work day to drive over and meet the banana boats expected from South America. And the good part is that he has to have me along, too.

Don't ask me how he finds these things out, a schedule for banana boats. He probably stumbled on one by accident the first time and then began to hunt for specifics. Arrival of banana boats isn't Gabriel Heatter's kind of good news.

As they unload the cargo, huge stems tall as I am, ringed with hands of green bananas shoot through a pulley contraption off the ship down a moving ramp. Dark gold men with heavy black hair and strong backs handle them as they reach dockside. All banana hands beginning to tip yellow are cut loose quickly and dropped on the dock. Too ripe to ship to grocery stores.

Here's where I come in, running all over picking up banana hands. Daddy has burlap sacks we fill. Reckon my quick eyes and rapid feet prove to be necessities for this operation, like Strelka retrieving ducks on the lake in Canada.

When we return to the trailer park where we live November to February, we distribute bananas to everybody. The smiling pink cheeked white haired couple from Ohio—they look alike—and the widow who walks her bitsy white dog every morning. Even the grumpy man with a scratchy looking beard. His wife died since we were here last year and I have to admit that when I heard about his wife I whispered to myself, *Who wouldn't want to head on into heaven with an ornery man like that at your breakfast table*. But Mama said, *Bless his heart*. She's right of course. It requires extra helpings of goodness for his dried up heart to keep on beating.

Miami winters mean banana bread—that other people bake and share, us with no oven—banana pudding, banana cream pie and bananas on porridge or anything you're eating. They take a while to ripen, some now, some later. It's a regular festival.

There's an irregularity about winter in Miami, too. No church. Not only every night, but sometimes not even on Sunday.

Local pastors hold certain suspicious attitudes toward traveling preachers if they haven't personally invited them to be at their church house. Why? Well, as a matter of fact, it's pure foolishness on their parts as Daddy points out when he and Mama discuss it, since he is *no way* and *never* interested in being a pastor. He demonstrated that fact again in Jasper. But that doesn't stop pastors from entertaining the jitters when we show up.

Always some friendly greeter finds out our True Identity and that sets the Strelka quivers going from top to toes—pastor's pompadour to his shiny white shoes—and what a pity. You'd think we were from New York, rather than fans of Real Florida People. I don't roll my eyes on account of Mama's assuring me that a gesture like that wipes away any doubt about my being a decent sort of girl, but inside, while keeping my eyes straight ahead, that's exactly what I do. We find ways to be in church while we're here, just not every night or most Sundays.

Besides, Daddy's *plum wore out* by the time he's upholstered furniture for rich people living in penthouse apartments—in hotels on Miami Beach—four, five, or six days during the week. That's why he does not put himself through trouble and suspicion on Sunday.

If people think it's strange that a preacher can work a day job, too, they'll have to review the Apostle Paul and his making tents. But personally I think it's his own father that Daddy takes after. During the 1920s, specially after '29, Daddy tells me that Deede—which is what the grandchildren call his father—trolled the docks of San Francisco just like we do looking for banana boats, but he was looking for jobs. Any job. Daddy remembers how wretched it was when his Papa didn't have work.

The sounds of Worry and Fear tell that story in Daddy's voice so loud and clear, I figure he decided he'd have a trade he can do anywhere. He learned how to upholster in San Francisco when he was sixteen to pay for his violin lessons at the San Francisco Conservatory of Music. But now *spitting tacks*—as he calls *upholstering*—keeps saving our lives on the road for Jesus, paying for our cars, tires, gas and close to everything else. Or, takes care of us when we settle down for a spell like Mama and Daddy did in Sacramento when I was born.

Those *love offerings* fall short. Folks generally do their best but some pastors where we hold meetings have the same twitch ailing them as the ones here in Miami even though they, themselves, invite us to their churches. Scared we'll be wheeling a barrel full of dollars out the door. Daddy's been heard to say *Don't they realize stinginess is not the same as godliness?* And Mama lets it go on by with, *Have mercy.*

'Course Daddy doesn't buy so much as a pack of *Wrigleys* without a good reason and that's only a nickel. Love offerings stretch further along the highways we travel than any ordinary person could expect them to go. When Daddy says we are completely out of cash, there's no doubt a hundred dollars in small bills rolled up inside a sock somewhere.

We'd stay at the Fonts' for winter if it wasn't so far from Miami Beach hotels. Josylyn Fonts took to Althea's music when she heard her play at Assembly of God Camp Meeting in Lakeland. The Fonts live in a palmetto patch stretch of sand more toward the center of the state that any northerner looks on with contempt. When we met them at camp meeting, their thin, freckly girl recognized Althea's talent right away. "Josylyn like ta swooned!" her mother, Sister Fonts—nodding her head so vigorously her sandy blond holiness bun loosened up—told our Mama, "that vibry harp 'mpressed'r ta no end."

It's nice to see my sister enjoy being appreciated. Ordinarily she ignores her own *musical gifts* as we call them, given to us by God our Creator and Heavenly Father. You still have to practice, let me point out.

At any rate, Josy's appreciation made friends with Althea's shyness. They keep in touch, letters following us around everywhere we go. Josy takes guitar and piano lessons her mother describes as *preparin our girl to be a fine lil preacher's wife* which causes Josy's heart shaped face with its turned up nose to smile in pure delight. She wears too many pink ribbons for me, but sometimes I have an attitude I dare not express.

Josy is one kind of sweet South Florida native. Other Originals like Arden Gilley, not so sweet, trace relations back to the 1800s. As a general rule they're the ones who've been here since ever and don't plan to leave. They farm the poor sandy soil for celery and grow oranges and grapefruit, grove by grove. Maybe run cattle. One road cuts across a piece of Florida that used to be for driving cattle, called *The Florida Cracker Trail*. Runs from Bradenton to Fort Pierce.

Another thing about Originals, you can pretty much count on their loving Jesus and go to a Holiness church like the Assembly of God, Pentecostal Holiness Church of God, or some branch of Baptist. They talk blunt southern talk and let you know as soon as possible that Jesus is all the world to them. When you meet them you know in an instant they don't have Minnesota tags on their cars or pickup trucks. None of their grandchildren prefer oven roasted chicken over floured chicken fried in deep fat in a cast iron skillet or English peas over crisp cornmeal coated greasy hot okra. Around New Year's Day there might be a big pot of Creole gumbo speckled with okra cooking on their stove, too.

Real Floridians talk about the Glades back in the 20s. *'Member when they was no bridge t'Key West?* an oldtimer might say. Mama and Daddy remember that time all right. They were living in Key West—1934, his first mission church as a pastor—on Florida Street.

Happiest place on earth to hear Daddy tell it. People in Key West agreed that he grew the biggest tomatoes on the island with his method of putting tiny cheesecloth sacks around the yellow blossoms to protect them from the scourge of bugs that troll the tropics. Neighbors all trouped through their yard to see his invention. *Ah'll be*! I can hear them.

A fine early December Sunday morning in Florida dips us into the wide waters of the Atlantic, one of God's most beautiful waterways. Heading south along the causeway toward the keys we find a stretch of sand with the fewest people.

Mama declares, "Atlantic Ocean's salt water is Bill's full immersion baptismal tank." Makes sense when you consider how he loves the island of Key West. He believes salt water heals him, whatever ails, but especially when poison oak or ivy grabs ahold of him. The welts of that scourge come close to killing him and he knows for sure that's a time to head for the healing waters. But scourge or no scourge, Daddy takes pleasure in rolling around in the shallows. Covering his arms and legs with his own brand of holy water. Never had the chance to learn to swim.

Today I'm searching the sky for clues. Rain arrives now and then, but the sky over Miami and the keys has cirrus clouds this morning, looking as if God's been picking cotton balls apart high overhead. Calvert science lessons teach all about cirrus, nimbus, cumulus and stratus clouds. Knowing their names makes me feel more at home.

All right, I realize *this world is not my home we 're just a passing through* like the song says. But while I'm here? I like to be friendly enough to know what's around me.

Althea, Mama and I take walks in the shallow surf. But what I love best is building sand castles just out of reach of the water.

As the tide comes in, my castle may wash away with one slurp of a wave but every room stays in my mind. Friends play there, friends I've never met but are real to me anyhow. And Peggy, my buddy, who doesn't live with me any more, but I don't like to talk about that. Even though I don't have a doll that travels with me now, she's still in the rooms of my sand castle.

As well as Peggy, the genuine girl I met in Pennsylvania. What a good news surprise she turned out to be—and her name!—but she's not as good at writing letters as Josy. That may be on account of Peggy's definitely not being interested in growing up to be a preacher's wife. Enough to be a preacher's daughter, she'd probably say, so she doesn't care to be connected to an evangelist all the time like Josy. That's how I see it.

Not another living soul is on the sands when we find a place at our Atlantic Ocean Holiness Sunday School. Mama spreads a cotton blanket out, leaving the loaf of whole wheat bread, bologna, and carrot and celery sticks in the car until lunch time. Mama's fair skinned, Althea too, so the blanket is half in the shade of a banyan tree, which change my idea of trees whenever I see one. Roots stretch up to make branches or vice versa, fall down from branches to make roots. It beats all. There is no other tree like it. Whichever direction it goes—limbs down or roots up—a banyan tree radiates shade.

After our bologna, bread, and carrot sticks at noon, a dark blue Ford pick up arrives with three kids in the back, two rowdy boys, one my age and one about Althea's age, thirteen maybe, plus a girl who's probably fourteen or fifteen. She's what Mama and the women she discusses such things with while dinner's being fixed call *blossoming*. Her brothers grow oversized crooked teeth, wear blurred-together freckles, and hurl peevish words—such as *ain't gonna, cain't make me,* and *he done it, did too, did not*—back and forth at each other.

I figure these people don't have a church home. Their *Ma* and *Pa*, as they call them, don't take kindly to *foreign* license plates. Our tags are from Florida—Wildwood in Sumter County where our friends the Browns live and where Althea was born—leading Ma and Pa in the dark blue pick up to choose this as a safe place to go to the beach and not be exposed to a bad influence like northerners.

Ma, I'll call her *Rosie* since that's the color of her skin, hasn't seen a swim suit other than one that fits her like an inner tube stretched beyond its capacity for a long time. Probably since she was *Teeney's* age, which is what the girl's being called. If it was *Tina*, real Floridian talk would sound like *Teener* so most likely Teeney, a nickname from when she was born.

When people pop up in my sight, stories begin to unfold. I see details settle around folks as if they were telling me about themselves. You might say I make it up, but sometimes in revival nights what I see around folks turns out to be right. Sometimes I think it's because I talk about them to Jesus and He fills me in—like I used to talk about them with the Lion?—but now I'm not so sure how that happens.

Rosie, the Ma-person, totes around bosoms about twice the size of Aunt Lucia's pillows. She swims out into the ocean and becomes a black dot on the horizon, then returns with the happiest face, dripping out of the water and calling to her kids, "Hits s'fine! Y'all gotta git on in!"

Pa leaning against his truck, fixes his bristly mouth around one cigarette after another, which is what leads me to suspect they're people who don't go to church but no doubt love Jesus on the side cause their Mamas loved Jesus all their lives and they know that's the right thing. You won't find most church folks on the beach come Sunday, even in the afternoon. Sunday dinner, then rest, and after that, the evening service being the order of the day.

"You know how t'float, Suga?" Rosie sees me lolling on my stomach in the shallows after a wave took my castle for a swim.

"No, not without the help of an inner tube," I say, friendly as can be.

"Well, it's s'much fun! Lookee heah," and she goes out a little ways, stretching her deep and wide body on the waters, looking as if she's an easy part of the waves.

She lumbers back toward me, water flowing off of her pink self and her brown pin curls appearing as wooden nickels under the clear plastic cap she's pulled on over her hair, shouting, "Na don't at look fun, honey chile?" Rosie teaches swimming at the Y, she tells me, imitating the woodpecker toys that dip into a water glass as she talks, bobbing and grinning.

I glance at my Mama sitting back on our blanket. She's smiling, accustomed to my making friends with all-out strangers wherever we go. So I say to Rosie, "Sure does look fun, all right."

"Wanna try?"

We wade out a little way, I don't need quite as much water as she does, and she takes over, giving me instructions about our bodies being mostly water and no wonder we're all a part of it? And no wonder how easy it is to float? And no wonder we loves it soooo much!

Rosie places her hands underneath me, saying, "Lay down, uh huh, na ya gotta trust me!" Her giggles cascade along with a running stream of orders. Naturally I think to myself of the "everlasting arms" the little boy song writer David sings about in the Psalms. I'm smiley inside and feeling full of sunshine with Rosie's plump fingers spread under my back, my suit is the blue one Althea outgrew a while ago, stretched out so much it skims my knees. I'm a little tense, maybe, wanting to get it just right, but prepared to float like clouds high in the sky.

"Relax, na jus reelax, arch yer back . . . arms straight." I do all of it. Well, I think I'm doing all of it.

Suddenly her hands aren't there and in a split second I sink, heavy as a conk shell. Quickly gulping breath, but instead of air, stinging brine flows into my nose and mouth.

Panic. Arms flying, feet scrambling for a place to land.

Though I can't be sure.

Straight out of the storm in Kansas, that blank sheet of paper takes over, only this time the white comes from salt, liquid salt, burning up my eyes, nose and throat. Rosie grabs me—she's not that far away—saying the few words filtering in that sound under water, over and over. At least it seems to be what's happening.

"You aw right! Sweetie pie—yeah, na—you fine!" Turning me on my stomach on the beach while I cough and hack. Then turning me on my back again, sitting me up to breathe, "If ya din't relize I's gone? You woulda shor nuff gone on afloatin!"

The lady's trying to smile, my first sort of normal thought out of the roaring white, coming to with my Mama kneeling beside me, her hand at my back. I've been capsized on the beach, you might say.

Jonah is no joke.

That's my next thought. Salt water still drowning out every single word. I'm breathing sandy salt through every pore.

Don't ask me how I made it back to our trailer. I don't have a clear recollection of the rest of that afternoon.

Daddy's out of sight on a little inlet of beach, rolling around in a shallow salt bath, Althea says. She runs down to fetch him. Mama and Daddy don't make much of tragedies in our own family, just other people's hardships. That's the usual way. *This is ordinary.* That's how they treat most everything except what they see as sin and that's a whole other barrel of crabs.

Since my recollection pages are blank, I'm guessing that Daddy, casual as can be, decides it's time to go home anyhow. Mama agrees. They smile and speak sweetly to Rosie, thanking her for her kind help so as not to make her feel bad about drowning me. They—my Mama and Daddy—will never mention it again, I can guarantee that. And we'll go to the beach like always. But I won't be easy in talking to strangers that want to teach me to float. Even folks who most likely love Jesus by way of their mamas.

Worn out canvas signs we recognize from seeing them last year and the year before, begin to show up along the Tamiami Trail in front of scruffy cinder block churches heralding *Christmas Program* along with a tacked on date of the big event. During the couple of weeks churches celebrate Jesus' birth with musicals and plays, we put in enough church time to equal several months of Sundays. Some on Sunday morning or in the afternoon or evening. A few on Christmas Eve.

The Sunnyside Holiness strings sheets across the baptismal tank opening—usually covered by a faded blue drape—and around the sides of the platform. White. Dazzling, if you fail to notice the pink that faded from something red in the wash along the side of one or the rip that's patched with black thread on another. A single light bulb dangles in the left corner over the platform. Daddy whispers *that's the star in the East* in case I miss the meaning.

One larger angel announces that this Holy Child will save us from our sin. Other lesser angels, smaller, and not up to learning lines, flutter through in additional white sheet bits and pieces. A shepherd who's watched his sheep long enough begins to agitate for change. His face contorts at first, then grabbing on to the belt of his shepherd's costume bathrobe, loudly wheezes under his breath, "But I hafta gooooooo . . ." to his mother seated on the front row and leaves in a hurry, missing the Holy Child's appearance.

The point of the stories we see and the songs we hear is always the same of being saved by the baby Jesus, and the boxes of treats every child receives at the door hardly differ at all. I do look forward to the doorway—*Merry Christmas, God bless you!*—custom of giving out treats.

Each box front or back is the dimension of a letter envelope that's three inches thick. The design may be blue with a big white and gold star beaming from one corner. Or it may be yellow with straw as the theme, a manger on one side. The contents shake loose—Althea's, mine is mostly eaten on the way home—with the orange rolling out first. Then rectangular or square sparkling white, green and red hard candies, mimicking the designs of flattened tree ornaments shrunk to Life Saver size, follow. Some, taste of cloves or wintergreen. Others, unidentifiably sweet, porous in the middle. If they're packed the day before, the orange peel will have turned them damp by now. At least that's Mama's theory of how it happens, though Florida humidity carries enough moisture to creep in on its own and clump them together.

These candy ornaments would fit just right for our tiny Christmas tree if they were hangable. Not a real tree, mind you. Where would we put it? Althea found a craft book when we were visiting a friend of Mama's and Daddy's in Goulds, Florida. "Nothing will do til we find an old Reader's Digest, Bill," Mama tells Daddy, "Althea wants to make this Christmas tree . . ."

"More junk!"

"But Bill," Mama lowers her voice, "We can throw it out afterward . . ." and the response is his form of the *dirty shame* sound only it's a *more foolishness* grunt.

That's how our customary tree—a Reader's Digest with the right top corner of every page turned down to the center until it can stand cone-like—came to be. Althea found some gold paint and glitter at a Five and Dime, which could cause more grumbling about expense and lead to added *foolishness* disturbance. We avoided that through Mama's secret saved up change. And when it's perfect, we stand our tree on the built-in bureau drawers to the right of the doorway.

Then! Wonder of wonders, our little tree acquires a grand reason to be when Auntie Dorie's traditional box arrives three whole weeks early. Her lavish red and royal blue ribbons with silver foil-wrapped boxes in back of our little bit of sparkle-plenty brightens the whole trailer house every bit as much as the elegant trees in windows we pass.

Daddy doesn't believe in Christmas presents due to the foolishness idea but on the 26th of December, he comes home from upholstering wearing a look on his face I've only seen on Aunt Lucia's cat with a mouse tail dangling from his teeth. Mama has our favorite supper on the stove, canned corn beef, potatoes, carrots, and cabbage, and Daddy announces, "Here's the dessert!" As if sweets are normal every day when we only have one day, besides Christmas boxes at pageants, that anything sugary visits this trailer house and that's an occasional Sunday afternoon. A quart of vanilla ice cream and a bottle of root beer for floats. I even missed that little bit on the day of my drowning by not being able to swallow a single thing.

When I investigate Daddy's catnip grin, I find two pounds of Whitman's chocolates. Marked down to 99 cents, you understand, since holly berries and red ribbons decorate the box.

Now the secret of a Whitman's box is the diagram on the inside of the lid. Every piece sketched, the shapes of caramels, creams and chews, with the nature of the filling printed underneath. So, no *accidental* poking in the bottom, then leaving the lemon cream, for example, and continue looking for a walnut fudge with additional pokes.

Daddy knows how to shop bargains, but even so this surprises me. Something must be making him feel real good. Or he remembers that his youngest child nearly went to meet her maker in God's baptismal a few days back and he wants to treat her well. That's the thought I keep.

All this talk about God's baptismal, the Atlantic Ocean, including a mention of the holiness church baptismal tank behind the pulpit covered by sheets for the Christmas program, yet never a mention of my own baptism last August leaves a gap. Started thinking about this when I woke up this morning. Especially since my own baptism announces a smiling celebration instead of a very wet *dying with Christ* as it's usually called. Good thing my baptism happened before Miami.

You can say it all starts while we're coming home from Aunt Lucia's and Uncle Mike's farm in Canada last year. Being out of our usual southern trails—driving in Kansas, North Dakota and points north—puts Pennsylvania to the east and Daddy's good friend David Bennett in mind. He pastors the Assembly of God Church in Williamsport.

So Daddy wrote to him when we landed back in Alabama, but at the time, I didn't know about his children. Arriving in Williamsport for the revival meeting this past August, there she stands: Peggy, Brother and Sister Bennett's youngest daughter. The best friend I will ever have.

Plus, not knowing her until that very minute, I already named my doll for her, a mystery. And I take it as a good sign that a real live Peggy shows up as a perfect playmate even though my doll baby was already living somewhere else since May.

Peggy and I made tents with checkered table cloths in her back yard, got sick on tuna fish sandwiches served with too much grape pop and ice cream, and then with surprise and ceremony, we were baptized together in the Susquehanna River on the last Sunday of our revival. That meeting blessed me for two whole weeks while we're there and forever after in my heart.

First, I overheard Mama and Daddy discuss whether I am ready for such a sacred event as being baptized. Mama saying I surely am a willful child (bad) and Daddy saying I'm a witness for Jesus whenever I have a chance (good). Then Mama saying I love to sing (good) and Daddy saying I've been known to ask a lot of questions (bad). And sometimes there just doesn't seem to be an answer for some of those questions (very bad). However, they don't hear about most of them these days. A girl learns. After a silent spell Mama does come up with the idea that Calvert School encourages curiosity. Daddy kind of *humphs* in a frowning yes.

Finally Daddy says maybe they should ask me. Mama agrees.

It's no secret that Peggy is being baptized so the idea blooms bright for me. Jesus enjoys his friends. Easy choice.

The day of our baptism we stand in a row with all the other candidates. Questions about rejecting evil—who wouldn't?—and *living a holy life acceptable unto God which is our reasonable service* come at us.

Peggy and I stand straight, holding hands real tight. Her braids are plaited close to her head, the chestnut brown and sunny blond strands pulled together and tied with yellow ribbons to match her yellow polka dot pinafore. Brown eyes reflecting more gold than usual, smile sideways in my direction beaming a powerful song of happiness. Except, naturally, when the questions about sin and evil are being asked. Doesn't bode well to be pleasant in an atmosphere full of Satan and his minions.

We pass the tests. And right after the Sunday morning service all the people troop down to the river, singing, *Shall we Gather at the River.*

Peggy and I each have a cotton blanket around our shoulders as we wait in line on the banks of the muddy Susquehanna—there are five of us—to *follow our Lord Jesus Christ in baptism.* Brother Bennett wades out into the brown waters with his dark haired young deacon who's along to help. I mention hair because Brother Bennett has none. Easy to tell them apart even chest-deep in water by the sun reflecting off the pastor's head.

Sister Leona Harvey, plump with fruit preserves she makes herself and all the good things that go with it, wades out first to meet her pastor and number one deacon. Both of them—pastor and deacon—will be necessary with Sister Harvey's dunking. She came down to the altar to be saved last Tuesday night and everyone rejoices with her older daughter, a member of the church. Kind of unusual for a daughter to get saved before her mother. But Sister Harvey had to be delivered from cigarettes, that was the main problem.

Brother Bennet and his helper both place an arm under Sister Harvey's back while *Bennet*—as Daddy calls him—says *Dying with Him we are also raised into His Glory. I baptize you in the Name of our Lord Jesus Christ,* then swiftly dunks her under as one of her hands holds her nose and the other is placed over her heart. Her arms raise up as the two men on cue pull her out. *Effort.*

Now that I consider a little more closely this baptism of the Lord event, I sure am glad it occurred before my drowning. I don't know that the words *dying with Him* and going under the waters send the same message to my heart, brain, and body now as my fearless self experienced them. In fact, I'm pretty sure that lining up, holding hands, and fidgeting as we wait for our turn might be a whole lot more nerve wracking to the point of saying, *No thank you.* Then I'd really be known as *bad.*

Peggy and I are last, after Bobby Seymour who's Althea's age, a skinny little person even shorter than my sister. He appears downright malnourished, his Mama constantly assuring anyone who'll listen that he *eats like a horse, boy has a tapeworm, I declare.* But, most important, he loves Jesus and he's decided to follow Him in baptism. She always adds that she's *praying he'll be baptized with the Holy Ghost and fire after this here water baptism.* That means that he'll talk in tongues. The language nobody understands except God and the people chosen by God to translate if such a person turns up to prophesy. So far I haven't overheard anybody in my family say that about me. Good thing. I have enough to worry about already.

Coming up with a *whoosh* out of the river, Bobby's grin lights up just as the sun slips under a pale sky cover overhead. His face is a proper substitute for all the sunshine we can use at this spot on the river. Somebody begins to sing *Showers of Blessing* and a tambourine clatters to the beat as voices raise.

Our mothers take our blankets to hold while Peggy—her braids wrapped and secured by barrettes around her head—and I trudge through the water toward the pastor. The mud squishing between our toes, occasional rocks slipping under foot, make the going slow. If it wasn't such a worthy moment we would have to laugh uncontrollably, but the earnest singing and faces there to greet us correct any rising foolishness.

She stands with Brother Rennsler—sounds like that's his name—as Daddy wades in and Brother Bennett places a hand on my back and begins his words. Daddy saying Jesus phrases like praying all the time as I clasp my nose with my left hand and place the right hand over my heart. Looking up, Bennett's head is a halo of light which nearly sends me into a fit of laughter—*an angel!*—plus the squish of my toes in deep mud. Come to think of it, I didn't see any angels during my drowning.

The folks who aren't singing have another chorus, a chant, saying the same words over and over as each person descends, "Help, Jesus. Help'er Jesus. Go with her now." Then a shower of tongues, the other language, falls through the crowd just as the waters flood over me, blocking all sound and sight.

It's harder to be *raised with Jesus in newness of life* than it looks from the shore. A heaviness pulls from the water. Maybe it's the thought that flits through as I fall back into the waters on Brother Bennett's arm, *What if he's plum worn out?* A wonder having to do with his ability to lift me out, but he doesn't seem to have a problem, heavy as I feel. Squishing toes distract me from the *dying with Jesus* idea and I go blank inside my head. Falling back blank works fine. It's the raising to newness of life, like I said, that's harder.

Next, Peggy. But the blank mind dying with Jesus still fills my head. Outside, dark curls down to my shoulders resemble seaweed plastered flat. Just my toes move, working the mud as I watch my friend descend.

Brother Bennett gets a little hitch in his voice as he assures his youngest child—Peggy has an older brother and sister—that she is *dying with Christ*. His voice strengthens, raising her into new life in Christ. Even in my blank condition I notice that.

Folks turn up the volume singing *Leaning on the Everlasting Arms*, with the beginning words, *What a fellowship, what a joy divine*. Just for us, dripping and dragging ourselves back to shore—me in my best yellow daisy play dress and Peggy in a white cotton slip like dress her mother made for the occasion—hands gripped together like we're holding onto a lifeline.

Holding hands? That's close to the best part of baptism for me. We're a couple of wet mops bumping up and over a few rocks to the shore. Mama has my dry blanket ready and wraps it around me in as close to a hug as Mama ever gets. This is the best part of the baptism. I cozy into Mama's arm, still holding Peggy's hand, and her mother drapes her in a blanket.

Peggy's eyeing me sideways like she does. Her grin getting louder and louder. When we're dry enough, she whispers *look at you!* picking trash, twigs and leaves out of my hair, showing me each bit caught in my curls from the river's flow. It's a pure miracle we don't bust up laughing. *Bad*, considering the serious nature of the event. And her whispering, "You look more like a girl sneaking through our front hedge than a girl going down to the river to pray."

We can't really laugh out loud since this is a holy moment when we're meant to be rejoicing and praising Jesus like Bobby Seymour is busy doing, but we're squealing and turning summersaults inside.

Later while we're sposed to be asleep—Mama said *yes* to sleeping over, a miracle, on this last night in Williamsport—I ask in a whisper if Peggy feels any different now that she's followed our Lord Jesus Christ in baptism. There's a longer silence than we usually have between us. Then she shines the flashlight we have under the covers in my face and says in a low spooky voice, "Yesssss. I doooo."

Pause.

"Whoooooooooo . . ." blows her growly wind, "Noooow I knoooow, it's nooo wonnnder my best friend's hair currrrls . . . she's a *sin-nerrr* sneaking around in hedges when she's sup*posed* to be down at the *river aprayin'.*"

We giggle so hard we both fall out of bed.

Thud.

Tip-toes down the hall to the bathroom to pee. Good thing it's not Opp. We'd have to go way into the woods to a dark outhouse. That'd sober us up.

When our car pulls our house trailer away from it's spot between the church and Bennett's house the next morning, Monday, my heart can only sing, *If We Never Meet Again This Side of Heaven.* Tears flow enough to put the Susquehanna at flood stage, but the promises to write to the list of *General Delivery* towns for the next couple of months will be quickly forgotten.

I'm just a kid, but I already know that. Peggy writes one time, then no more. A Christmas card comes from her family a couple of weeks ago with a family picture Mama lets me keep. The kind of card our family detests, only signed, no letter, with their names and *Lord bless you real good.* That's all.

A long day of travel on this Monday, a good time for every detail of the past two weeks to march merrily along in my memory. Including the radio time Bennett bought to surprise Daddy. I loved that part, too, though it always causes a fit of nerves for Daddy.

I put some time in on blasphemy worries, too. Do you think our laughing over our baptism could be a sin against the Holy Ghost? That's the Unpardonable Sin. Wouldn't a body have some warning like thunder or lightening striking right through the ceiling? Maybe that's the falling out of bed part. But then I'd be scared, not tickled. Probably? But maybe not.

Really, we were laughing about me, not the baptism of our Lord. And certainly not discussing the Holy Ghost. Although, our bodies are the temple of the Holy Ghost.

Snow birds start arriving after Thanksgiving from Ohio, New York, New Jersey, Minnesota, Indiana and Wisconsin and every place in-between. But by late December the New York delicatessen on Miami Beach is full to over-flowing *dawn to midnight*, as Daddy says, with New Yorkers, and Miracle Mile in Coral Gables needs one. A miracle: to keep rude people in check. The real Florida people complain that these northerners, *invade . . . reckon this here sunshine b'longs ta them. Like as if they done bought it.* Starting in January, new car makers target Miami for the place where people flock with enough money to buy a new car.

So Daddy says *let's go* to the car show at the convention center. Who knows, we may need another car, trailer pulling wearing ours out like it does. Not that he ever buys a brand new one, but knowing what's coming soon helps bargain for an old one. That's his out loud reasoning. Me, I know my Daddy and he just wants to be up on everything that's news.

Driving down to the Miami Convention Center, Mama and Daddy discuss a subject I have not heard before. Althea going to high school, a school in a town. So she can go to college with no problem, seems to be the idea. They aren't including my sister in the conversation and that means I'm to be quiet, too. Daddy says Sacramento upholstery shops provide plenty of opportunity for work. He knows people in the business. Mama says maybe she can work for the State of California, typing.

They talk about Daddy's father Dedee, too, and his need for care. Aunt Dorie invited him to live with her as his health declines. But she works full time and she lets everybody know what a burden this is for her and Uncle Hugh. *Maybe*, Daddy says, *maybe we can help.*

Will we live in the trailer still? That's all I can think. This is another foreign language to learn, I can tell that at least.

The car show is about more than cars. Seeing the new undivided wind-shield Cadillac, the gem of the show, slowly revolving, its burgundy coat glistening under the bright lights. A tall, tanned, skinny girl—bright red lips—with legs long as a ladder, dressed in a bathing suit and filmy beach robe, acting as if she's about to sit in the driver's seat makes me feel as if I'm watching a living movie. Observing her behavior explains the sin part of moving pictures. These days, according to the news, even theaters fear being replaced by drive ins which from what I hear are even worse. Anyhow, here at the car show, Daddy murmurs to Mama under his breath thinking I'm out of earshot, *sex sells*. Whatever that means.

But here's the big news: the advertisers at this show have plans for the future. *Cruise control*, one promises. You will set your car and it will drive itself. Another one says there will be an electronic map to guide you with a voice telling you where to turn. I'm not kidding. Then still another declares there'll be an oven that cooks things in a flash—say, instead of a baked potato taking an hour, only ten minutes—that is, if you have an oven.

We're all quiet as we start home to our trailer house.

Daddy breaks the silence, "Lord'll be comin back to take us as His own. Right outta here, Doris. 'Fore all that happens."

More silence except for Mama's "Have mercy."

Daddy goes on with, "Before any of these things come to pass, cruise control? Who needs such foolishness! *Instant ovens*? What's the hurry! *Foolishness*. Those people are going to be surprised by something greater than their inventions."

When we're in revivals, Daddy often says, introducing our family to a new bundle of Christian folks, "Now Brothers and Sisters I can't tell ya where we're from in one or two words. Found Doris in Olympia, Washington; picked up Althea in Wildwood, Florida; Audrey—our Spark Plug— joined us in Sacramento." He gives them a minute to appreciate our foot loose status in life. Then his talk turns rapid fire. Not quite like news with Walter Winchell but close.

"Hallelujah! we know where we're going! Amen? We're goin up *yonder*. Gonna be with Jesus when He comes to claim us as his own, take us on home to Glory!"

The shouts start right up even if it's not much of a shouting kind of congregation. Then Mama sounds a chord on the accordion and we start singing *I'll Fly Away*.

The Preacher exhorts them with a mighty thunder in his close, "Now this week go out in the streets of Laverne, Opp, Florence,Beaverton, Sayreton, Bessemer, Frisco City, Clanton, Columbus, and invite sinners to fill up this church house. For Jesus! We don't know the day or the hour! Will it be this week? How bout tonight! We'll be caught up to meet Him in the air!"

That's when it strikes me that Daddy either sounds like a lot of other people when they talk or they sound like him. 'Course he has a different way to set it, not having a home on earth and all, but the phrases are like the menu at the family table. Different every day but the same as last week. I'm in the back seat quiet as a clam while Daddy talks on the way home from the car show, and I know this is not the time to ask questions or make any comment whatsoever about the Rapture.

Could it be I have too much time to think when we're in Miami? Just like Daddy has too much time to listen to world news. *Good evening Mr. And Mrs. America and from border to border and all the ships at sea, let's go to press.* Walter Winchell booms through our trailer house every Sunday evening about five o'clock. He's a talking typewriter going as fast as only my Mama is capable of going, one hundred words a minute. Daddy agrees with his attitude *against* communists and *for* Senator Joe McCarthy. That's the main thing.

Winchell talks about Hollywood stars, too. He even reported on Jascha Heifetz, Daddy's hero violinist, when Heifetz was married a couple of years ago. Other newscasters refer to Winchell as a gossip columnist for his movie world connections, but gossip or not, Daddy still listens. It's all about his antagonism toward Russian communists: as far as Winchell's concerned, world war still goes on even though it's 1950 with artillery headed for the same enemies Daddy claims.

Nineteen forty-two, the year of my birth, another newscaster, Gabriel Heatter declared, *There's good news tonight* about the United States Navy sinking a Japanese destroyer. Mama says that's when he began saying that phrase every time he opened his newscast, *there's good news tonight.*

What's good about war news? Somebody always gets hurt, killed, blown up or sunk. Daddy told me after I asked—a long time ago when I was only six—that war's good because it does away with our enemies. *God's* enemies. But that doesn't make much sense to me. I've a mind to mention what He wrote on those tablets that Moses brought down from Sinai. *Thou shalt not kill.* Then Daddy would just get disgusted with me and ask why I have to be so difficult. Hard to find a place for me to fit where there aren't prickles. Sand spurs.

We're on the road to tell the Good News of Jesus. Come to save us from our sins. Which this world certainly has plenty of—*sins*—demonstrated here in Miami by people parading their flesh up and down the sidewalks. But sometimes I wish we could stick to good news everywhere.

Mama always calls me a *war baby* since I was born when goods were scarce. No rubber teething rings, for one thing, and that's how I developed a taste for the carrots I gnawed on instead, plus violin music Daddy played to distract me from my pain and suffering. No rubber for tires, either, so we couldn't travel. We had a house, then.

I've a mind to ask Mama politely to please find another way to talk about 1942. I don't want to be a *war baby.* Sounds too much like I hurtled into the world as a bomb—the day Pearl Harbor happened, 7th December 1941 being the day she discovered she was expecting me—and I'd rather be known as walking into this world holding hands with Jesus or an angel. *Just a Closer Walk with Thee*. Like that.

When you think about it without war attached, *Pearl Harbor* sounds wonderful. Say it slowly. Roll the words around with your tongue. A warm gem of a place and like my neighbor here in the trailer park says, *a jewel*. A jewel developed by adding iridescent satiny layers of shell around an irritation—a grain of sand—rather than blasting the annoyance into oblivion. Leo, the pink-faced man from Ohio, tells me that's how pearls happen. He set about studying where his money goes since his wife began to collect pearl jewelry.

The *Pearl of Great Price* is the one Jesus talks about. A treasure, worth giving everything you have when you find it. Now that's my idea of grand and beautiful goodness.

Why, I could be a whole string of pearls considering all the grit I swallowed. I've been pondering this for a while now, and it comes to me that this pearl is expensive and Jesus doesn't usually lean toward extravagance. What can he mean?

I don't know. But I like it.

Maybe something Aunt Dorie appreciates. *Foolish*, but lovely. I'm beginning to think that's a good thing to aim for now that I survived my own drowning.

News

1952 • 1953 • 1954: *Sacramento Elegy*

1952

Jesus wept.
John 11:35

- *Queen Elizabeth ascends the throne at age 25, the heavy crown sure to cause headaches; her wartime service as an auto mechanic much heralded, hardly believed.*
- *Winter Olympics in Helsinki; Russians move back into competition after forty-year absence.*
- *Tornadoes tear up five states in the South.*
- *Summer in Sacramento, California, 4925 Roosevelt Avenue, home of people formerly known as the Skondeen Family Evangelistic Team, next door to the Minetti's and grandson Sal.*
- *Church experience becomes random for Skondeens; local Pentecostal Holiness or Assembly of God congregations prove unsatisfying for the Preacher to merely attend.*
- *Skondeen Family-time passes in fractured minutes—Audrey, Fruitridge Elementary; Althea, Sacramento High School; Doris, typing in a California State office; Bill spitting tacks (upholstering) at a furniture warehouse on Two Street—far apart. Scattered.*
- *Fifth grade classroom for Audrey in September with squat, colorless Mrs. Reynolds, rumored to be a teacher, screaming at children all day long; not much learning.*

- *Louise, the only colored girl in fifth grade, Audrey's designated playmate, plus neighbor Sal.*

- *Audrey and Louise shunned by Popular Girls—tiny, blond Janis and tall, dark Beverly—class queens.*

- *Headaches.*

- *Noises in the night, unheard in prior times—parent's voices—loud, raised in argument.*

- *Audrey arrives home one Saturday afternoon from neighbor Sal's expecting her family to be there but sees only a pair of her mother's shoes in the kitchen doorway.*

- *This is it—the Rapture!—anticipated everyday of her life. Terror seizes the child's heart, everyone taken and she, Audrey, the only one left behind.*

- *When the family filters back into the area, amused by her fright, her trauma heart resumes its normal beat; the child resolves in silence never again to care about the Rapture.*

1953

Do not suppose that I have come to bring peace to the earth.
Mark 10:34

- *General Dwight D. Eisenhower—war hero who brought the campaign against Korea to a successful end—as President of the United States continues fight against Communism and corruption.*

- *Magazine stands light up with a nude photo of Marilyn Monroe as the first cover of a new magazine, Playboy.*

- *Gentlemen Prefer Blondes, the hit movie of the summer for people who go to movies.*

- *IQ tests administered in Mrs. Shelton's sixth grade class—an upsetting test that can't be studied for—a frenzied mix of rational and irrational questions designed to frustrate, confuse.*

- *Fruitridge Elementary School Principal calls in the Skondeen parents to discuss Audrey's IQ score and new grading: if Sal gets 88 percent, he receives an A; if Audrey gets 88 percent, she receives a C, measuring "ability and potential" her scores must be 97–100 percent for an A.*

- *Janis, one class queen, declares Audrey her New Friend, telling her "the first time I saw your dark curls and blue eyes, I hated you," laughing.*

- *Audrey continues to value her True Friend, Louise.*

- *Moving the Skondeen Family to a new old house—23rd Street near Stockton Boulevard—the reason for loud voices in the night.*

- *Doris Skondeen unconvinced, "This looks like a lot of work."*

- *The 23rd Street house has an apartment upstairs; renters help with the mortgage, not the upkeep.*

- *A library two blocks away in another old house becomes, for Audrey, a perfect refuge as well as source of forbidden information.*

- *Wide shady streets to roam for Audrey and friend, Billy Butler—a boy from Bethel Temple, large Assembly of God church nearby—who faithfully drags his sister's bike along so Audrey can ride the neighborhood with him.*

- *Billy pretends to be a race car driver, a stuntman; lanky legs stretched over his handlebars and a wiseacre grin so big, bugs die there; ripe dandelion blond hair blowing, blue eyes sparkling like headlamps in the dark.*

- *Audrey bakes her first cake—for Billy—applesauce cake with lemon frosting.*

- *Parents, formerly known as Mama and Daddy, band together to prevent a $10 used bike from being bought until Audrey can hold her temper for 30 calendar days.*

- *Audrey fails; both parents constantly waving the words, "there she goes again . . ."*

1954

"Lazarus! Come out!" The dead man came out.
John 11:42, 43

- *The Ford Foundation donates $34 million to education.*

- *Ike—President Eisenhower—signs into law the addition of the words, "one nation, under God, indivisible . . ." to the Pledge of Allegiance.*

- *Unification Church founder Korean Evangelist Sun Myung Moon, 34, claims the Bible is written in code and he's the only one who's cracked the code.*

- *Seventh grade at California Junior High includes Miss Eakins gym class; bullies on the ball field undaunted in beating up smaller students.*

- *Learning to sneak into dances and out to the ice skating rink with Sunday School friend Lee Ann and her older brother become Audrey's preoccupations.*

- *Althea says No! to college.*

- *Deede, William Skondeen's father, dies while living at his daughter Dorie's house.*

- *Bill Skondeen resurrects his sermons; orders the family back on the road early in the new year, headed toward Route 66, returning to the South.*

9

Sayreton, Alabama 1954
Dancing with the Devil

- *Pius X becomes 70th Pope to be canonized by the Vatican.*
- *Senator Joseph McCarthy under growing pressure by CBS commentator Edward R. Murrow who claims McCarthy engages in half truths and confuses the public about the actual threat of communism, convicting people through rumor.*
- *GM Produces 50-millionth car.*
- *President Eisenhower—Ike—proposes interstate highway system for atomic defense as well as for general use.*
- *A bill to destroy the Communist Party as a political and legal entity in US signed by President Eisenhower.*
- *Formation of Tobacco Industry Research Committee seeking to counter scientific reports linking lung cancer and cigarette smoking.*
- *Joe DiMaggio, Yankee baseball hero, marries Marilyn Monroe at San Francisco City Hall.*
- *To celebrate turning 19 on January 8, unknown singer Elvis Presley brings his guitar to a Memphis studio; pays $4; records "Casual Love," and "I'll Never Stand in Your Way."*
- *TV stations now total 360 in US; 231 opening in 1953.*
- *Sinkholes are an inescapable fact of life in places where the bedrock consists of limestone, sandstone, dolomite or other rocks and minerals that are soluble in groundwater. May be acts of nature, but many collapses are attributable to acts of man such as mining, quarrying, and pumping well water. Also, vibrations from machinery, cars and drilling*

equipment, can trigger the development of sinkholes. Alabama Geological Survey estimates that there are more than 4,000 "manmade" sinkholes in Alabama, "most occurring since 1950, corresponding with the period of greatest economic growth" [quoting Scott Brande, PhD].[1] They swallow roadways; cars; porches.

- *Audrey Skondeen is eleven.*

THERE SHE IS. I see her as I come through the church house door, curls bouncing, one hand on her ruffled hip and feet slapping the floor in shoes fresh out of the Magnin's box from San Francisco. She's such a story for the family, it's as if my younger self turns into a Shirley Temple doll, wound up and set loose in front of a dim, scratched up mirror, never leaving this Sunday School room. "Mischievous child, using Aunt Dorie's gift—new shoes!—for devilment."

Nobody around the Sayreton Assembly of God Church remembers exactly how the tall, narrow beat up mirror landed in this room, tacked to the supply closet door. Folks shy away from vanity. Women are meant to be modest and unadorned according to Apostle Paul's Bible. Maybe a bride lugged the smudged reflecting glass in here? Adorning for your husband's OK. *But shun profane and vain babblings . . . their word will eat as doth a canker*, words stuck in my brain I've heard them so much. Vain anything, even a little girl twirling in a mirror, is always considered rank, no good.

Used to be, anyhow. Before California.

Just inside the door I plop onto a short-legged wooden chair fit for the little kid I was and watch the dancing child turn and turn in dizzying circles. This time, she has my permission to kick up her heels with no interruption by a scolding, spanking mother. Lunchtime events at Cal Jr. High taught me how good tapping, shuffling feet really feel and I'm not about to stop grinning, either.

Sayreton's the northeast corner of Birmingham that accommodates miners, housemaids and waitresses with humble places to hang their helmets, jackets or hats between work hours. Not many of those free hours, though. Especially not for men in the coal mines, since plenty of them head to Murphy's Irish Bar whether they come out of the mine at 6 AM after the night shift or 2 PM after the first day shift. There's another one or two shifts in there I've never been able to keep straight.

Talk about the mines sputters quietly in between all other conversations. Triple explosions the year I was born, nearly 12 years ago now, still

---

1. Yount, *University of Alabama at Birmingham Magazine* 22.1, 2002.

hang *Danger* signs and breathes a no nonsense kind of fear in every woman who has sons, brothers and husbands or fathers blackened by their work underground. "Nerly 30 odd kilt. Cain fergit a thang like thet. No siree." Pastor here, Brother Bowins said today at dinner.

The Bowins strike me as twin pastors even though Sister Esther Bowins does not preach, preaching being wrong for women by Apostle Paul's standards. Pentecostals get around that one, though, with licks of Holy Ghost flames ablaze in the air over women as well as men on the Day of Pentecost. But in the Bowins' case, I say twins by their looks and attitudes. Both about the size of my father, 5'5", hair the color of walnut shells. His, flopped over a low forehead and hers bound up in twists pinned with a hundred hair pins that begin to fly when she starts dancing in the Holy Ghost. They welcome you with blue eyes always smiling, whether into the church house or to their rosy brown living room. Always ready to praise the Lord.

Remembering the way to their house after we park the trailer behind the church proves no problem for my father. Maps ride around in his head: left turn out of the Assembly of God church parking lot to the pig iron refinery, then right turn, going along two full blocks of tin roofs, smoke stacks and train tracks. The street ends at a ridge of humble wooden houses looking as if the acres of machinery across the street nudges them further away every year. Even the trees strung together with kudzu vines in the back yards wear coats of industrial grime, smudged by smoke billowing from chimneys below.

But after we've climbed the seven cement steps to the inside of Bowin's home, *Glory* shouts from every corner. Blessings fall as you walk through the door. Sister Esther and Brother Bobby love my mother and father. We girls rate high, too. Althea, for her musical talent and ability to be quiet constantly. As for me, I think it's mostly for the Spark Plug stories that circulate, getting better as years go by. This travel time proves that with only three months on the road. I never realized I was notorious before this.

The shrill whine of the twelve o'clock whistle sounds off as we arrive and feels as if it cuts through and clears the murky air. But of course it really doesn't. Anyhow, dinner will be served at 12:30, sharp, Sister Esther not being one to slack.

Soft mottoes on wooden plaques brushed with handpainted roses or angels overseeing small children and words, "Raise up a child in the way he should go and he will not depart from it," or, "Honor thy Mother and Father," adorn the walls. Next to the doorway entering the kitchen, Jesus leads the way as the Good Shepherd holding a lamb. Their son and daughter, we learn at the table, married and moved away since we were here four years ago. That's after the blessing's said, of course.

"Gracy met 'er a farmer at Toccoa Falls Bible Institute. Can ya beat thet? Figured 'er fer a preacher's wife, piana playin an all. She's a workin fer auvr Lawd nearby to Nashvl." Esther opines. But Brother Bobby finishes her thought as he passes the first round of fried chicken in a wire basket fit with a well-worn yellow checked cloth matching the table covers and Sister Esther's apron, "Na, Estha, honey, w'needs folks on em benches, too, don't we Brotha Skondee?" Nobody south of the Mason Dixon line seems to be able to pick up that n on the end of our name.

"Praisa Lord, Brother Bobby!" The visiting preacher has to pause a minute to say it, already tucking into the hot wedge of cornbread Sister Esther dropped onto his plate from her cast iron skillet.

Bowin's son, Bobby Jr., went to business school and sells insurance in Montgomery, "Workin is way up? Doin good. Says he rather live on a pay check than on a hope chest like we done all these yars!" Bobby Sr. laughs, "Loves a Lawd, tho. Prais'im, prais'im."

My surprise at the size of my plate and glass, a saucer and a jelly glass, among the settings on the round table they've pulled from the corner of the sunshine yellow kitchen goes unmentioned until Sister Esther realizes just before we sit down and says, "My lands!" blushing even beyond the warm glow of the oven's glare, "plum fergot ya growed up, girl!" But mother covers up for it saying, "No, no, it's fine. We can all eat a little less."

Well, I never. Sure, my sailor dress from last summer is tighter in the waist than it was, but it's small across the shoulders, too.

Talk drifts past families, thank goodness, and on to the church folks we've known here.

"Yesirree, Brantley got 'im a job—praisa Lawd, finely—'n Deetroit." Brother Bowins reports, "Cousin calls'im? Whole famly takin outta here, dumps what's leff inna mishnary barrel atta church hass? They gone, all right. Jan'yary."

"Ever rebuilt their burned out house?" my father enquires.

"No 'surance. No hass." Bowin's shakes his head, hair free to move about about now that the water-slicking he starts out with everyday has dried. "Squeezed a fam'ly inna brotha's hass. Two olda boys livin atta aunt's hass. Cindalee onliest one leff with em."

"My, my," Mother chimes in, "Bless their hearts."

Of course all I hear in *Cindalee* is Peggy. My doll, sent from Aunt Dorie for my best Christmas ever. Always by my side as my only true friend. I told her everything on our long travel days and sat her on top of the built in chest of drawers where I could peer over my bunk bed's edge and say good night to her porcelain face and sparkling eyes that matched mine. Eyes that opened, shut, and knew everything. But there's no time to think of her right now.

Talk drifts to Virginia's and Owen's Daddy, then, with, "Good news in Sayreton Assembly, Brotha. 'Member Sista Phoebe?" To my parent's blank looks, "Ginia 'n Owen's mama, works cleanin offices 'n Birm'nham? Nights? Drunk husbin saved a las night a revival."

"Oh yes. Yes!"

I sure remember. Every night praying to Jesus for those little kids sleeping in that barren house with a drunk daddy. Asking the Lion to stand guard, 'course He always "guarded" by cozying up and comforting a kid. At least He did with me back then.

What if they had a fire, I'd think. No chance a drunk'd have sense enough to get them out.

"Wal, Lawd A'mighty done a good thang w'thet maan. Prais'im prais'im. He's servin a Lawd, inna church hass ever Sunday, Wens'dy, 'n onceta month, Satiddy? Whole fam'ly cleans uppa church hass!"

After all that praying I did for their Daddy, he shows up the last night of revival as Brother Bowins recalls, and I spotted him—came in late—while I was singing the altar call. Midway through *Softly and Tenderly*, I slipped away from the pulpit while my mother and sister kept playing the music and went back to the last row where he slumped, stench of rancid sweat, smoke, gaseous mining chemicals and alcohol coming toward me like waves as I approached, "How 'bout tonight," my hand on the hunched over shoulder of his canvas jacket, his sooty hair covering grimy hands pressed hard to the back of the bench in front of him.

Waiting a spell as he snuffled, struggling to control himself, attempting to burrow deeper into his hands, I added, "Virginia and Owen love their Daddy. They want him to meet Jesus tonight." With that he raised blood soaked eyes blurred with tears and I took his hand as he struggled to stand.

Headed up the aisle my mind goes blank, too full to allow one word over another. But folks all along the way jump, shout in the Holy Ghost. Celebration for a sinner holding tight to the life line. By the time we got to the altar, tongues peeled out with firey eloquence showering us with unintelligible power while words of encouragement from the men who received him into their circle rose to greet him.

"Evehlastin ahms, Brotha, evehlastin ahms! Allluuu!"

"Ya comin home, na. Prais'im prais'im."

That was a night for the ages. And he's still faithful.

From my place at the table, facing Sister Esther across from me, I begin to study the softly faded bluebird scattered cafe curtains at her back, a ceramic bluebird holding a pot scrubber in the middle of the window sill.

Talk continues to swirl, as a sense of old life, new life, where to next, settles over me. Happens often these days, since Sacramento.

On the way back to the trailer from Bowins, stashed in a corner of the fake mohair covered Dodge seats—Daddy says the DeSoto's grill looks too fancy for an evangelist nowadays so we've made a switch—scenes from the Brantley's house fire play back in terrible memories. Their family was walking up the church house steps when Betsy Brantley turned and saw smoke swirling into the sky in the direction of their house. The two boys, straggling behind as usual, kicking grimy Sayreton gravel at each other at the edge of the street. Sirens swell right about then and the scene freezes, a chief's car and hook and ladder truck careening round the corner going east toward the smoke. Air charged with lights, motion, pulsing sound and sudden fright yet still as a graveyard all at once. It is their house.

Hours later, commotion and emotion so confused it's impossible to say what happened when. What's sure is that there's nothing left. Nothing but blackened rubble. Resembles most of Sayreton, come to think of it.

Church house itself, once white clapboard, slowly turning the color of soiled snow through the years. A motto from the Bible fit for Bowins' living room hangs over the door, "Come unto me all ye that labor and are heavy laden and I will give ye rest."

There were some mighty weary people on that firey night. Good people hearing the fluster and fragments of news reports clumped together murmuring prayers and making plans of who can give what to the Brantleys. Their somber conversations began my own interior dialogue.

I don't really have anything to give.

Oh yes you do

No, not . . .

Uh-huh

Peggy.

But that's my only . . .

Yeah. Well, Jesus demands our best.

But not . . .

You're eight, getting old enough not to need a doll. Cindalee's only six.

All that first night even through my sleep, the debate raged on. *Jesus demands our best. Our best. Our best.* Those words ended the debate.

Morning sunshine burning through heavy air convinced me that Jesus has to be right. Every day. And that night I wrapped Peggy in her ice blue satin blanket, same color as Aunt Dorie's wedding dress I now know, and presented her to Cindalee. The child stared at me blankly through strands of hair the color of weak tea.

She's just quieter than usual 'count of being in shock, people said. And I wondered why giving your best doesn't feel better.

Our car stops at the turn into the church, interrupting my reverie. We wait for a coal dusted man to cross the parking lot's driveway. Could say he looks like a licorice penny candy, wearing the day's underground labor as he is, but there's no sweetness in his desolate shuffle. Cap pulled low over his head and shriveled face, hiding all but a few oily strings of dark hair, at least it looks dark. Shoulders aiming for the roadway, empty mailbox shaped lunch pail slapping his side. *At least he's going in the direction of what must be home, away from Bailey's Bar*, is the most positive thought I can muster considering the misery of the man.

We're breathing the same air he is. It always smells like tar in these parts. No sidewalks here. Trudging along in the gutter's normal.

"Lord help him," my dad murmurs.

"Yes, Lord," mother's echo.

Anxious as they are to set up our instruments and practice—revival starts tomorrow night—they have time to say a prayer for a weary man. I do like that about my parents. Cranky as I feel about them most of the time.

The cranky streak in me? Now that's all caused by California. My parents argued with each other over the second house we bought, over Althea's romance with a boy from Youth For Christ, and over Mother's teaching a Bible class for older ladies at Bethel Temple, the Assemblies' church near that house. My father was strictly against anything she did besides working for the State which brought in a pay check. 'Course a wrinkle creased that Sunday teaching debate: his calling her a *preacher* like he did. But she learned pretty quick that if she took his part over whatever I asked, she'd be in his favor. She hopped right on that one.

Oh, she arranged shopping for us with her stash of independence earned at the state offices. And when I rode bicycles—mine always borrowed—with Billy Butler, she'd let me leave by the back door in pedal pushers instead of a dress. Both shopping and girls wearing pants being perverse in my father's world of holiness activities. Her gestures were never enough to restore my faith in her, to trust that she wouldn't join my father—even when she knew he was being unreasonable—just to set up his smile for her.

In the sunroom of the library near our last Sacramento house, I sequestered books I'd never take home, learning about adolescence one subject at a time. Sex, sure. The parents of adolescents, a more complicated lot than I'd ever guessed.

The rest I picked up at a news stand on Stockton Boulevard. Small papers. Exposé kind of information with Marilyn Monroe and her new husband Joe DiMaggio who doesn't seem to mind that she was displayed wearing nothing but her birthday suit in Playboy magazine last year. They were married where my Uncle Hugh works—the office right across the hall from his—in San Francisco. No such news stands exist in places like Milton, Florida, where we held our first meeting the end of February. Or Bonifay, De Funiak Springs and Marianna, for that matter. Sayreton's revival #5.

After Althea said *no* to college and I turned in *I hate school* reports for junior high (except for the dances which I did not mention) my mother's and father's arguments shifted to discussions of going back on the road. We'd all be under one roof all day everyday once again.

When the verdict was in, my father exhaled.

My mother *in*haled. Swallowed her words and slipped into silence. There's no debate over serving Jesus.

The redeeming play my father made to comfort me in leaving a house with a bathtub plus tiny daisies and purple johnny jump ups along the walk, arrived in the form of a standing bass fiddle. For me. Boom. Smack dab in the middle of doodling around with piano lessons comes a lovable creature I can hold close and dance with to my heart's content. And with my parent's approval, besides.

The bass showed up in October after our house was already on the market. By the time we were packed to leave, I was ready to pluck those tough strings as backup for our singing. I never felt more powerful, callouses and all. Not just the *Spark Plug* any more, but part of the engine taking us to that home beyond the blue. Hallelujah.

January 1954, a trailer in the driveway on 23rd Street followed the *Sold* slapped over the *For Sale* sign stuck in the lawn. While my father customized our mobile home to be living quarters, I took big gulps of Calvert 7th grade, jamming the fall semester into six weeks instead of three months. But I have to admit that was exciting. After the dusty classrooms and dull teachers of the past two and a half years? No doubt about it.

Elementary school turned downright mean, peevish and unjust when IQ tests ratted out my "ability." But that's comparing a rolling pin to the steamroller the start of seventh grade turned out to be.

My last day of California Junior High prison began with rain dense enough to flood gutters at Stockton Boulevard and William Land Park Drive where I walked to school, and ended at Christmas vacation. Bedraggled, surly kids sloshing out of mulch brown doorways where worms sought higher ground only to be stomped into oblivion.

Thoughts running through my mind were as muddy as the rain water rushing along the sidewalk's edge. Mostly had to do with freedom as I recall.

Free of Miss Elkins in PE Class, brassy gray/brown/blond chunky patchwork braids wrapped around her head as if to keep it together. Her bow legs in year-round shorts always recognizable in the twenty-four inches beneath the shower doors when she stood outside eavesdropping on three of us sharing the space. "Self control!" She snapped at me across her desk after I spoke harsh words about kids who harassed me on the ball field. Later they punched me in the stomach in an empty hallway.

Free of boring English and endless history classes. The red-faced one-time jock football coach imitation civics teacher, feet perpetually propped on his desk, round belly anchoring him to the chair was especially hard to bear.

Free of fellow students clumped together in neighborhood groups. You have the High and Mighty from the nearest houses in Land Park, then the Angry Outsiders from Oak Park mostly dark skinned and ready to fight, and the huh? Geeky Kids who try not to be noticed. I didn't fit anywhere and I figured that was a good thing.

Calvert days beat out boredom any time, even as hard as Latin is and as demanding as Composition with real writing assignments such as newspaper articles or profiles of people in history. Concentration never lags over classic poetry's Yeats, Whitman and Dickenson. My attention hones in and the hours fly.

We drove away from Sacramento aware of what we call *worldly goods* left behind, however. At least I'm aware. Nobody talks about it. But how can you not remember your bathtub when you're soaping a wash cloth in the sink of a church bathroom?

A long goodbye in San Francisco for the first two weeks of February where Aunt Dorie, my dad's younger sister, and Uncle Hugh live. Also Burlingame down the Peninsula, south of the City, Uncle Al, dad's older brother, and Aunt Dena. Some bits of this are awkward as I'm learning all relatives tend to be. I don't get why that is. We rarely see my mother's sister and brother. They live in Oregon and Washington and by my father's attitude, unexpressed, is that it's about right to see them once every five years, if that. But mother misses her daddy, I know by how anxious she is to receive his letters and packages of his home baked cookies tied in yards of string.

Reveling in the loveliness of my Auntie Dorie's life reels by like a dream. Althea and I slept at her house both week ends on white sheets ironed smooth as silk, down feathers filling our pillows, rosy satin comforters over each of us in matching twin beds. Details roll around, gathering secret pleasures our family never mentions but are as real as the maps we follow over so many roads. A crystal pitcher of water and a glass etched with violets on the bedside stand sooth me as if I'm being led beside still waters. Restores my soul. And the sheer pink fabric finished with ivory lace covering the sheets before the comforter's added. Beauty where no one can see, always there.

Aunt Dorie's high gloss black window boxes spilling red geraniums cause the front of the pale gold brick house on Belvedere Street to stand out from the rest. And when you walk in the brilliant black front door, brass knocker in the top center and frosted glass panels along each side, an aroma fills you with the scent of a warm pine cone fire in fall and winter, or hyacinths and roses in spring and summer.

She's tiny, I think to myself, even though her presence fills the room. *Petite*, that's the word people use. Dorie's version of our family curls attempt to be reddish blond with help from the beauty parlor, a layer cascading around her face, then caught into a fashionable scroll across the back. Her white shirt, smooth over full bosoms, tucks into the narrow waist of a dark, flat-pleated skirt. For our Saturday shopping spree she wears a burgundy sweater rather than the usual suit jacket reserved for work at the bank. Aunt Dorie and Uncle Hugh both catch the trolley car at the end of the block on Carl Street every morning, Monday through Friday. She, headed for the California Bank downtown and he, for City Hall.

A midnight blue hat, one plume from a bluebird's wing shot along the left side, perches slightly off center on her head before she dons the swirling coat colored for the sky a second after sunset. Demure as Dorie Hester intends to be, her forget me not eyes twinkle and flirt from a kittenish face as she adds one touch of lipstick—not as red as my Calvert teacher's, Mrs. Kellerman's, but close—in the oval hall mirror, gold cherubs in attendance around the edge.

Sundays, we spent at Uncle Al's and Aunt Dena's house in Burlingame with Dorie and Hugh coming down for dinner after we've been to church. My parents came to pick us up in San Francisco from the trailer park in Daly City where the trailer stays for the time being. Awful place, rutted and run down as most temporary arrangements are. Cold, rancid bath houses with scary showers sheltering spiders.

"Dena's too fancy to have a trailer in her driveway," my father groused while we looked for space.

They're just in time for bacon and waffles in the curved breakfast nook in Dorie's sunny kitchen. Uncle Hugh has already come back from "early mass" bringing the Sunday paper with him. Did I ever wish I could stay and read instead of go to the Burlingame Assembly of God Church. "More hoity toity people, Doris. In this town they're bound to be."

"Well, Bill. Now they do love Jesus or they wouldn't be in church."

I felt like piping up, "Even a Roman Catholic Church?" But I knew that would start a war I'm not prepared to fight. We passed Saint Cecilia's Roman Catholic when Uncle Hugh took us for a drive late on Saturday afternoon. That was after lunch at the Pig 'n Whistle where waiters wear bellman's uniforms complete with pill box hats. You can hide behind the tall menus. Aunt Dorie pointed out his *parish* as they call Saint Cecelia's, adding that they were married in Old Saint Mary's Church downtown.

"Smaller sanctuary, right, Hughie dear?" to his broad smile that takes over his sweet oval face and lights up the dove colored eyes. His hat, a Fedora, Aunt Dorie calls it, matches his eyes. Square shoulders and tall stance, still left from his years in the Navy even though the softness of peace time has rounded his six-foot frame. She never just calls him *Hugh*.

Of course I say nothing to my parents about that little trip. My father already being so torn up over Dorie's *losing her soul* by marrying a Roman Catholic, he spent that day in April of '49 weeping and wailing in the Alabama woods. I was so scared about the goings-on I didn't even write about their wedding. Now, seeing the photos of the two of them toasting each other with glasses of champagne, I only wish I had been there, part of the revelry myself. Champagne glasses look pretty good.

On the other hand, Aunt Dena, a hawkish woman who's about five inches taller than Uncle Al, teaches a Bible class at the Assemblies church as if she knows all about Jesus when if she really did she wouldn't act like she does. Rude to children in general and mean to my cousins Danny and Fay, Uncle Al's kids from his first marriage. Sure, we know divorce is wicked but those little kids didn't cause it. And just because they're born from a no-count mama—which makes me think of Donny Johnson—doesn't mean they're no-count, too. But that's the way Dena acts, which, like I said, leads me to believe she's not on speaking terms with Jesus.

Now if I were to say this out loud, my parents would land all over me: *Do not judge* lest *ye be judged.*

Entirely neglecting what I've learned from my father's *gift of suspicion* as he calls it, "When you see a black hog cross the road there's no judgin to it. It's a black hog." Quoting him back to him is dangerous, however.

Last thing I'll say about those short days of long good-bye comes from Aunt Dorie and Aunt Dena doing the dishes. Being careful enough with the *bone china* which Dena never fails to call her cups and saucers, means only Dorie is allowed to wash them.

"That crazy Billy, dragging these kids all over the country," Aunt Dorie says just above a whisper, hands immersed in suds.

"And blaming the Lord with his foolishness. As if . . ." Aunt Dena's voice trails off when my mother walks in asking how she can help.

Old friends come to see us when we're on the road again. Colemans, Donald and Betsy, from Pensacola show up in Milton, a sand spur of a town in West Florida. Bonifay, DeFuniak Springs and Mariana follow in quick succession. One week meetings and only two days off in-between.

"Gotta build up that preaching muscle before summer camps, Doris."

"Singing, too, Bill. We're rusty." They mutter in quiet talk up front as our car and trailer traverse two lane roads, sand and palmettos along each side. Occasional scrub oaks strung with moss the only change of view. She's right. We're not quite in sync.

"Lakeland Camp Meeting, first? June?"

"Lord willin." My father's there already. Going through the motions of introducing us at an evening service, splicing in a tiny sermon as he does, "Sayin a *few* words? Hmph. Takes more 'sperience than a revival night," he wags his head in wonder.

Being back on the platform serves up both familiarity and strangeness. Science fiction strange. Spaceship to an another planet. Part of me stands off to the side assessing the whole scene. I don't recognize myself.

Especially when visitors tell Audrey Stories. "Tha chile s'fearless! Fer auvr Lawd n Save-yer. Mmmmmmhmmmmmmm. Runs out inna aisles a *re*vival? Yas, brings 'm in—frumma trailsa sin 'n damnation!"

"Na she cain be a pill, too, ya know. Oooo eee!" The word *pill* drawn into several syllables depending on the one speaking.

"'Memba at o'ster eatin atta beach? Yeah! Fo yars ole and eatin em o'sters raw wi hot stuff dab on em? Yeah! Beat all! It idn't enny raison ya cain't still lob em o'sters right own in, Sweetie Pie!" I doubt if I've had a raw oyster since then, when I was four. Took me til the end of March to learn how to listen to *Southern* being spoken again. I do love the music of this language.

But talking *Audrey*? When it finally dawned that they were speaking about me, a kind of creeping shock suffused my body, no sign from the outside, but bones slow lit as fourth of July sparklers. And I'm just sitting there, small smile pasted in place hearing about this child so foreign to me now.

Coleman's a fount of information. A Florida highway patrolman—former military man—West Florida brands him with facts about every one of its little towns. Milton, the town, he says is named for Governor Milton. Civil War governor. The man had a thousand slaves on his plantation. When conversation turns to slaves and race my brain goes on alert. I know we can't make any comments so I keep my mouth shut. My parents have been very clear about that. "All these communists stirring up the Negroes," as my father puts it.

But the faces of Louise and Zorneely pop right up. Not the girls from phys ed class in Sacramento. They'd be thugs no matter what their skin color and they don't need any *communists* to fuel their rage. It's about a connected heart I figure. Connected to people who matter to you even when you feel cranky. The joyless mean girls don't have ties to much of anybody except each other.

Marianna? When he finds out that's our next meeting, Coleman assures us that we ought to be thanking our Sweet Jesus we got white skin. Yessirree. Had 'em a lynching few years back. Negro man accused of . . . well . . . His dark eyebrows shading flinty eyes shoot up as he leans in to tell us that it don't pay to have no dark skin around a town like Marianna. He glances around the yard of the cement block church where we're balancing ourselves in folding chairs steady as possible, set up on sand and patchy sand-spur-crab-grass under mossy oak trees, his eyes skating over Althea and me and shrugs, "Ya know. Crimes 'gainst wimmins?" Must mean rape.

Our last overnight stop was with Bebe and Rayleen Harvey—farmers in Brundidge, Alabama—before arrival in Sayreton. The Harveys, according to my parents, have the *common decency* to keep writing to evangelists even when the preacher's settled down for a spell. Chester, their hound dog guarding the acreage just inside a cattle crossing, rises to protest our car and trailer's rattling across the metal bars late in the afternoon.

Rayleen, even while recounting the blessings of our Lord poured out so rich upon us, manages to maintain a face that's sad as the crucifixion. Her mouth straight as the cross bar, her tiny yellow teeth mostly hidden, and blank hazel eyes without sparkle or any hint that she pleasures in walking with Jesus on the inside like she mouths on the outside. Braids thin as string loop down in back and twist back up again. Un-plaiting it, washing it, plaiting it back in place guarantees a half-day's work. Bebe's moon face stirred with sunshine on the other hand, catches all the happy as he describes her hair reaching nearly to her knees.

I want to say, "Why?" Oh, I know the Bible claims a woman's hair is her glory, but this just looks like a headache. What I do is smile and appreciate the big pot of rabbit stew with buttermilk biscuits she's prepared.

She reminds us as well that last year after the "crops was laid by", she spent another month "a'cannin an preservin."

"Strang beans a put up lass summa? At's all we got by na. But we thankful." She heaps a crockery bowl with heated beans, a hint of pride creeping into her left-sided grin, straight mouth twisting up as a turn signal for a hint of pleasantry. Maybe traveling preachers are good for people like my father contends.

The worn out R E V I V A L sign, creases counting out the years, draped outside the Sayreton Assembly front door brings bench loads of people inside on the first night. The Preacher's ready.

> Secret of Praying is
> prayin in secret!
> Now the sinning man—sinning woman—*stops* prayin.
> You know that?
> No secret there . . .

And the shouts raise folks off those benches into the heavenly places they're promised in Holy Ghost messages. Sometimes the promises arrive in the unknown language with a later *prophesy* and sometimes they're left in the untranslatable language of hopes, longings, and heart's desires.

I can't report the sounds of *tongues* itself. Speaking often starts out with a *hundaiashandala* . . . kind of sound then elevates rapidly into words too hard to explain on flat paper. The Preacher keeps on preaching when that happens during his time in the pulpit. Tongues interrupting his message don't work for him.

> Three people live in us—one
> we think we are
> one other people think we are and
> the one God *knows* we are!
> Amen?
> Like the preacher doin his best to color-up a
> man's life after he's layin there—front of the
> church house—stretched out in that pine box.
> Preacher's tryin to make him fit one of those people
> he *wished* he was, you know, Brother Bowins?
> Talks about his good deeds. Fine father.
> Loving husband. Man of honor in the town! Hard worker . . .
> Yes! Yes! People are shouting *amen* and *hallelujah*,
> encouraging the preacher to decorate this man

even more, *Why he loved everbody! He . . .*
Before the preacher can go any further, wife of the dead man
leans over to her boy, says, 'Son—would you run up yonder
n check if it's fer sure yer Pa in at box?

Laughter spins through the crowd as readily as Jesus-shouts. Weeping, laughing and shouting blend into what people call a *heavenly chorus*. A *fore-taste of glory divine* as the hymn *Blessed Assurance* sings.

God knows the groaning—tears—weeping,
all! Rewarded in heaven, hallelujah!
He knows our secret prayers—
Prayer is our supply line to the Eternal Source.
That's why he died—praise His name—that our supply line
might never be destroyed by sin or the devil!

Owen's daddy jumps to his feet shouting, "Praise Jay-zus—iss true! Iss true!" His round face fringed by hominy colored hair I'd never have guessed could be so bright those years ago, thin rumpled and dirty as he was. His name is Owen Sr., I've learned, so now they just call little Owen, Junior. Both of them being in church *ever time a doors open.*

Lord knows the man's a walking witness of Jesus turning barroom whiskey into kitchen-table milk. Never mind the water into wine for the wedding at Cana.

Returning to a familiar place for revival guarantees rewards not built in anywhere else: we'll be received without suspicion or competition from the pastor and word will already be spread without our having to talk it up the first night. Sweetest of all, there'll be people awaiting our arrival. The Welcome Table, already spread.

Come Sunday, Sister Walker's one of the people *rejoicin, pure rejoicin!* to see a Skondeen walk into her classroom. She works at an office in Birmingham during the week. Buses run too late to get to service on time.

"Audrey, Sweetie, you grown!" She smashes me up agains her powdery scented pink cheek, soft as the flannel board she uses to tell the Bible story lessons. Audrey stories come rolling out like spilled Necco wafers:

"'It wasn't such a big trouble. M' daddy made this here traila n' he can fix it!' Memba? When ya'lls traila hass tore up from a lumba truck comin too close?" Shaking her head, she slaps the side of her navy blue dress, long sleeves, high neck above tiny tucks from the belt to the top button. The silvery bun in back of her head loosened with finger waves around her face, a distraction from her long narrow nose, her face widened considerably in these minutes of laughter. "I bin lookin forard t'seein ya chile since Brotha

Bowins sur-prise us, 'Skondees onna road agin!' Whooee, I can tell ya there's shoutin all round!"

She sits down on the adult-sized teacher's chair in the room, smoothing her dress over her lap, ready for catching up on the years gone by, "How ya doin, Hon chile?" tips her head, leans in, lavender blue eyes steady behind their thick round lenses.

I tell her as kindly as I can that it's good to be here again, standing before her in my robin's egg blue Sunday dress Aunt Dorie bought me in San Francisco.

"You practicin a piana?"

"Yep, sometimes, but there's something new!" My description of the bass meets her wild exclamations, "Movin on fer Jayzus!" Followed by a hint of an exhale, *ah, here we are.* "Took va-cation nex week, fromma job? Ah can be heah ever night. Then Eastah! Eastah Sundy. Thass gonna be s'fine." She nods with satisfaction. I add that we're singing with the Morning Doves of Dolomite after our regular service that Easter night. Every time we're in town, we manage to get in a visit to the *Morning Doves*, the happiest singing group you've ever heard from I don't know what kind of Colored church in Dolomite, a few miles away. We don't stay for the whole time, it's liable to go on for hours past our bed time. We just sing a trio, a solo, and scoop up their blessings and appreciation.

Music acts like Jesus does in the song they sing at their church in Dolomite, *Fix Me Jesus*. Music mends hateful people. I've seen folks visit that church and sing along in the sweetness of the Holy Ghost who might call *colored* by that hateful word *nigger* on other days, but they will not say any such thing when singing's involved. If we'd sing more and stop the talk from commentators such as Fulton Lewis Jr., who's always full of bad news, we'd be better off. Can't say that to my dad. But honest to goodness, he always walks around real mad after he listens to men like Fulton Lewis on the radio.

Sister Walker isn't finished. "Na you mus 'member iss heah insdent. Ya was s'little, itty bitty thang no more'n fo, five? Firs time y'all 'n Sayreton? Ah tole at story s'many times. Calls it *dancin w' the devil*!" Ripples of laughter follow, making a few attempts to stifle, saying, "Ah know y'mama don't think iss funny."

This Audrey story I mentioned earlier belongs in a set of tales resembling the Grimm Brothers collection. About Aunt Dorie sending me new patent leather shoes she calls *Mary Janes* like the ones I have on now. Only then, trying them on, I preen a bit in the scratched-up full length mirror tacked to the supply closet door, noting the fine sounds my shiney shoes made on the cracked linoleum floor. Slowly at first, I begin to tap tap tappity tap.

She replays the legendary whipping, one that she's positively certain I'll never forget. Sister Walker slows down to more of a chuckle, now, from the high pitched laugher. I smile and join in her merriment as well as I can.

But I did forget, I've a mind to tell her. The lunchtime dances at junior high cost a dime and I'd give up milk any day to dance. But as the mirth settles around us, dust motes in the morning sun streaming through the Sunday School room window, I smile ever more sweetly and keep my mouth shut.

Sunday's shutdown of mines and refineries quiets Sayreton to distant church bells in Birmingham. Occasionally a passenger train's whistle sounds far away, but that's different from the daily screech of nearby box cars chugging into industrial sites for loading. Birmingham's named for her sister city in England, with plenty in common, including drilling and mining and the sinkholes they sometimes produce. Whirring pulleys, rock-splitting and grinding apparatus; the pumping power-up and fall of hydraulic lifts; the roar of refinery fires two stories high, all, quiet for one day. Absent are the dump trucks and their clattering shower of fine rocks they strew along the roadway in front of the church. The belch of black smoke that billows from smoke stacks coloring the sky a jaundiced gray, today is nowhere to be seen.

"Slave lab'r on 'r heads," Brother Owen tells the Preacher after tarrying a long time at the altar. "Ah lay m'burd'ns down right heah . . . iss heah bench a prayin. Ats where! Praisa Lawd." Tears squeeze out of the corners of his eyes. I'm standing one step above on the platform ringed by the same faded purple burlap fabric as ever over a pipe-like railing, an opening on either side of the pulpit so preachers can immediately access the altar. Tonight, I'm singing *Softly and Tenderly*, a song whose refrain pleads, *Come home, come home, ye who are weary, come home.* Who doesn't want to just go on home? Especially if you've forgotten how to get there.

Brother Owen keeps talking, but it starts sounding like a prayer.

"Ah lay m'burd'ns down, yas Lawd." The Preacher has his hand on the man's shoulder as he shakes his head, continuing, "Don't know what ah'd do 'thout a Lawd." Then, with a quick motion, he reaches over and clasps my right hand as I stand there, my left hand still resting on the pulpit, and says with a fresh sob, "Don't know what'd come a me 'thout iss heah lil chile . . . leadin me t'this prayin bench." The Preacher says, "Thank the Lord, Brother! Thank the Lord."

Here I stand, motionless as moonlight, quiet as breath. Finally I slip away when he goes on to praising God for mercy with the Preacher still in attendance.

What can a person do when something like that happens? Talk about glued to the spot, that's me.

People tell their tales about my being a problem, laughing at the "girl who has at lil ole curl downa middle a her fore-head" and "she some kinda trouble." That's normal. Every place we've ever held a revival meeting knows what it means when my father glares at me and starts saying, *Help us Lord* more than two times. Haven't heard that yet this time on the road.

But being singled out as a blessing? Don't ask me what to do with that.

Same when folks run on and on about what a gift I have. Back when I was that little kid Sister Walker recollects, I basked in talk like that. Never occurred to me to think *gift of what*? Well, what do you reckon. Gift of suspicion like my Dad? *Gift of mischief* is how he described me one time. Laughing, sort of. That was when Ernestine Bees was hugging me up calling me a *gift* as we were leaving Selma, Alabama. My father made his *mischief* comment quietly so only I could hear him.

At least I seemed to know what to do with the gift of mischief or blessing in those days. Use it. Say *thank you* and wear it with pleasure. But I seem to have mislaid it now, whatever it is. Left it in a cupboard of my little girlhood. I'm not even sure where I am. Not exactly a kid but certainly not a grown up either. Definitely not treated like one.

My dad just worries about pride. "Spiritual pride, more evil than any other sinning, Doris," he said when we were leaving the tent meeting of a TV healing preacher who boasted about his gifts.

He'd probably say that believing the praise people heap on your head resembles a sink hole folks get used to in mining territory. Besides creosote air breathed in from the outside to coat your lungs on the inside, a sinkhole from an abandoned mine shaft or well can swallow your back porch, yard, or car even as it rolls along the street.

Life's uncertain when it's perched on mining territory, and if you perch your character on praise from others instead of keeping your head low, studying to *show yourself approved* by Jesus, you'll have nothing but swirling dark waters in an empty abyss. Suddenly. When you need that sterling character most, which I'm sure my father would say is when you stand before the Father Almighty on Judgment Day. But I'm not going to ask him. He'll lecture me soon enough.

Easter morning's coming through the rolled-up vent in the trailer's top when the first church bells float into my sleep. *Early in the morning, first day of the week*, words that call up the dark beginnings of the resurrection story.

Beaming in with the early sun are memories of *Easter Eight*, which— this being Easter Eleven, since my birthday twelve is not until July—is how I think of our detour into more northern reaches, Frederick, Maryland. Easter dinner at the home of a judge my parents knew since he was a boy somewhere in Alabama. A farm boy. And here he is in a fine house near Washington, DC.

For some odd reason the new automatic washer and matching drier fascinated me more than any other finery in their home, imagine such magic. And the judge's willowy blond wife, nails shocking in their peachy perfection, can't be bothered to run them. She leaves it to the housekeeper.

Dotted swiss ruffled dress from Aunt Dorie also marks Easter Eight, plus the judge's wife making sure my Easter basket leaves nothing to chance: chocolate eggs, jelly beans, marshmallow chicks and a fuzzy white bunny right in the middle, cellophane drawn to the handle with a giant yellow bow. Complete enough to make even Aunt Dorie proud. None of that *foolishness* had long to stay around but I loved it for a little while and forever in remembering.

Mother taps my reverie short by her insistence that I hurry to wash up in the church bathroom before folks start arriving. We're parked right outside the back door. I know she misses her bathtub as much as I do but the only indication she ever allows is a small shadow that glances across her face. Then, efficient as she is, she gets on with the job for the day. Resurrection.

I can do my part on the bass for *He Lives* and *How Great Thout Art*. Those songs are just ahead this morning, guaranteed, along with Easter Sunday finery and Hallelujah, He is Risen! shouting. Miners, maids and the rest of the people who slave everyday for Birmingham big shots don't go in for very fancy Sunday Best. Wearing white, alone, sends a shiver along some spines and blossoms into faces full of grins. Years old straw hats decorated with new artificial flowers from the downtown Five and Dime, Woolworth's, show up on happy people. But the most important thing is they're here in the church house and they fix their minds on Jesus for pure delight.

Sister Walker arrives decked out in pink. Pale pink, with big 'polky dots' as she calls them adorning the soft skirt. Puffy long sleeves looking downright girlish. White straw hat showing some seasons, but the pink roses fresh from the Five and Dime. I love Sister Walker.

> He's alive and
> He's with us today!
> Hallluuuuuuu!

Brother Bowins starts the morning worship after the shuffle between Sunday School and church with a shout causing folks to get so loose I begin to think service might be over before it begins. But my father motions mother to play the piano—the regular piano player Effie Willis twirls in the aisle, hair pins flying, her straw hat ringed in daisies landing on the altar—and as mother starts the music for *I serve a living savior He's in the world today*, Althea makes a run on the vibra harp and I pick up the bass to join her.

This Preacher is not going to let Easter Sunday slip away from him that easily. He has some things to say, especially since this is our farewell Sunday.

But after threading together the Easter stories from the Gospels, speaking of the rolled away stone, the excitement and fulfillment of promises that the beauty of their living Master brings to Mary and the other disciples on that first morning, he goes some place I never expected. Sayreton bore a message to his heart this week.

> I see loved ones right here in Birmingham
> still underneath that stone. Can't seem to get up.
> Looking for fulfillment in Bailey's Bar!

The church house suddenly gets real still. Husbands and sons drag themselves onto these benches for Easter Sunday morning who might not be here the rest of the year. Preacher's pulling out all the stops.

> Minute that mine whistle shrills through town, they're on their way,
> away from their babies, their wives—their only hope!—for what?
> *I drink because it relaxes me.*
> Sure it does, right into the gutter, a garbage dump. Everything gone.
> You'll be relaxed, all right.
> *I drink because I owe everbody.*
> You'll never drink your way out of debt.
> *I can take it or leave it.*
> But you always take it, don't you? Same with cigarettes.
> *I drink because my job gets me down.*
> Keep drinking and you'll soon have a new boss. Or no boss at all.
> Drink kills more than all the wars put together.
> *Be not drunk with wine but be filled with the spirit*, says Apostle Paul.

Brother Owen's shouts himself straight up off the bench and his wife Sister Phoebe waves her handkerchief in praise as the Preacher heats up. Plenty people here love somebody who's a drunk.

Yancys, Sister Bertha and her mother Beatrice, have shown up faithfully every night and she looks mighty serious with this preaching. They're new since we were here last and I'm not sure about their story. From what I hear, Bertha Yancy's husband, Darrold, was crushed when a timber fell on him in the mine last year. When Sister Bowins mentions it to mother, she's too quiet to indicate a heavenly landing. That stillness around her words means there's a heap left out. Like maybe the bar room. And the way Bertha Yancy weeps at the altar makes me think she's praying the good Lord will build a by pass around hell.

But the indictment on strong drink only begins the Preacher's confession from his own life. Now I'll have to tell you, I've never heard him go on like this before.

> I know what it is to look for satisfaction!
> All my life I've suffered disappointment,
> my school days shambles. Fear. Anxiety over those books, exams.
> Frustration. Barely finished grade school.

"Ohhhh Lawd!"
"Yasss, Jazus, hep auvr chillrun."
"Hep! Hep Lawda mussy. Hep!" Calling for mercy for children who hate school. Easy to quit when you can start working the mines. Takes a strong will to decide that will not be your way when your family lives on the mines. Lives with the soot and the sweat of coal.

> Looking for a job—not satisfied—*no way satisfied.*
> Started music lessons
> never satisfied!
> Heard Fritz Kreisler play, but that didn't satisfy me.
>
> One day I read *This Is That* and
> went on off to Bible School. Not satisfied.

(Stands quietly, shaking his head)

> *Never satisfied.*
> Got married—now you know this wonderful woman—but
> look around these United States, does marriage and children
> satisfy us? Never!—problems everwhere—have mercy!

My mother's face looks a trifle pale about now. He's never given people information about him and his wife, even if he's making it sound kind of general. Can't help but wonder if their arguments changed them over the last couple of years. Their loud voices sure enough caused my attention to go on the alert.

> Evangelistic work, some glorious days but days like this of parting, too.
> They always come, days of parting,
> facing a cold world and in the
> next meeting, folks we don't know, hard to gain confidence.
> People sit back looking at you,
> disappointed.
> Disappointed with church people!

Until now, he's been on the platform, his voice building louder and louder, but now the Preacher jumps—yes, jumps—down the one step beside the pulpit, his jacket's off, and he begins to roll up his white shirt sleeves, his deep blue tie with thin yellow diagonal stripes shining like sun streaks as he shouts *Young People!* And heads into the aisle, speaking as rapidly as his feet are taking him up and down, then up again, fairly running, jumping back up onto the platform, both arms in the air for the finale.

> Young People!
> Don't be deceived, struggling to be like *So and So.*
> Only True Satisfaction is when we will
> "find ourselves in His likeness"
> *raised up* into newness of life.
> Holy Ghost comes to breathe the character of Christ in ME,
> *Then I shall be satisfied!*
> Holy Ghost comes to breathe the character of Christ in *you*,
> then shall *you* be satisfied!
>
> Then shall we be satisfied havin new bodies
> raised in His likeness—
>
> that meeting in the air?
> I'm not going to miss it!
>
> *Then shall I be satisfied!*

Folks are in the aisles since his last run up to the pulpit. Even my lovely Sister Walker in a kind of jig speaking tongues, her hat flung across the front benches. Brother Owen's wife—Virginia's and Junior's mama—Sister Phoebe says nothing, but with her arms in the air above her jonquil gold-yellow dress, auburn hair shaking loose it's tight roll from one side to the other, tears glistening on her smiling face. The woman wears her satisfaction all over her tiny, dancing frame. She's never looked so beautiful and by the way Owen and Virginia are staring in awe, they must be thinking the same thing.

I'd say this *is* the rapture.

Mother's wearing the accordion, Althea chimes in on the vibra harp by the time I have the bass in hand and we're already singing, *Going to be a meeting in the air in the sweet, sweet by and by*, adding form to the fullness of *Holy Ghost outpouring* which is what most people here would call it.

Now here's a gift. The Holy Ghost. But do I want the gift of speaking tongues? Watching ecstatic words work physical wonders in people satisfies their longing. Or it seems to from the outside. But for me, loving the plunk of each string that backs the singing and giving voice to the song, I have plenty of Spirit. Don't I?

Participating, I'm still an observer. Like a reporter writing a news story in my Calvert composition book this week. It's just that I'm stumped on how to investigate what can't be seen.

10

Jennings, Florida 1954
Nothing but the Blood

- *Boeing 707, four-engine airliner debuts in Seattle; William E. Boeing, 72-year-old engineer witnessed the maiden flight.*
- *$30 automatic coffee makers introduced, able to brew two cups in four minutes.*
- *Observations of 800 galaxies demonstrate that the universe was born in a giant cosmic explosion 5 1/2 billion years ago.*
- *Princeton makes computers available for rent to private corporations.*
- *President Eisenhower—"Ike"—calls communism a global peril that cannot be checked by armed strength alone.*
- *Senator McCarthy charges Communist infiltration in CIA and atomic plants.*
- *Senate votes to condemn Senator Joe McCarthy for conduct unbecoming a Senator in controversy surrounding his tactics; McCarthy vows to continue investigating defense plants but the consensus is that his stature has been greatly reduced.*
- *Ike signs Atomic Energy Act, opening the door to private exploration of nuclear power.*
- *Lassie has pups, making her TV show even more enchanting.*
- *Record 120,000 people attend last night of Billy Graham's crusade in London.*
- *Robert Jennings settled Jennings, Florida, Hamilton County, in 1860 operating a farm and general store. George Jennings comes, 1884, on a raft*

by way of the Alapaha River: shipping point for Sea Island cotton before WWI and the coming of boll weevils.[1]

- *Sharecroppers are tenant farmers especially in the southern US who are provided with credit for seed, tools, living quarters, and food; they work the land and receive an agreed share of the value of the crop minus charges.*[2]

- *Audrey Skondeen is twelve years old.*

FIRST I HEAR *SNAP, plunk* sounds on a tin basin—used for dishwashing most times, now in the service of preparing a mess of black eye peas—plus the hushed conversation of Sister Bernice Rogers and my mother, heads bent toward each other, snap peas between them. Their quiet voices alert me to important information being passed.

"Like ta bled ta death . . ." An image emerges of the striped ticking mattress we've seen airing in the yard on a summer's day, soaked through during a birth: one of Sister Rogers' sons being born. My mother's low, mournful sounds of have *mercy, bless your heart*, empathy gathered around women's ways of knowing each other's suffering.

"Life costs us. Sometimes life costs a lot," mother says. I don't often hear her talk that way. Bernice Rogers ranks high on our family's list of all time great people. She may be at the very top. Well, maybe tied at first place with Sister Mary Watford in Scratch Ankle over in Franklin County, Alabama.

When this conversation passed my way the first time, I was six years old. And though the image I registered is indelible, *indelible*, the facts that tumbled out didn't hook together with any logic. *Birth blood.*

Blood flows in torrents through Pentecostal songbooks: *Saved by the Blood of the Lamb*; *There Is a Fountain Filled with Blood*; *Nothing but the Blood of Jesus*. And blood has a powerful place in most church meetings. Everything from messages and scriptures intoning the absolute necessity of being washed in Jesus' blood for salvation to pleading the blood of Jesus Christ over one's self, family, household, or friends as protection in time of danger.

But a mattress? At six, salvation language rushed through my senses without touching down into the physical messiness and meaning of human blood. As if Jesus wasn't human. As if I wasn't human.

---

1. *Wikipedia.com*, s.v. "Jennings, Florida."
2. *Merriam-Webster's Collegiate Dictionary*, s.v. "sharecropper."

Now, twelve years old, it's different. My library education has cleared me up on how babies happen and what I have to look forward to if I venture into Babyland myself. That's a large *if*.

Althea talks quietly to me about what it means to be a woman. I respond with *you mean having a period*. She blushes. She's fair skinned like mother.

Fussiness over being female escapes me. I'm born a girl. That can't be a surprise by now. Sometimes I think *Billy David*, the boy my folks meant me to be, still shadows me even though I gave him the shake at my birth.

My *menses* as the books say, starts like all other females—which is what my sister is patiently explaining, probably prompted by my mother—and now I'll have this going on every month for the next forty years. Except when I'm having a baby. That's an unlikely thought, but my sister and mother talk about babies in the no-doubt zone.

Have mercy.

We love this place, Jennings. Just barely inside Florida, nearest town of any size being Valdosta, Georgia. Everything from Mayor Holland who also happens to be the sheriff and judge in town—our loudest fan, "Cain wait ta heah em girls sang!" even though dad joins in when he puts down the fiddle—to the Roger's family, their Alapaha River farm and even the Jennings kind of green grass. Something about the color of this churchyard catches my eye every time we drive into town. Fern like in color from deep in a primeval forest. I credit the river for nourishing roots beneath the land as afternoon rains keep it watered from above.

Sometimes in early spring the water way runs high, sending everybody—including livestock—for higher ground. One of the Roger's boys, Donny, remembers waking up and finding worried cows gathered at his bedroom window, gently mooing their concerns.

Alapaha's a tributary to the Sewanee whose mysterious characters nudge up against each other on long nights of telling tales around campfires along its banks. But what this river contributes to the earth, the crops, and the people here is incomparable.

Folks gather on the front porch of the mercantile, a colonial-looking store front with big peeling-white-paint pillars on a narrow wooden porch. At least it looks narrow compared to the pillars. Everybody stares at our car's pulling our trailer into town like it's the most fascinating parade ever. Around the corner sits the sturdy brick Assemblies church. Few windows and those, frosted, built flat to the ground without even one step up to the front door from the simple white-framed porch. Odd, in a way, but my guess is that no random tornado could disturb a single brick.

Church house looks to be the strongest building in town. Well, maybe the elementary school made of cement blocks painted a painful shade of green rivals it. School has more windows, more light. Church aims for keeping light and sound on the inside.

Here comes Sister Rogers, first thing after we pull in on Friday afternoon, bright as sunshine cutting through the old oaks hung with curly moss. Pot of chicken n dumplings in hand to make sure we are well fed our first supper in town. Growing four boys and a hard working husband teaches her to have a pot full of something at all times on the back of the wood stove out at their peanut farm.

The Alapaha runs right along their acreage at the end of a wide unpaved road across the railroad tracks and through the piney woods. Straight as arrows, pines pointing at the sky and mossy oaks gather round the pioneer homestead itself. But the road into it resembles a paper mill's reserve with only those arrow-pines. Not even shrubs to speak of, or other trees.

"'Member that visit we had, comin into your place to surprise you?" my mother says. The only person I ever catch her speaking Southern to is Bernice Rogers, "Not a soul around, but I declare I never got over how neat as a pin the place was. Not a broom straw on the floors. Like you scrubbed it from top to bottom before you left for the fields that morning, an ah know ya go out by five AM." Mother shakes her head, still under the spell of Sister Roger's near perfection.

At the time, I thought it looked as if somebody left that day believing Jesus would be there when she returned. Wouldn't due to be found wanting. That's when I was still very nervous about the Rapture.

Roger's farm could be, piece by piece, set up on a Saint Augustine Museum's replicas of early Florida homesteads: sugarcane grinding shed, the tread of the donkey's feet leaving a circular path; sorghum boiling lean to, all the pots cleaned and up turned, ready for use come harvest; clothes wash shelter, now, more than only wash tubs and scrub boards, though there's still one of each along with the wringer washer. Even the garage has the feeling of a barn, one extra lean to for a pick up truck used for hauling hay. All structures the same unpainted, weathered gray wood capped by corrugated tin roofs. Against that green, green grass, they're a sight.

First question from my dad for Sister Rogers, "How bout them turkeys, Sister? Leadin any turkeys to the pen for fattening?"

"Brotha Skondee, got yer season outta place. Farm boy like you? Em turkeys ain aroun til Setember."

We laugh at his lapse in farmerly timekeeping, recovering with Sister B as she says, "This heah sprang time? Musta deliva some dozin a calves.

Trickin turkeys—at trail a corn to a trap door inna pen?—hit don't compare ta job like that'n."

"Doin the job of a midwife, huh?" My mother chimes in, to Bernice's vigorous nod, followed by, "Twin calves atta neighbor's farm. 'At mama cow so tore up ova it, she wails all night long. Donkey's onliest one safe from givin birth iss yar. Ah declare."

"Boys help?" Mother asks with a furrowed brow.

Mouth set in a wry kind of grimace, she answers, "Oldess one? When a can keep im awake early inna mornin. Iss yar, coulda hung outta sign *Midwife Fer Hire.*"

Sister B's eyes gently mix brown and green, like leaves falling from their trees in November. Her hair, color of a brown squirrel's tail, pulled back in the way of a holiness woman, a spray of fine strands loose around her small, oval face that reminds me of a delicate gold locket, and dress a shade of distressed blue dungarees. Fit for work. Bernice Rogers is not one of those people who wears holiness like a badge on her sleeve. She lives it deep inside her small sun blessed frame, muscles in arms and legs stringy, hard, from vigorous hours on the farm.

Some kind of thankfulness hovers over their 300 acres. That's how it feels.

"Firs suppa we share as man n wife—me n Harley?—onna up turn wash tub," she laughs when talk turns to the farm land. "Por ole shah crop-pas. All w'were."

But sharecroppers who managed to buy the land one acre at a time. My father never believed he'd meet anybody like that, I'll guarantee: *No way to get ahead* being his opinion on sharecroppers.

Harley Rogers doesn't tarry at the altar. May be he never even gets there. Smokes many cigarettes quietly out by his pick up truck in the dark. Reckon a can of Prince Albert tobacco and pack of fragile white papers are carefully stowed on a high shelf at the house. But I've never heard a word of discussion about "Mr. Rogers, Christian?" The evangelist calls him brother with affection and respect, not breathing a word of doubt about his eternal soul. Unusual.

Quietly, Harley stands with his Bernice. A fearless pioneering team. His determination and grit pulled together dollars for each acre by clearing cypress trees from swamps and selling the wood for lumber. Not a tall man but strong, sleeves rolled high over square arms hard with heavy lifting. His eyes that are also a mix of brown and green, but darker, turned inside, straight pecan-shell colored hair close cropped.

Sister Bernice begins to rise from her perch on our folding canvas chair, ready to leave, "Five minute rule, that what it is? Can't sit longer than that?"

"Nah, vangliss. Hungry mouths ta feed. Ah can heah em callin loud b' na. Big growin boys. Ya won't rec'nize a one a 'em boys." Sister Bernice rattles off toward home in her dusty pick up once a well worn red, now barely showing a hint of original color.

Revival begins here on Sunday morning, but the blessing begins when a woman you love sits with you in person once again. A visionary flood of *whens* sweep through—singing together, standing side by side; frying a mess of catfish; eating boiled peanuts around a giant tin pot; being surprised when the Roger's family shows up in Augusta, Georgia; Samson, Alabama, and Winter Haven, Florida—every scene that merges with the next, a reason to smile inside and out.

River may feed the peanut crops and cattle, but Jesus and the people who preach Him fuel the Roger's family by sustaining their mother. Besides, she prays *without ceasing*, just like the Bible tells us to do. In the house, preparing to get herself out to the fields and in the fields toiling through hours of dusty heat. "Nevah 'lone." I heard her tell my mother one time. No, never alone.

Surprise hits town on Saturday, the day before revival opens, when the Daytons from further north in Georgia show up. They say they're headed to a family reunion.

"'Reck'n w'needs some time w' th' Skondees,' ah say t'Erline.'" So really, having a destination in mind or not, they'd have wound up here anyhow, that's what Ernie Dayton means.

Thin hair barely stretches over his round and rosy head. His body another form of round n rosy, but carried on a six-foot two-inch frame, so it works out swell. Erline Dayton, about a foot shorter than he and perpetually smiling. A laughing blue eyes kind of woman with corn silk hair slipping out of knots, braids or any arrangement she attempts. This dear woman unfailingly reminds me of the strawberry shortcake for which she's famous. See Erline, see two round shortcakes dripping in strawberry juice and slightly lost in clouds of whipped cream. Can't help it. Pinks and reds are her favorite colors, too. No holiness drab for her.

Besides the Rogers and Mayor Holland here in Jennings, the Daytons (Georgia), the Bowins (Alabama), and the Browns (Florida), rate our full schedule with the card we send at Christmas. They're the folks who follow our band, though this one's only a ragtag family of singers, players, and one preacher. Any one of them just might pop up in the neighborhood when you least expect it. Holland came to see us in Miami one year. That really was a surprise.

The Browns don't travel to see us, though, come to think of it. We're the ones who show up to park in their yard when we're traveling toward or away from Miami. Unless, perhaps, we're in a revival meeting very close to their place, Wildwood, Florida, a town like Leesburg. Theodore Brown's running a general store every day of the year except Sunday of course, ties up most of their time. They were friends with my parents before any of them had kids of their own. What everybody knows is that their oldest boy Albert's sweet on Althea even though she ignores him. Pretends she doesn't notice a thing.

Saturday afternoon, Holland's sitting with us out in the church yard, gold and silver handlebar mustache picking up any stray sunbeams filtered by the sprawling oak tree overhead, his wide smiling face a burnished trademark of Jennings good will. Ten gallon used to be white cowboy hat tipped back just like he is on his chair, braced in the deep grass by one of his feet which can always be found in battered used to be brown herding boots. You can tell those boots've kicked a few clods of horse plop. He's fixing to tell us a tale about hunting alligators in the Okeefenokee Swamp when Daytons turn up. They already checked into a Valdosta motel, nearest guest rooms around here. They're anxious to surprise us.

Daytons remind me of the Rogers. Folks able to make something out of nearly nothing. Ingenuity. Uncommon smarts tethered to endurance. Brother Ernest Dayton started a trucking company with a beat up third hand one ton flatbed truck he learned how to fix for himself. Wiring it together when everything else failed, using a screwdriver for a starter, "Nevah felt s'safe in somethin s'shaky," Erline says. They now own a fleet of dump trucks that work out of Augusta gravel yards in a crunchy spot on the road near Sparta, Georgia.

Erline Dayton right beside Ernie, feeds every hungry driver who either doesn't have a home or just prefers her food. Also stray evangelists who wander in. With a six foot diameter table built with a four foot lazy susan revolving at the center to hold the bounty, food craves to be part of breakfast, dinner or suppertime in her setting. They have a locker at the ice house storing berries, peaches and all the vegetables left from summer's garden. Shortcake and much, much more. Year round.

When it comes to storytelling, Dayton gives a good run for anybody. Ernie addresses Holland after my dad has introduced them, "You a judge, too? Wal, wal. Mayor. Judge. Shar-iff. I'll be. You got you some kinda duty roun' heah."

Holland grins his satisfied cheshire cat grin and says, "Don't pay t'be caught w'ma shirttails a hangin out. Know what ah mean." They laugh as if everybody knows.

"Wal, na," Ernie keeps on, "Ya have a man rat chere—Vangliss Skond-ee?—he can hep ya' out." We know exactly where he's going with this one. Back a few years. Hot summer night close to Augusta, but still country. Girls wearing soft colors in gingham dresses, hair tied high in pony tails or braids. Young men—some young women, too, the ones whose parents weren't on the church benches most likely—out in the friendly dark on pickups backed to the open church windows. Testimonies popping up, inspired by the music *Won't It Be Wonderful There*. It's wonderful here, too, don't you know.

"Youngins was singing ther hearts out," Ernie shakes his head remembering the pure glory, "back bench, jus inside a open door, strong young guy—twenny sumthin?—jumps up while folks still a shoutin affer Skondee fam'ly done sung, prolly a SparkPlug!" He winks at me, "An a guy, strangah, nevah seen im afore, says he bin livin in sin. Man goes ta cryin, wringin is hans. Livin in sin n shame n *Mi*ami. Rat out inna aisle, na, cain't miss'im."

Brother Ernie's correct. The guy was right out in the middle of the center aisle as he trips into his testimony, head low down, bowed at first. A catch in his voice describing a life of debauchery in Miami's night clubs. Such a wayward life, wagging his head in misery. But then he raises his hands, his eyes surprising pools of deep blue set in a square jawed, golden face, shock of sunny blond streaks in dark hair swinging back above his high forehead, straight full brows raised in expectation of more rejoicing, praising Jesus for deliverance from sin. Praising Jesus for bringing him on in out of the darkness to the glorious light and—hallelujah!—sending him home to Tennessee where he's gonna live for our Lord and Savior Jesus Christ forever more.

By now he's up five or six rows toward the front, still center aisle, and people rejoice with this sinner born again and washed by the blood of the lamb.

"Wal, Vangliss Skondee's standin rat neah," Ernie nods, "han on iss guy's arm, real friendly like. Asts 'is name, when Manny Partridge—deacon?—sprangs t'is feet n says, "'Less take iss heah man a off-rin. Hep 'im get on home a Tenn-see!'" Ernie adds that crops was good that year, people feeling generous. While the offering basket's rustled up and starting the rounds, the Evangelist, after hearing the man's name is Sammy Steele, says, "Well, Brother Steele, sing us a song, now, won't you? Come on up."

Sammy hesitates with a shy smile, then says, "Ah'll sang a song ah've change a words to, 'Oh Happy Day.' M'words can tell y'all good folks about a happy night. Night ah found Jeee-sus." The Evangelist nods, walks up front with him as shouts surround them and sits on the front seat as Sammy sings, standing in front of the altar:

> *Oh happy night*
> *Oh happy night*
> *When Jeeesus washed*
> *M'black heart white*

Hand over the heart side of his rumpled blue and red plaid short sleeved shirt tucked into hip hugging dungarees, his well built body speaking loudly of showmanship. When the words, *He taught me how / To watch and pray* come out of his earnest mouth, his voice cracks, streaked with emotion, he shakes his head as if to clear himself yet again of sorrow, *An live rejoicin everday!* Ah, the relief.

People are already standing with frenzied clapping when he finishes, bowing his head, first, then bowing low: *Oh happy night! When Jeeesus washed my black heart white.* Some of the women are shedding tears, applauding, waving handkerchiefs, "Jayzus, Jayzus, bless im blessim real gooood." Wishing they could take him home and feed him, no doubt.

Manny Partridge, saying, "Lord be w'ya as ya go on home. Come back ta see us, na," empties the offering basket of its bills and change into Sammy Steele's hands, sending him on his way. But Ernie says here, his voice lowered, "What folks inna church hass don know is Vangliss Skondee whispas ta Deacon Bailey, 'Foller at man!'"

Bailey leaves real quiet like by the side door and tracks the guy back to his rented room. The police later find ledgers there revealing a history of visits to churches all over the Augusta area: where, when, how much. There was a trial. The deacons testify against the man whose name turns out to be Joe Brady.

Holland says, "My lands, why!" He and Dayton, both, caught up in the drama. Ernie says, "But heah's a bess paht, w'say t'Vangliss, 'how'd ya know. How'd ya guess?' an a Vangliss says, 'Cain't sang! A guy cain't sang—no *Mi-ami* night club's gonna hire a guy at cain't sang!'"

They're engulfed by guffaws, wiping tears from their eyes. Holland goes from slapping his dungarees accompanied by roaring laughter to fanning himself with his ten gallon hat. Never thought I'd see the working white felt, sweat ring under turkey feathers around the crown to prove its substance, off his head outside the church house.

"Marcher time," Holland saying *time* as if it has three syllables, "brangs along folks a plenny ya cain't prepare fer meetin," shaking his head as the laughter slows to random riffs.

"Wal, at air judge. Adam Olds? He got some eyebrows. Not a hair on iss head, nary a one, but em brows, why if he's up onna watch tower inna prison yard—em brows n big ole horn-rim glasses—ya know im from at far 'way!" He's telling about the sentencing. "Lookin ova from high up onna bench; shoulers hunch up unner em black robes, an em brows—'Ahm jus a judge inna muniss-pl coaht hass, but ya gonna stan afore a Judge on High one a these days. Bettah get yerseff save, Boy!' an sent im outta town. Nevah seen im agin."

After they fully recover, Brother Ernie adds, "Know what ahm a sayin, Judge Holland? Ya gotta a helpa heah in Vangliss Skondee. He gotta gift a suspiscion!" And after a chuckle or two, he adds, "Na, if Erline'r me has auvr doubts bout sumpin, jus nods a head an says *cain't sang!*" It's code.

Everybody knows the Evangelist's habits come late afternoon, Saturday. Study time, preparing for Sunday. Stillness settles over even the joy loving Daytons. Mayor Holland heads for home. They gather us one by one in smothering hugs declaring their need to take a rest for tomorrow's marathon Welcome Back to Jennings Sunday.

My parents, Althea too, for that matter, stay clear of most hugging options. They wave, smile their gladness over seeing and being seen with as much heart felt enthusiasm as they can muster without physical contact. I never used to notice that. But nobody escapes the Daytons.

As they drive off in their latest model Chrysler—my father praying silently, I'm confident, to be free of covetousness, this being the car perfect for pulling a trailer he tells Ernie, slapping the glossy blue fender—my mother's already assessing how many carrots remain in the vegetable basket. Enough for tonight's supper?

Our main meal is dinner at noontime, but later we have something to *tide us* over as mother says. That's supper, and except for Saturday or travel days, it has to fit with the evening service. A couple of hours before church starts, a meal has to be simple as an apple and a piece of cheese, or maybe just those carrots. Mother concentrates on what's good for us, nutritious, and she often throws in the admonition to Be Healthy! Our bodies being Temples, of course.

We always sit together for our meals at the table that lets down between two seats in the front of the trailer. Dad fitted this traveling home just like the one we had before, *customizing* he calls it. They pull together at night to form a double bed for my parents after the table is hooked securely to the ceiling.

We always ask the Lord to bless our food, too. Blessed or not, though, my father still gets indigestion from time to time. His stomach definitely rates as delicate. When that's going on he moans a lot, says *Help us Lord* quietly and mopes. But in Jennings we have no bread and milk, warmed a little and kind of stewed together. Here, he's content.

Buttered carrots work fine for me as a simple supper. May be my favorite. Mother cooks them in her waterless cookware, a method she's confident causes food to hold their vitamins. Doesn't boil them away in a lot of water. "Cook vegetables to death, most people. Leave the best of the ingredients in the water then pour it all away. What do you have then? *Fodder*. Pure and simple. You're eating fodder." That's her little lecture. She finishes up with, "Might as well use that stuff to slop the hogs."

Her pans are stainless steel with tight lids that steam the food instead of boil it. Besides the one quart size for cooking rice or vegetables, she also has a stew pot. Since there are only two burners on our hot plate, there's no use having any more than that plus a frying pan for eggs. She usually poaches those to avoid added fat. Paring down to just these few kitchen utensils again after being in a big house was a job, though, I can tell you.

But she did it. And she keeps her sense of what's important: *waterless* cooking. A person has to appreciate my mother and her bitsy points of pride. She'd never admit to being proud, of course, but there's a thing she does with her mouth. A smile that makes her face turn up to one side as she cocks her head, like she's winking at a butterfly that's flitting through.

That look indicates that what she's doing is *correct*. She knows best.

We still have some peaches left from the half bushel we bought along the road. Daytons brought a cooler with frozen berries, too, nearly thawed by now. We'll have some of those tonight after our carrots and the rest of the fruit with our oatmeal for breakfast.

This time on the road, my parents have found a song written by Ira Stanphill, *Suppertime,* they sing as a duet. The words speak of the end of the day as it is about now. One of the phrases *the shadows length in fast* we thought at first was a mistake and meant to be *lengthen*. Then a man from Ireland explained that's their way of speaking. The song brings a tear to my eye some nights:

Many years ago in days of childhood

I used to play till evening shadows come
Then winding down an old familiar pathway
I heard my mother call at set of sun

Come home, come home it's suppertime
The shadows length in fast
Come home, come home it's suppertime
We're going home at last

Sky glow comes on at evening in humid weather like this. Calvert science might describe it as *particulate matter* in the air catching the rays of the falling sun. Holding the light in a glow through the trees, the sky pale before a quiet radiance suffuses the air without a sound.

Near dark except for fireflies, orange heads and slender black wings etched in orangey red, tiny artists playing among leaves. Landing on shadowy branches, dashing the dusk with sparkle and shine.

Air unmoved. Then gentle and sweet, imperceptible in the appearance of the trees, the slightest breeze passes by. I'm glad to be in the right place at the right time just for this delicious minute.

Sunday opens wide favor's doors: not too hot, even for August. No ants or wasps molest any more than usual for the dinner on the ground or afternoon sing.

Our music by Redd Harper—from the Billy Graham campaign—leads the way into favorite requests everywhere we travel this time around:

At the end of the trail
where dreams come true
we'll live forever in the
home of the blue . . .
beyond the river at the
end of the trail.

The Holy Ghost hovers over these benches the same as the spirit of Thanksgiving hovers over the Roger's Farm. I don't speak in tongues, never seems like a tarrying project I want to begin, but there's no doubt about the undiluted majesty felt in God's own Ghost reigning supreme. Personally, I sense it as the man Jesus. *God* seems too far removed, somehow forbidding. This Spirit, this Holy Ghost, churns, rises, sweeps you up, impossible to name or figure how. Better not try too hard, that's how I figure it. Pure, welcoming potency, untouched by selfishness, control, or stinginess, moving to higher ground.

And doesn't it say in Genesis that the Spirit breathed over the waters of creation? So the Spirit breathes through us too, natural as that.

Any chance of making progress with forgiveness, trust, faithfulness, or plain old getting past grudges—Phys Ed teacher, Miss Elkins, comes to mind—hangs with the Holy Ghost. This nearly windowless church fills up every time we're here with what a person in right mind recognizes as Heavenly Power. *Holy Ghost Power* people might say. But it feels like love.

The Preacher gets loose in Jennings. No bother at all finding that word folks can hear. And his *gift of suspicion* takes a rest as well as his sour stomach, like I said. But for a Sunday evening service after a long day of Sunday School, morning preaching and an afternoon of dinner on the ground followed by more singing, he's no fool. Something that will surprise people is in order. He's been working on a sermon of Letters and it looks as if they're ready. He pulls out papers from his worn imitation leather study case and slides them out across the pulpit top.

> Folks may not read the Bible much,
> you know, Brother Holland?
> But they're reading *You*, I'll guarantee!

"Ha! Hep us. Mussy, mussy, oh ma Lawd," Cletey Gaines calls out, fanning herself with a McClane Mortuary fan, Valdosta, Georgia. She's rocking her full frame in its butter-yellow print dress as if she's sitting in a chair on her front porch. Straw hat still hanging on to the topside of steel wool hair loosing its bun-shape gradually since early morning.

> Question is, what is your life telling them? Look at this one.

He reaches into the pile of papers on the pulpit and pulls out a neat envelope.

> Traveled a distance by the looks of the beat-up paper, but wait!
> There's almost nothing written: one page, few words,
> *Enoch walked with God and he was not for God took him.*
> That's it? Unremarkable. Nothing important . . .
> But God.
> *God took the man.*

The Preacher steps off the platform walks up to the front row, talking to the people there, then walks up the aisle:

> Now tell me. Are you living now?—today?—so
> if the Rapture happens this very night,

in a moment, in the twinkling of an eye,
God will be taking you on home?

I have to admit my mind starts to wander about here. Back to my very bad no-good experience in Sacramento when my family thought it was funny because I was scared when I returned home to find no one there. Sal's house, where I was playing, was only next door. Seemed to me if something important happened I'd be aware, but here was a pair of my mother's shoes in the doorway between the kitchen and the living room. And no one was to be found, anywhere. When Althea and my parents reappeared—they were picking peaches across the street—they laughed at my fright. Since then I don't put a lot of stock into Rapture stories. Well, that plus the tornado incident. I nod and think *hmmm*.

By the time I rejoin the preaching, the Evangelist has a letter that is in the shape of a scroll. He's back on the platform now and tumbles the rolled paper away from him. It unfurls across the front, electric fan perched on the railing ruffling the edges: *Methuselah*.

Lived over 900 years, but look at this!

He examines it closely inch by inch. Then, with a look of bafflement, continues.

Blank!
No stories about his life at all!
What's the use of a long time on this earth with nothing written?
God says your tears are bottled up, each one precious,
recorded by God's own hand.
What happened to Methuselah?

Holland acts as pastor, here, too, though he'd never call himself that. More like an overseer, time keeper, property manager. Could be the land belongs to him. A lot of it around here does. He's loving these letters. Hat at rest on the bench beside him as if it has its own presence and place to keep.

Now, here's a beauty. Look at all
that's written in this one: *The Lord is my shepherd I shall not want.*
This man has poetry in his life. Music, even.

But wait.

As the Preacher unfolds the pages of script, a huge ink blot mars the writing. Scratches and black smudges stain the paper.

What could have gone wrong here? Besides the Psalms,

First and Second Samuel writes details about the reign of King David.
Anointed! By the Prophet Samuel, the oil of blessing dripping down
over his head, his shoulders, his arms,
those hands that tenderly cared for the sheep and
played the harp.
Why, he even calmed the evil spirit that shook King Saul,
'Little David!' What a blessing his life has been!
Until. That split second when sin looks sweet, reaches out,
trips that man dancing on the edge of *his own willfulness* . . .
I like it . . . I want to see . . . to touch . . . nobody needs to know.
Then begin the lies
the cover-up that takes not only the lives of others,
but his own. Lost!
If a man powerful as King David is no match for temptation
who do you think you are?
Prophet Nathan goes to David . . .
Saying,
Thou art the man.
Thou art the man!
Don't think deeds done in secret fail to speak out loud
about who you are.

You think you can fool God?
You're the fool.
Your life is a letter.
People may not read this here Bible I have in my hand
but they are reading you!
Lord have mercy. Have mercy.
They are reading you.

Singing tonight won't be long, but it is beckoning. *Come home, come home, ye who are weary come home.* I always feel this song, *Softly and Tenderly*, with a particular twang to the heart. I miss home.

What a week of welcoming, singing, and even a sinner or two rounded up and brought on 'home ta Jayzus', as Sister Gaines says. *Morning by morning*, the song sings, *new mercies I see*: red birds, cardinals, scouring the bushes for seeds and berries, flitting here and there, the brilliant male finding sources and leading the way for his mate to dig into the bounty.

This week, Holland's constant request was *It Took a Miracle* and I sang it with these gentle nights inside:

It took a miracle to put the stars in place,
It took a miracle to hang the world in space,
But when he saved my soul, cleansed and made me whole,
It took a miracle of love and grace.

The hum through pines and mossy oaks continues past sunrise. Nervous Katydids—cicadas—making their music, still, though most retired hours ago. These must be the night shift, holding on well into the morning. A beautiful collection of nights and days.

Wednesday, after Latin II, algebra, science are finished and our noon meal cleared away, we're invited out to the Roger's farm to do our laundry. *Bless their hearts.*

Folks who know us never take for granted that we have access to services hearth and home provide. They ask. Humble as the Rogers' homestead, she recognizes the kind of *less* we live when she sees it. Where else would we scrub our everyday wear, single set of towels, sheets, plus the Preacher's shirts, and hang them out to dry. Bernice Rogers will be thoughtful enough to put the ironing board and iron at mother's disposal, too.

Rolling onto their property and seeing the feed lot where the silos stand in the distance, hearing the clucking from hens as every egg is celebrated, I can't help but see in my mind's eye the other ways those hens give: their lives. Pushing those images out of sight doesn't help much when chicken and dumplings arrive. Honest to goodness brutal killings. Catching them first in the hen yard, that, I can hardly stand, knowing what's going to happen. Then the neck wringing or chopping block. Sharp ax whacks through the delicate bones and a murmuring sort of squawk moves through the hen yard, raspy sympathetic gossip of the day. Hanging the corpse to drain the blood, pitiful wings flailing, from a tree or post high enough so the hunting dogs aren't tempted. But maybe the worst is dunking them in boiling water to begin the plucking of wet, smelly feathers. It could ruin your taste for any form of chicken. Aunt Dorie can't imagine such a barbaric routine as she stands in her blue feathered hat and prim coat at the butcher's shop on Taraval Street in San Francisco. I won't be the one to tell her about it.

Althea and mother tend to the wringer washer out under the shed where there are drying lines protected from sudden showers. And far away from the hen hanging site my father and I soak up the quiet on the front porch of the tin roofed cracker box house. When you approach the gray weathered boards from either side, it appears precarious, a simple no windows structure set on three cement blocks in the middle, and one large, solid block graduated in size from the bottom, smaller at the top, at each corner. I'm occupied with tomorrow's history reading in the swing at one end of the front porch, and the Evangelist settles into the rocker with his Bible and note pads at the other end.

No words pass between us at times like this. Studying and Studying. Understood. The peace on earth of these grounds flow in and around us as easily as summer air passes through the wide breezeway at the center of this little abode. One side holds the kitchen and rough rectangular table that doubles for workspace as well as for family meals, the other side of the open space serves as sleeping quarters, divided for parents—the smaller part—and for the four boys in the other. No space is wasted. And the outhouse, located a short walk away at the edge of the trees, takes no room at all.

Only three steps up to the porch from the grassy yard, shaded by oaks, laurels, pines, and one mighty pecan tree where high in the branches a swarm of gnats swirl away this summer day. "Paper shells" that come off this tree go to make the best cake in all the land. Created by Bernice Rogers' hands, both the cracking of the pecans and building of the cake, this dessert carries considerable honor in three dense yellow layers loaded with pecans, enhanced with caramel icing between the layers and over the top and sides. The only treat our family consumes to the very last crumb. No worry at all about sweetness or fats. She's promised us one for dinner on Saturday.

As we leave, my father points out the stakes in the ground near the day lilies and roses outlining the new house they're planning to build: a real house with windows, bedrooms and an indoor toilet. That good woman's waited a long time for ordinary convenience.

Refreshed after an afternoon of high breezes, add the aroma of clean clothes stacked in-between Althea and me as we travel back to town. A fresh start.

Tonight's singing cuts loose. I'm slapping out *There's Power in the Blood*, on the bass when Holland leaps up on the last verse and goes to *extendin the pow'r* as he puts it:

> *There is power power power power power power power*
> *In the precious blood of the lamb.*

Usually, there are only two powers in the chorus. We sing it over again, the whole song,

> *Would you be free from the burden of sin*
> *there's power in the blood, power in the blood*
> *Would you or' evil the victory win*
> *there's wonder working power in the blood*

You can see how that jacks up the energy. People like that word *power*. And don't you know it means power in their own blood with no need for a tonic like Lydia Pinkhams. Why else would you drag yourself out of the house after working in the mill or in the fields all day long and show up at revival meeting.

Every bit as much as the preaching, music hooks folks up to a surge in an *I can do all things* attitude. Hard as taking a breath at the mill sucking lint into your lungs. Impossible as the note due on the farm appears with the current price they're getting for peanuts. Discouraging as a donkey coming up lame, or a horse that has to be put down for colic. *There's power in the blood.*

Saturday dinner at the Rogers, but we head over there long before noon, mother saying she surely does intend to lend a hand to Sister Bernice, considering the work that woman handles every day. Dad's anxious to prowl the river front with the boys and a fishing line, or help Harley bring back a stray cow. Whatever comes up.

Althea generally sits at the bricked area between the day lilies and roses, near where the stakes for the new house are in the ground, underneath the high, willowy laurel tree decorated with a frieze of moss. Little outdoor water pump is right there, too, iron handle, sturdy spout dependable as can be, yet the look of a toy. A bent metal lawn chair, two of them, function as a tiny park Sister B has arranged. But too far from kitchen central for me.

Fried chicken dinner today. No wonder the vision of local hens giving their lives jumped up when we were here to do the wash: telling what's ahead. Not exactly warning, but a way in. Be Ready. Seems to work that way for me. Sometimes I wonder if everybody's brain operates like this.

That night, Wednesday, when Holland turned up the powers of *Power in the Blood* and we sang it again and again—which was good practice for the bass, I must say—folks went right into *There Is a Fountain Filled with Blood*. I took a breather on that one, lay the bass down carefully but sang out all the same. The words are arresting. Get this: *there is a fountain filled with blood/drawn from Immanuel's veins. Immanuel*, a name for Jesus—meaning *God with us*—but I never noticed those words before now. *Blood . . . drawn from Immanuel's veins.* I nearly quit singing. And here I am moving into the song from memory. Known the whole song all my life. *Drawn from Immanuel's veins?*

Why would words like that be in music. What's to sing about? Followed by, *and sinners plunged beneath that flood, lose all their guilty stains.* That purely gives me the heeby jeebies. I don't know what to do with draining veins / flooding stains. I want to ask somebody *howzat work*? But who, that's the real question.

Everybody acts normal as pecan pie about all this. Soon as the singing's over, they jump up and testify. Take Benny Hinson, "Ah member th'day, jus a lil ole barefoot boy, bout ten yar ole? M'deddy died at yar. We's livin at m'grenny's hass." Here an *Amen* catches in his throat, he swallows with a sob and raises his hands in praise.

Really touched my heart to think of this child at his grandmother's house, missing his daddy. Finding Jesus. But still, why all the blood? Does being washed in blood comfort a child about his dead daddy? Most of this goes through my head in pictures, not words. Small sad child, graveyards, blood. And all the scenes swirl back around circling a question mark. Gives me a shiver, I admit. Like a chill. *Washed in blood.*

The mattress covered in striped ticking airs outside on saw horses today.

Right under the pole where they hang the chickens to drain.

But then bring that image back up. Sister B's own blood when she delivered her boy to the world. Soak those mattresses through with blood and that changes the scene considerably.

On Wednesday night they go on and sing the last verse of *There Is a Fountain*. Listen to these sentiments: *by faith I saw the stream / thy flowing wounds supply.* Wounds . . . flowing. When a woman gives birth everybody rejoices except the woman. She does that later, I hope. With faith, I reckon, faith that this live birth and her life surviving it are worth the pain.

But I hear these stories ten, twelve, twenty years after the child was born. From what I can tell no woman forgets her wounds even though her son or daughter may never even realize how their own birthday story happened. At least not as vividly as the photographs that are forever alive inside their mama's body. They never go away, those pictures. Those images storm through these women and pour into my hearing.

"Cain't show no weakness. T' yer maan? Wimins cain't 'ford ta do it. Uh uh!" Here's some news. All this time I've been told men are to guard and protect the weaker sex. Isn't that what we're called? *Weaker* sex.

Sure, there's evidence otherwise. Maybe I just like the idea of protection in spite of what's in front of my eyes everywhere we go.

Images telegraph experience like the dots and dashes of Morse Code. Emotions, too. I didn't recognize the words when Sister Bernice's birthing stories filtered through still air around women bent to their tasks six years ago. But they're forever with me. Now the stories make plenty of sense.

Today it's feather plucking that's going on outside the kitchen door in the breezeway. The stench of seared pin feathers reach me on the front porch, sitting on the floor next to the corner of the breezeway having abandoned the swing due to excess squeakiness. Bent knees propping my literature book as I dawdle with memorizing an Emily Dickenson poem: *Tell the truth but tell it slant.*

This company of women, Bernice Rogers and Doris Skondeen, remember stormy weather of hard health times. Their stories of major physical events—birth, death of loved ones, being kicked by a mule—bubble up into all forms of loss and discomfort. And every one lifted a little higher by the other in the telling. And the retelling. Seems as if stories of their trials wear away the sharp edges as they repeat them, making the burdens they count up day by day easier to bear.

"Bein fair? Maan cain't know what wimins take on." Her *on* sounds like *own.* Sister B chuckles a humorless little laugh, "The'd run 'n hide, any maan hava idee what bringin out one chile's about, Sista Dor's!" Though I can't see them, I guess mother's nodding, murmuring her assent.

Scenes of fury rise up suddenly in sight and sound through my mind: my mother's tear-streaked face, my father's sullen frown, but most of all his deadly silence for days at a time. As if my mother isn't there, that's how he acts. Then her reluctant shift into a woman entirely agreeable. Mouthing his words, his opinions. Nodding. I've watched her body melt into his will, like when we left our home.

Here in the breezeway, quiet reigns for a time. Then the murmuring begins again. As if the lull provided time for refueling.

"You can catch you a buncha scorn. Showin yersef weak? 'Course a kind man a likes a auvr husbins don't say much aloud. Ya jus feels it."

"Feeling shame for being needy," mother confirms.

"Um-hmmm, but lettin em know ya down low ain't good like a said." Sister Bernice nods with her words.

"Maybe," mother continues, "Maybe they fear need in themselves most of all. Their own weakness embarrasses them . . ."

"Mmmhmm. Ah know'd thet fer im." Bernice says, "But what can ya do? Spect they fraid ta look too small."

Dawdling with slanted truth, my ears pay keen attention but a piece of my imagining flits off to the church house. Watching men shout and sing. Watching them strut their hallelujahs and amens. Not Harley Rogers, but maybe he's just more careful than the rest. Everybody talks about loving Jesus but not many care to listen to the heartaches of their own families.

Especially their women. Women have to be strong, enduring, and especially mind their men's frailties. Protect men from themselves. Is that the way it goes?

Turning the other cheek, treating even enemies with kindness sounds good until a man's own behavior comes into question. That goes for the Preacher, too.

Along with this dose of reality, Sister Bernice slips a kindliness note, "Course not the Preacha . . ." as if she's reading my mind. Her voice trails off, small to begin with then silence. Mother sounds as if she's holding an uncertain smile, "Meanin' to be what the Lord wants us to be. That's some kind of hard job. Doesn't mean we skip bein human."

"Ats true sayin!" adds Bernice Rogers.

Then an odd thing happens. Staring into the pages of my Calvert textbook, Mary, "Jesus' Mama" as Sister Watford up in Scratch Ankle referred to her when she and her Papa "carried at lil ole baby, eyes wou'n't open?" Taking that child over to a healing preacher's house. The baby's name was "Mary, fer Jesus' Mama . . ." Funny how the way somebody says a name— and she always says it with a long a, *Maary*—trips pictures in my head from the baby Mary with stuck-closed eyes to a San Francisco church and a life sized woman statue. Mary. *Jesus' mama*, there, always the same.

She wasn't always made of stone, Jesus' mama. She gave birth and we keep telling the story every Christmas. Just like Bernice soaked birthing blood through that mattress. Only difference was Mary's blood saturated the hay where she brought Jesus into the world, like the calves midwifed out of their mothers by Sister Bernice this spring.

Althea, born breech—bottom first—must have caused a fair amount of blood. And I tarried so long in the womb, mother says, Dr. Sox came close to carrying her over to the hospital instead of letting her stay at her mother's and father's house on Percival Street in Olympia, Washington, where I finally made my appearance. My grandmother, an RN, was assisting the doctor. No doubt plenty of blood involved, messy as can be.

So that's when I *was born the first time* as we say in church. How is it Jesus, a man, *His* blood cleanses us from sin being *born the second time*? Born again. But what about Mary. What about Jesus' Mama's blood?

Is it just that I've inherited my father's *gift of suspicion*, I wonder? He wouldn't like the shape of questions brewing here.

I hear talk, preachers and Bible teachers going on and on, believing there's comfort in explaining *what the Good Book says*. Maybe it helps others, even though a lot of it doesn't make a lick of sense to me. Being born the first time sheds plenty of life's blood for another life, I get that. But I don't know about that second birth. I sure don't know about that.

As for me, I don't believe it's just suspicion, but I am stubbon. I'm holding out for that miracle I sing about, the *miracle of love and grace*. And the child I was, soothed in the curve of the great Lion of Judah while the storm came for us in the night. The Lion's soft warmth, my pillow, as I was carried—tumbling—through the tornado. There was only rest with nothing to resist.

11

Waynesboro, Mississippi 1955

What a Friend

- *Mississippi: tornadoes kill twenty-nine in February.*
- *President Eisenhower proposes $101 billion highway development plan, one-third federally financed.*
- *McDonalds hamburger fast food restaurant founded by Ray Kroc.*[1]
- *Albert Einstein, physicist and humanist, dies in Princeton, New Jersey, heart failure, age 76. He likened faith to physics, saying, "If you asked me to prove what I believe I can't . . . There comes a point where the mind takes a higher plane of knowledge but can never prove how it got there. All great discoveries have involved such a leap."*
- *Marilyn Monroe's famous photo—white pleated skirt blown high over her legs—a scene from "The Seven Year Itch" shows up everywhere.*
- *"Lolita" by Vladimir Nabokov, sells outrage in a story of a twelve-year-old sexually bold girl.*
- *Rosa Parks refuses to sit in the back of the bus in Montgomery, Alabama, an act of civil disobedience.*
- *Reverend George Lee, Belzoni, Mississippi, uses his pulpit and printing press to urge others to vote; white officials offer protection if he will end his efforts; he refuses and is murdered.*[2]

1. *Wikipedia.com*, s.v. "McDonald's."
2. Southern Poverty Law Center, http://www.splcenter.org/GeorgeLee.

- *Emmet Till, 14-year-old from Chicago, visiting relatives in Money, Mississippi, kidnapped and brutally murdered; his killers acquitted by all-white, all-male jury.*[3]

- *Heat treating process for making steel includes the most common of annealing—heating to high temperatures, softening it—then quenching it in water or oil; rapid cooling results in a hard, brittle product needing to be tempered.*[4]

- *Audrey Skondeen is thirteen.*

HARD TO BELIEVE THAT this dusty two lane road bumping along in front of the Maynard Creek Assemblies Church near Waynesboro, Mississippi, has a number, 84, and connects to major highways. The elementary and high school buses pass by early mornings and mid-afternoons, kids all sizes and shapes yelling out the windows and tumbling around inside, a crazy automatic washing cycle gone human. Doesn't look like anywhere I'd like to be, but for these two weeks I'm living along the road they travel.

Beyond the church house yard the road bends and disappears into woods where signs of autumn already appear in the sweet gum trees. Their green to pale gold flares into orange and red in a couple of weeks. Something about fall pulls at my senses. Nudges me to sing *Just a Closer Walk with Thee* holding hands with everybody I've ever loved. *Everybody*. In a long line that snakes from here to San Francisco and loops up through Washington State and across Canada.

But no, not so grand a gesture for today. Instead, I'm learning to play *What a Friend We Have in Jesus* on the piano.

"Don't forget one instrument because you're learning another," mother warns, referring to the piano and the bass. Miss Guernsey taught me piano, coming to the house in Sacramento when we lived on 23rd Street. Her serious, broad face surrounded by a tidy bob of gray hair. If she'd had any verve at all in her voice, her face, her eyes, the music might have stuck. Inspiration. But she's a *Let's Begin* kind of lady with perfect posture even when she sleeps, just a guess.

What a Friend We Have in Jesus, like most songs in the Southern Gospel hymnal, fit right into intermediate level for learning piano. Four part harmony in shaped notes, and mother's showing me how to do left hand chording.

---

3. PBS, "Murder of Emmet Till," American Experience series, http://www.pbs.org/wgbh/amex/till.

4. *Wikipedia.com*, s.v. "steel."

A cemetery reads off the eastern slope of the Maynard Creek church property where headstones tell how long folks lived before the rest of the family followed them into the rectangular chain-link fenced graveyard. Husband or wife, mother and father, young man at 37, a child. A baby. Takes me back to Wetumpka and the memory of a little white casket.

Lonely as the cemetery feels, I tend to skip around that and go straight to the woods. Kudzu vines are missing here, no sign of their tangling together and smothering, the trees. Light and shadows play through pines made of a thousand spinning pinwheels in breezy sunshine. Hickory, sweet gum and mountain laurel cooperate as neighbors. Lacy, delicate leaves of the vines here, in varying shapes, reach high, and one has a fragile white flower that mimics a tiny morning glory waving through limbs and leaves.

Walking the edge of the trees listening to the mocking bird gather sounds and twirl them high into the sky draws me through late afternoon. The quiet cardinals, loud only in their red feathers, gather information for good nesting but don't socialize like other birds. Crows, jabber mouths of the forest, command attention or vie with stellar blue jays for most audacious.

Besides walking the road and the woods for exercise afternoons when my schooling is over, we practice our music or learn new songs. Although here, variety's not so necessary since no one has heard anything we've sung. Beginning the week singing *There's Room at the Cross*, a new tune from Stewart Hamblen, guarantees I'll be asked to sing it almost every night of the revival. I don't mind. Every time I sing a song sends it deeper. That's all I can say about that though I'm not sure what I mean.

A while after the high school bus passed today—maybe 4 or 4:30—I was returning from my walk in the woods, going toward the church house for some piano playing before supper, when a bicycle speeds up the road from the direction of the high school. He almost darted right by, then he did a crazy braking motion, whipping the rear tire around in the gravel at he edge of the road, heading him the opposite direction. He grins a lopsided grin, eyes sliding sideways with his upturned mouth, "You that Vangliss girl a heard 'bout?"

"That's me, all right."

"M'Aint Tattie an Unca Jim come to meetin las Sundy."

"Well where were you?" I ask the boy who's skin says he's seen this summer from the sunshine side.

"Wal, ahm s'wore out affer football practice . . ." he begins with a swagger.

"On Sunday?"

He shows his white teeth with a laugh that abandons good sense. Impossible not to join in. "Ya got me there, girl."

"Well. Show up, then." I look right into those giddyup green eyes without a flinch.

"You a pistol!" He says, swinging his agile frame back on board the bike, spinning tires cutting a swale through gravel as he takes off.

I walk on in the church—by now it's nearly suppertime—and play *What a Friend We Have in Jesus*, chording with the left hand. Play it through twice without a pause before I hear mom call me for supper.

At the time we met Waynesboro's pastor, Petey Simmons—camp meeting last summer—we were booked up through this spring. He liked what he heard and finally, we're here.

There's a lot of Jesus in the rolling hills of this county. Strewn through meadows where cattle graze you'll find three crosses in a stand of trees and wrought iron twisted into messages—*Today is the day of salvation*—stuck into lawns or decorating the side of the road. Billboards proclaim *Jesus is the Way, the Truth, and the Life. Prepare to Meet Thy God.*

Wayne County looks well ordered, religious. Even righteous in a country that's upset about communism and civil rights demonstrations raving through big cities. My father's newscasters harangue about the mingling of the two, Communists and Negroes. Small town Mississippi breathes normalcy unless you notice that over half the people in the area are Colored.

Remember Aberdeen? I sure do. Zorneely, too. It's a couple hours up the road from here, and Negroes are seen but not heard there, too. One bar b que place in Waynesboro buzzes like a hornet's nest slapped by a broom handle. Noon traffic flies in and out of the rickety screen door and the back entrance for Colored swings, too, besides clusters of folks at picnic tables outside. It's as if the sound's turned off on a TV screen. You see the people milling around mostly with their heads down, eyes averted, cooking, eating, sweeping, loading and driving delivery trucks. Busy part of the community but seldom heard. Like a pen's dark ink underlining a long, complicated bunch of verbs: The letters dance pulsing words, and the mark make it loud on the page, but there's no sense to it.

When we go to pick up the mail, details of a town show up both in the trip there and in the post office itself. Riffs of conversation snag on my curiosity as we wade through clumps of rough workers paused to roll a cigarette, trade ranch gossip or lie about their exploits.

Not entirely rough, of course. The sugar candy church ladies, prim faces and bless your heart hugs, trade words of blessing and gossip by way of prayer requests. *Ya know a Dillons shor needsa prayin fer.* They'll follow that up with a detailed outline of why, exactly, this family needs so much prayer.

In our address—*Skondeen, General Delivery, Waynesboro, Missis-sippi*—the town's the only part that changes, but you could lead me blind-folded into any post office in the US and I'd be able to tell you what kind of place it is by the aroma. Some people would say *stench*, maybe, but the mix of tobacco, dirt and sweat, plus a whiff of oiled wood, paste and papery cardboard never fails to soothe me everywhere I've ever been. A trace of bad perfume or powder sometimes streaks through but the overall effect doesn't change very much.

Clangs here and there from the numbered, sturdy 4x6-inch metal gates on the post boxes keep a rhythm in the place, opening and slamming after local people check for their daily dose of letters, papers and notices. Large windows in a row of wrinkled gold glass behind bars, face the front door and raise up during hours of operation. Heather blue uniformed US Postal employees stand in these windows at wooden sills worn to smooth, shallow valleys: General Delivery & Packages; Stamps & Money Orders or C.O.D. (Cash On Delivery) at another when there's more than one window.

Standing in line at the General Delivery window in Sylacauga, Ala-bama, a slope-shouldered man in dungarees still full of the fields who was ahead of us waited to receive a C.O.D. package in the wrong line. The post office person treated him with uncommon kindness. Didn't make him go to the other window but let him sign his X on the line and pay the money to receive his small box right there. Maybe the Postmaster knew him. Touched my heart.

Neither snow, nor rain nor heat, nor gloom of night stays these couriers from the swift completion of their appointed rounds, my social studies teacher in Sacramento wrote on the board as a reminder of the importance of the US Mail. Words engraved in the marble Post Office building at the corner of 8th Avenue and 33rd Street, across from Penn Station, he said, in New York City. I intend to see that building some day. Instantly, when the teacher chalked that message on the board and displayed the pony express symbol in a sideways oval, the oiled wood/sweat/tobacco, plus that whiff of paper/cardboard and paste welled up and the warm rush made me grin though I didn't say a word to anybody else. Too much to explain.

Rural route carriers here act out that New York City engraving every-day, trekking the mail along the sorriest roads, their beater trucks jumping sideways or up and down, with a *US Mail* sign stuck in the back window, sometimes driving up the wrong side of the road to load the boxes. Occa-sionally making deliveries in official mail trucks that have the pony express insignia on the side.

Sacramento friends don't write. Billy Butler sent one letter. After that, he no doubt became distracted like other people do. What's so hard? My troublemaking buddy Lee Ann from Bethel Temple Sunday School who was happy to sneak out to the coffee shop up the street, or, when we were at her house, go to the skating rink with her older brother and his friends, somehow leaks out all her Audacious when it comes to buying a stamp and sending a letter.

Truth is, people who never live far away from Normal have no idea how important mail can be. Letters equal friends and possibilities, learning lessons and keeping track. But I keep that to myself. Who else would care that much, anyhow? I admit this to me and me alone. The General Delivery window explains who make up our list of friends. To everybody else we're just strangers passing through.

All my dad has to say is "Ready?" and we're on the way, usually about 11:30, so we'll have mail to read at the dinner table around noon. Our first request at the window when we arrive reaps a fine harvest. People like Auntie Dorie, Pauline Brown in Wildwood, Florida, and lately her boy Albert writing to Althea, label their letters in advance of our arrival, *Please Hold*. That assures us of a stack when we ask, *Any mail for S-k-o-n-d-e-e-n, General Delivery*? Always have to spell our name.

Air's as clouded with tobacco smoke as with half eaten words spit out through brown juice. Two louche buddies wasting time. Loud, slurring their conversation in half sentences while they slap people around they don't even know. Then they reach for snarls.

"Em commies . . ." echoing the headlines on the local paper, the usual stack in a bin at the door blaring *Ike Warns Red Threat*. When talk kicks off with communism and winds up with bombs over the US being the President's rationale for a national highway system—safe evacuations to where, I don't know—you know talk at the Post Office will pump itself up.

As we leave, ignorance still holds forth. A grizzled little guy with stained bristly muzzle hurls out a string of epithets, *pinko yankee nigra lovas* you can hear fairly often around Southern towns. He promises his tall, skinny buddy, propped up by a post office wall that all these people are doing is "stirrin up trouble, 'n leaves us nuttin but trouble when they packs up they bus and heads noth."

Buddy nods, "Thems's happy, yeah, em darkies perfeckly satissfied, til em commie yanks show up."

Can't help but wonder if their lawns have *Jesus Saves* signs on them, considering the number of crosses, scripture verses and signs of righteousness turning up along these dirt roads. Hang around long and you learn that advertised salvation might have some twists and turns in it. All you have to do is listen.

When the subject of race arises, my stomach tightens and Zorneely's stricken face flashes a warning light. What to do, what to do. Freezes me every time. Seldom see Colored people in the post office. Usually I notice their entrance but in a small mail room there's not enough space for that. Just a window off to the side or certain hours where they come and go like shadows against the light. They're better off staying away.

Friday night's date night, driving gaggles of Wayne County teens into the churchyard. Backed up at tall open windows, snuggled close, giggles preparing summer air for night fall sure as roosters wake up the morning. All the while, the church house chugs out sounds wild as the dance hall we passed in Birmingham one spring night. Besides our music, a nineteen-year-old boy with unfortunate facial skin who's wishing for Althea's glance, plays his guitar, and a man whose willowy height confuses his blond hair with currents from the 'lectric fan stands at the edge of the platform whaling on his ukelele.

The Evangelist makes it known that everybody's welcome to *play along* and by the sixth night of revival, which this is, the sound intensifies. Harmonica just showed up, a new guy. Maebell Hawkins pounds a mean, which is to say right-in-sync, tambourine. *Over in the Glory Land, In the Highways, In the Hedges, I'll Fly Away,* surrounded by clapping, foot stomping and singing on the beat ignites the warm night inside as fireflies flash the dark outside.

Never doubt there's dancing in the Holy Ghost up and down the aisles. Nobody's expected to hold back and the service hasn't even begun. I can see *Preacher Petey,* folks call him around here, immersed in the music and at the same time checking the aisles. He knew the Skondeen Family could bring on Revival. It's happening.

Green eyed boy turns up this afternoon, slower on his bike, but faster too. Slithering through the double church doors sideways—they were standing slightly open—and trotting up the center aisle, leaning against the piano as I finish playing *What a Friend We Have in Jesus,* ignoring him til the end. I let him be the first to speak.

"Heared ya slap a bass fiddle, too. Bigger 'n you."

"Mmmmhmmm, but I'm keeping up on learning piano . . ."

He slides onto the piano bench, "Teach m'sumpin, whyn't cha."

Sudden *boyness* impact moves me an inch or two toward the other end of the bench, the *pow* sensation I'm not sure I recognize. A mix of dust, sweaty heat and sweet mystery. Added space lets me turn a little, casting a sideways glance. "There may not be time. Enough. Time." the words swan out and circle him. That causes hard laughter, alerting me to the sound reaching parents who could charge in here any minute, even though the trailer is parked in back of the church and Sunday School rooms are in-between. For caution's sake I unfold myself in time to the words I just said and stand to lean against the walnut veneer of the ancient upright, grinning down at his boldness.

"Where ya goin?"

"Finding some room for me . . ." I begin.

"Ah sceer ya?" Sly eyes tilt toward me.

"Well, now, maybe we can start the learning, here, with some manners. Introducing yourself? You know. A name." After another bout of merriment, not so loud this time thank goodness, he rises at the other end of the bench, bows ceremoniously and says, "Ma'am m'name's James. Some folks like m'Ain't Tattie 'n Unca Jim calls m'Jimbo."

"James. I'm Audrey." Even the Evangelist rarely calls me *Spark Plug* any more. That would be awkward for a teen-ager. Sometimes he'll refer to me that way when we're in places that remember the younger Audrey. Not here.

A grin cranking out highlights for his angular, sunny face, substitutes as a sufficient handshake across the bench. Not one to allow much silence, James instantly launches into a tshirt declension, unleashing a past perfect description of the scrimmage that left this particular once white t shirt dirt streaked and torn.

As he rattles along I saunter toward him around the bench, bypassing him even while I give him my attention, leading him back out of the church house doors. Safely outside, I lean against one of the porch posts. Countering his rendition of football field glory with, "Sounds like they nearly tore you to shreds, too. Besides the shirt."

Everything I say strikes him as uncommon humor and while he indulges himself with a knee slap or two, I slide down and sit on the top cement step where he lands as well. Far enough away not to crowd me this time. "Na, ahm too tough fer em guys ta tar me up."

Late enough afternoon, crickets begin to scratch their way through the bird calls. Close to suppertime, too.

His lights go on with an urgent question, "Say, na, what ya do fer school . . . er . . ."

I launch my explanation of distance learning that's now turned into International Correspondence School for high school which I do not like as well as Calvert, but they only go to eighth grade and I'm at least up to tenth by now. Skipped two grades. He reckoned we quit traveling during the school year. People telling him that Althea finished high school while we were settled in California, he's decided this must be the solution. How else. But school in the trailer? Now that beats all.

"We did settle down for my sister's last year of high school, so she could go to college? Without a hassle 'bout credentials. But she chose not to go on to school." I offer a small shrug, "Here we are."

"Trav'lin a'gin," he finishes, "Ya like it?"

"Well . . ." I begin, when my mother's whistle calls me to supper. She probably imagines I'm walking in the woods nearby. I smile, jump up, saying, "Hey, now, James! Thanks for stoppin by. See ya," and wave myself away around the edge of the church house in the direction of the trailer.

His question, simple as it seems, stumps me. Never once gave any thought for an answer to words about liking it. When people comment they assume. "Y'all s'forch'nant, cain't say *lucky*, cuz it's fer Jayzus!" Somebody said something close to that this week: *Called. By God.* When the Evangelist decides to pick up and go, he doesn't ask his wife or anybody else, does he? He announces. Everybody starts packing when God calls, which sounds a lot like my father's voice. Since Sacramento, I know the difference and that's trouble.

Tonight, James shows up in the back of his Aunt Tattie's and Uncle Jim's pickup well before the start time of seven, the boarded sides for hauling hay appearing to be his cage though he leaps free before they've finished parking in the side yard. We're tuning up to play when they arrive and by now, revival night's on its way, speeding from *Gloryland* into full flight and winding up with *Will There Be Any Stars*, people singing the chorus over and over again. Don't even bother with the verses:

> *Will there be any stars, any stars in my crown,*
> *When at evening the sun goeth down?*
> *When I wake with the blest in the mansions of rest,*
> *Will there be any stars in my crown?*

Everybody's headed for the stars tonight and the Evangelist, playing along with his fiddle in fit country form revels in the excitement.

We took a chance on Waynesboro, trusting the pastor's promise that two weeks ignites a higher flame here rather than finally flickering out. "We run on Holy Ghost p'wr. Yessiree. Folks love a Lawd!" The Preacher's test driving those words tonight. You'd think he overheard the question about liking to travel and fills in the blanks right up front. With so many new faces, specially young people, he introduces our family again, then launches into why we're here:

> Now you may ask,
> Who needs an evangelist?
> Lookit all the music
> you've got here in Wayne County, Mississippi!
> Amen, Pastor Petey?
> Why Gloryland's right here n now!

People laugh and the local pastor, white shirt sleeves already rolled up, jumps up beside him from where he's seated on the platform, swiping his high, damp forehead with a man's faded blue kerchief, sandy hair roughed back above round headlight blue eyes in a pale but Jesushappy face, "Yassir, praisa Lawd amighty! Brotha Skondee," and he slaps the guest Preacher on the back, appreciating being appreciated. The Evangelist usually scoffs at such talk when he hears other people do it. Calls it *throwing fish* like we see the trainers do for the flapping seals in their show at the San Francisco Zoo.

Sure enough, Pastor Petey encourages a round of applause peppered with shouts for all their musicians, "An how 'bout y'alls sangin fer the glory a Gawd!" He says to the crowd, raising the flapping sound a notch higher. But the Preacher hits it harder still into the microphone.

> Well, why evangelize, then!
> Friends, if the Gospel really is a matter of life and death,
> Heaven or Hell!
> It's horrible to think millions even here in America
> will live out their lives 'thout havin a chance to hear n
> receive the Gospel of our Lord n Savior Jesus *Christ*.
> Now is the time to act!
> Not tomorrow!
> Even God can't make us happy, but brothers and sisters,
> *I Know Whom I Have Believed*!

And the crowd moves wave-like reaching a Glory shore into all five verses of the song, repeating the chorus, *But I know whom I have believed and am persuaded that He is able to keep that which I've committed until Him against that day. Repeating the verse, bringing the people into the sway of the song.*

Big a boom as he lowers at the start, he figures for a Friday night crowd, still, and the Preacher lightens up when his message comes around. He preaches on the Tater Family: Dick Tater thinks he knows it all, doesn't need anybody's help. Agi Tater, always spreading gossip tearing up families and running suspicion through the whole county. Spec Tater, like a sponge takes all kinds of blessings in but can't witness and gives nothing out. Imi Tater, on the other hand, has no back bone, easily swayed by junk as worthless as TV commercials, think of it! Common Tater has plenty to say but can't think for himself, and Hesi Tater tells everybody how well qualified she is but never does anything.

The crowd's in the palm of his hand with their laughing, shouting recognition. Then he brings the question, "But who are you? How does God see *you!*" By the time I'm up to sing the altar call, *It Is No Secret*, people are praying aloud, pleading for mercy, help, and pardon.

Bells of the vibra harp led by soft accordion brings up the music for Stuart Hamblen's song from the Billy Graham crusade. Just after the opening chords when I sing into the mic, *It is no secret what God can do*, the quieted crowd soars with the violin's accompaniment.

> *What He's done for others, He'll do for you*
> *With arms wide open He'll welcome you*
> *It is no secret what God can do*

Beginning with the chorus brings folks in, then the verse locates each one for the meaning:

> *The chimes of time ring out the news*
> *Another day is through*
> *Someone slipped and fell*
> *Was that someone you?*

The response tucks into the already saved with plenty of tarrying to do over those who reckon they've slipped this very day. Not as much speaking in tongues on a night owned by sinners and backsliders. Preacher and Pastor both worn out tonight, but the singer is secretly exhilarated. A warmth from outside the church house flows in, an unnamed, unspoken glow.

Saturday morning announces itself by bird calls through the raised vent in the trailer's ceiling. I'm imagining a wide-open day for wandering followed by reading or whatever I feel like, until mother says at the breakfast table, "Be sure the Post Office run is early enough to be ready when Pastor Petey and his wife come by. Bout noon? They'll show us the way over to the Wilson's for dinner. All of us invited for 12:30 or so." My father grumbles at both the restriction on a free day for study as well as the prospect of a local cook showing off for the Preacher with too much rich food. I can read his mumbles with or without words.

I have no idea who the Wilsons are and mother's vague descriptions of medium height, Sister Wilson shouts a lot and he's real quiet and sits toward the back while she's up front in the shouting corner, don't help. Maynard Creek Assembly fills up every night this week, some different, some new. Hard to keep track of the changes. But I'll admit to some distraction in looking for one specific green eyed tan face somewhere in the crowd.

Driving up to the church after being in town, Brother Petey and Sister Agnes brighten, seeing us from where they stand out front talking to mother. She calls Althea to come hop in the car and the other two head toward their 1955 Chevy pick-up. This pastor works construction, days, to support serving the church. "Workin fer Jayzus ain easy onna *finance*! Gotta carry more'n one job *praisisname*." Of course a lot of pastors do this but not all of them with this good attitude.

We're barely settled in the car and mother starts relaying the conversation between her and Sister Agnes. Or Aggie as some folks call her, a woman who wears her intelligence well, shrouding it as she does in just enough country talk and just enough good grammar to be any place she chooses. She teaches at the high school so she's able to fill in more blanks than just family circles and besides, she's well versed from every angle in just how those circles overlap. Example to her students and trusted, Sister Agnes turns into a prayer partner at the church house.

Seems that Brother and Sister Wilson rescued their nephew from being a *mothaless chile*. Says the Wilsons never had a family of their own and *Miz Wilson? Bless er heart! At Tattiebell grabbed a holt a that chile as if he's er own youngin*. Surprising to hear mother quote her just as she said it.

This story creeps up on me in an uh oh kind of way. As the description unfolds, a weightless live electric charge begins around my chest and spreads.

Now mother's speaking low and confidingly in the front seat and I have to strain every listening bone I have for her words, "Some folks." She pauses with meaning and starts again, leaning a little closer to my father, "*Some folks*' opinion is that they *spoilt* this boy, willful as he is, treating him like a *lil prince*. Says he never comes around church, surprised to see him last night at revival. But even with all their indulging the boy, to quote Sister Agnes, *cain't hardly blame em, he's such a cutie pie*. Imagine!" My mother ends with a note of undiluted disgust. In our family *cutie pie* buys you nothing.

And my father's response, completely unsurprising, "Lord help us, Doris, good Christian people can't keep the Word: Spare the rod, spoil the child. Gotta train up a child." He shakes his head, exhaling with disgust.

Unca Jim and Aint Tattie Wilson with James the willful, spoiled orphan prince in a ragged, dirty tshirt. Have mercy. The warning of a storm moving over the landscape and putting me on notice at least beats out total surprise. Questions begin to rise, *how's he going to act when he's being watched? In close company?* Sitting on the platform as many nights as I do, I know how to stare straight ahead, smiling faintly. Being Good. Pretty sure I can pull off being Blank Evangelist's Daughter. I've practiced.

Off the main dirt road where the lined up loaf-shaped mailboxes congregate on sturdy wooden stems, a long dusty track brings us across a rattling cattle guard to a chorus of three brown speckled hunting hounds, long ears flying as they race alongside. They bark our approach to the sunflower house trimmed in white, startling in the hazy air of late summer.

Porch swing's still in motion as Brother Wilson stands to greet the approaching guests, the features emphasized on his face of a grand size nose, eyes deep set into bushy brows, with a frowning-smile sort of mouth that's free of brown stains, all a little too large for the narrow, bony frame slicked on top with thinning gray hair. Medium build and I'm sure, to my father's relief, not a heavy man in girth. Maybe dinner won't be too rich after all.

He grins a gruff, "'Lo folks," as Aunt Tattie bangs through the screen door, wiping her hands on a checkered apron the color of a woodpecker's head she's wearing over khaki skirt and brownish blouse. Sharp nose, small dark eyes under round black wire glasses above pursed lips, tight lines mooring them to the rest of her face, giving the impression of a stern schoolmarm. A permanent look of skepticism I remember noticing when she's with the shouters—how out of place she seemed—yet the flood of excitement in the Holy Ghost smoothes her face to a shine once the singing and praising take hold.

Sister Wilson's hair bun is caught in a snare of brown netting that darkens some of the gray, but the fray of cooking all morning allows natural strands to show up around her face, "Praisa Lawd, Brothas, Sistas! An iss wonna-ful musical girl," nodding to the adults and taking Althea's hand, "You add s'much special to a meetin!" Althea blushes and manages a smiling *thank you*.

From across the driveway, direction of the barn, comes a motor-growl slowing to a halt as a tractor half the size of the house roars into view. High up at the wheel, James, parking the dusty yellow behemoth at the fence rail alongside the driveway, swinging down to his Unca Jim's, "Hey na, Jimbo, don chu leave at! Taker inna barn, ya heah?"

But James is already on the ground, bounding across the driveway in his uniform of tattered blue jeans and once white tshirt. Having made an entrance, now nonchalant in answering his uncle while denying the guests' presence entirely, "Nah, Unca Jim, ah ain sloppy w'the high n mighty tracta, ahm gonna putter right, donchu worry none!" Only after he's inches away does he say, standing at my elbow while pretending I'm not there, "Why lookit heah, a Vangliss an a Pastah Petey, too, hey y'all!" What an actor.

Sister Wilson opens the screen door to welcome us. One by one we straggle through the portal—me, last—James hangs back and whips around silently, catching the door just as I'm about to go through it, quietly suggesting, "Whyn't chu stay out onna porch?" I shake my head and go on in the house, ducking under his arm holding the door, dangerously close to his warmth, and sit on the worn brown matellassé foot stool where Althea's perched on a matching overstuffed chair. He stays in the doorway, hanging half in, half out, shoving it with his foot in a nervous gesture that won't let it close.

The busyness of dinner's final preparations are underway. Dishing up chop greens cooked with ham hock in a pastel yellow crockery bowl, bringing out the matching oval platter of already-sliced ham ringed in pineapple slices, heaping a sturdy red Georgia clay mixing bowl with potato salad from tupperware taken out of the refrigerator, shaking the green jello mold onto a pale rose colored dinner plate. Women guests help as Aunt Tattie loudly directs, and the whole busy production takes up half an hour.

The rest of us linger in polite, hovering conversation while the helpers buzz back and forth, kitchen to dining room, the other side of the wide dividing arch. Wooden bookshelves line both sides between where we sit stalled in the living room and the heavily laden table.

Sister Agnes makes finding a place around the oval oak table easy, smiling her teacher-to-new-student smile at me, not caring a bit about showing teeth crowded or crooked, set in her wild roses complexion, hair fluffed out like a golden angel's in spite of attempts to pull it into a ring in back, "Heah ya go, Sweet Pie," she says, pulling out the chair next to her and patting it for me. This room's one window on the outside wall lets in very little light thanks to a giant Chinaberry tree. So that means even in day time the small dim bulbs of a wagon wheel chandelier overhead turn out artificial glow for the table.

Last dinner option for the table, a tin covered with a cloth dishtowel, arrives with James' pronouncement as he casually slides into the chair next to me on the other side from Sister Agnes, "M'Ain Tattie's cornbread's a bess in alla world! Y'all sure lucky she's a cookin fer ya." His aunt smiles a tiny smile attempting to be shy, "Aw, Jimbo . . ." as we wait for the blessings, first from Pastor Petey, then, by request from the host, the Evangelist.

My father detests having to be in people's homes with the pastor there, too. "As if we're going to steal folks away, gotta keep a watch . . . ," he grouses in private. That doesn't seem to be an attitude belonging to Brother Pete, but you never know.

Anyhow, my father needn't be concerned about being watched at this meal because I'm the one under surveillance. Aunt Tattie's hawkish little eyes are on me every other second though she never says a single word directly to me.

Meantime, a hand brushes my arm, a foot grazes mine. James finds every way to get close. He could write an instruction manual on nonchalant moves in public places. I have to admit I'm grinning like crazy to myself.

But wading through talk and dinner weighs me with chores I've never handled before this. Smiling, saying practically nothing to everybody around the table, explaining my schooling to sister Aggie and being gracious, I hope. Meantime I'm acting as if I'm ignoring football boy with cheeks of tan, blond streaked hickory brown hair falling across his face and shrugged off now and then.

He can't be shrugged off, that's for sure. Pastor asking him about the team this year encourages a glowing description by his uncle of how many times Jimbo scored the year before this one. Still living on the glory. This, being his senior year and last season, Aunt Tattie adds, smiling at Althea. He must be at least seventeen. Hadn't thought about ages.

A clatter of dishes being stacked takes over the conversation, *Sister Tattiebell*, as Agnes calls her, announcing that she has pineapple upside down cake for later. And as she does, James declares, "'Nother treat, y'all. Ain Tattie, donchu reckon a Vangliss an a girls oughta see a creek yonder? How bout a walk, whatta ya say?"

She almost smiles, shifts from one foot to the other standing in the kitchen doorway, hands full with the platter of ham leavings, "Wal, Shug, mebbe afta we tidies up?" Her eyes flashing full bore into the side of my head as she turns and heads toward the sink. But I do not notice. Keep smiling at Sister Agnes thinking up nice things to say, "You surely must enjoy teaching." Never felt so fake.

As the women rinse and stack dishes over Aunt Tattie's weak protests, I linger just outside the kitchen door, hearing her shift out of, "No need to be a heppin . . ." and other kindly talk among Sisters in Christ, to raving about "At cheerleadin bunch at chases auvr Jimbo all a time. Ain neva seen nothin like it, girls got no sense a bein decent no more. Not your girl, Althea, Sista Skondee. Na she's purely fine. Holness Chris-like girl!"

Sister Agnes murmurs something about knowing two of the cheerleaders, "real good. They sweet Christians! Baptiss, course. Not yer holness."

James swerves back into the dining room, catching my hand, whispering, "C'mon, we leavin . . . ," letting go of one finger at a time as they slip out of his, walking through the empty living room and out onto the porch where the men are holding forth on Jesus. They're talking about the Last

Days. That means before Jesus returns in the Rapture to take us as His own. There could be Tribulation and it's lookin like it. Heads shake at the current news.

"Unca Jim, whacha say we git started on at walk we up to?" Uncle Jim looks startled and says, "Shor nuff, speck we'll be comin right along, Jimbo."

James walks backward in the direction opposite the barn and still un-putaway tractor where a wide path enters a wooded glen resembling those around the church house. He's facing the men, still, calling, "Y'all don tarry s' long, catch up perty quick, okey dokey?" I'm about as far away from him as I can be while going toward the same destination. My father's frowning, staring after us, starts to rise, sits back down. Says, "We'll be along, kids," his eyes stern, focused with a *help us Lord* kind of attention to my cheery, "See y'all soon."

I confess to some nerves about here. Feeling what shameless cheer-leaders Sister Wilson abhors might be like, even though I'm not the one who's making this plan. But I am going with it.

Out of sight of the house, James says, "Mebbe," linking two fingers with two of mine, swinging along the generous trail, jaybirds squawking and a chat-tery chickadee calling, "we can take a dip inna creek."

"Mebbe," I smile back at him, "we should keep moving." Mocking the challenge, he plants himself on the trail and twirls me around to face him, "Tha Vangliss girl's shor cute. And sweet. *Sweet Pie* like Sista Aggie says."

I laugh and run ahead of him, jumping over a downed log, pausing at a fork in the trail. "Issa way to a creek," taking his turn to run ahead of me. A *crack* from the sky sounding Pegasus' whip bringing thunder and lightening from Mount Olympus, arrests both of us. For a quick minute I consider telling him the story from Calvert's course in mythology, then reconsider. Slowed, looking up at clouds suddenly darker in their shuddering, and then tumbling with a streak of white light.

"Whoaaaaaa! din't see at a comin," James registers emergency on the run and rushes ahead, firmly taking hold of my hand, "They's a ole moon-shine still up ahead, mostly boards n junk, but 'nough roof ta shield froma rain." We stumble along toward the defunct still, yelling and laughing as big drops splat us, not stopping til the leanto is overhead.

"Whew," I look around the tiny ruin full of presumably happy spiders filling every available corner, random drops drizzling us.

"Better'n nothin," James grins, close up. Slides the hand that isn't holding mine up my back into the ringlets at the nape of my neck, a heated breeze with what feels like wind chimes running through me. "Love em curlycues," he says, real slow, as he bends to touch my mouth with his. Lightly. Smiling, backing away from me a little, then again, memory testing reality. And again, slower, moist clouds moving the sky above us in gentle motion. That mysterious boyness, sweet salty warmth settles in close.

A weightless electric impulse that began to spread in my chest back there in the car, alive, lifts and shimmers. Breath, brief as it is, returns. But grounding, too. At first it's just rain finding another missing shingle in the roof, then an actual busy feeling around my feet intervenes,

"Eeee! Ants!" Screeching, then laughing as scurrying creatures charge across my brown leather sandals and up my legs toward the hem of my blue flowering forget-me-nots sun dress.

James yells, "Stomp!" Can't quite stomp enough to get free.

"Let's get outta heah!" he commands, both of us running into the soft summer rain in the madness. We stand in the waning showers grinning. I say, "Wow, that was special, doncha think?" We can't stop laughing on a further dash toward the creek. He's pulling me by the hand but I let go to flop my shoes off, wading at the edge of the water to rid myself of creeping critterliness. The feeling lingers even after I can't see a single creature.

Or maybe it's a jumble of too many sensations. I just can't sort them out right here, right now. "We better get back, or . . ."

"They be sendin outta posse?" James supplies. Helping me over the rocks at the edge of the creek, he moves closer in when I'm on the grassy bank. Smiling, leans over and kisses me again, "What'm ah gonna do when y'all gone on outta heah?"

Swinging back up the path, I say, "You can write me a letter. General Delivery? Wherever we go. I'll give you the list."

He cocks his head sideways, looks at me, "Playin Post Offss, huh?" After we've tossed that around a spell, he sighs, "Awwww righty na. Ah might could do that. Ennythang ya say!" He runs a hand through my hair for a farewell to our secrets, and our tacit agreement's sealed by a smiling kiss on both my hands. We run most of the way back.

Being out of breath as if we're outdistancing the downpour looks better. Everybody's on the porch as James, first one out of the woods, yells, "What happen a y'all, *huh*?" Beating them out of wary looks, his rapid fire story of thunder, lightening and ants plows through their possible suspicions.

This guy sure can handle adults. His Aunt Tattie's even laughing by the time he's finished. A rare accomplishment any place except where James is concerned.

"We sorry ya missed alla fun," he adds, teasing, in Althea's direction. My reserved sister seems to find him charming though it's hard to read her. She offers a sweet smile, saying, "Can't say I'm sorry to miss the ants."

Rain floods the sky for about quarter of an hour, promptly at four o'clock on the following Friday afternoon, right about the time James usually swooshes in. He's missing. Minutes later, Uncle Jim's truck splashes along the road, bikes and boys helter skelter in the back. One lanky figure pretzled around the end of the hauling boards, leans precariously over the road grinning in the direction of the church house. I'm watching from the shelter of the inside of the church as the acrobat for the rattle trap parade rumbles by, perfectly happy not to be visible.

Still, where I sit at the piano, I'm not in the mood for treading the black and white keys any more. Nor can I free myself and walk outside to shake off an insistent reverie. Thing is, I can feel the soft approach of his visit on other days this week. The rest of the family was in the church practicing new music on Tuesday, so he rode by slowly and, hearing the music, kept going. But Wednesday and Thursday everybody else was, as usual, resting before supper and the evening meeting. Even in his absence a feeling of warmth turning toward me rushes through and overwhelms my senses. I'm still here when mother whistles me in for supper.

Now it's a full hour before the last Friday of the Maynard Creek Revival begins, but I'm ready. Fiddling with the bass, plucking imaginary tunes out of my head. Can't make myself be at the piano where I do most of my running up and down, making up melodies.

My parents dawdle in through the side door one at a time, mother tidying up our music books, *preparing to pack them up*, I think to myself. Trading ideas on special music, the Evangelist mildly complains, "Get s'riled up with hollerin', singin', stompin', need something to settle down before the preaching." An added edge of irritation, "They need to slow down 'n listen!"

Solo? Mother asks him and they agree, *Audrey, how bout There's Room at the Cross*, a statement whose answer is always yes, another song by Ira Stanphill, sung a lot at the Billy Graham Crusade. Everybody raves over it and I do love to sing it, too.

I nod, absent minded, not really here. Watching the air outside soften to that peach glow from last rays caught from the falling sun, air thickened with left behind reminders of rain. Leaves, wet, the woods shimmer and glisten in the gathering quiet of evening.

Random practice over, I wander back to the trailer. The screen's ajar, my father entered ahead of me, and he's seated so he's facing the door. He says nothing, but an alert, distant as an echoing bell, distinct, travels along my spine as I feel his eyes on me. An instant wordless experience of a memory of *being* his eyes arises as I carefully practice the specific art of being casual, going to my clothes laid out for the evening at my space in the back. He leaves so the girls can get dressed. I breathe easier.

Seems very long ago, that Spark Plug alert of always being at my father's service. Constant attention to what he needed to see. Now, he's watching me. Red dress Althea and mother made me after we saw one like it in *Seventeen Magazine*—it's two pieces and fitted to the pressed box pleats at the hip—rallies my anticipation for the evening. I shrug off the Evangelist's silence with one last trip to the bathroom, at least they have an indoor toilet here between the Sunday School rooms, not a miserable outhouse.

Instead of going straight into the church and onto the platform through the back door for the beginning music, I walk around to come through the side entry. Shadows near the steps come alive with a husky "Hey girl . . . ," James quickly hooking my finger with his as I pass, and me, attempting to keep my pace up toward the door and into the bright lights of the church house. My heart becoming a loud drum, ribs used as sticks, *thrumming*.

The prediction holds true. Music tonight sets a racer's pace and we've added a couple of guitars, besides. "Looks like ever country boy in a 50 mile radius bought himself a Gibson, Doris," the Preacher grouses under his breath.

Whether a church in these parts has indoor plumbing or not, certainly it has an ace sound system. This one has both. And Bubba Jackson keeps the amps turned loud and clear.

When I rise to sing *There's Room at the Cross*, the crowd begins to settle. Listen. The buzz in the church house and outside, too, stills. Am I imagining? I pause, standing there just a beat with no sound before I give my mother an imperceptible nod to begin. No, that's not my imagination. There's a hush.

From the first words, music soft as warm honey pours around the heart that pounded tympani earlier, soothing. Beginning with the chorus:

There's room at the cross for you
There's room at the cross . . . for you
Though millions have come
There's still room for one

Then the verse, and a difference emerges. Not a single sound or movement, even from outside.

Though millions have found him a . . . friend

Maybe it's the slight pause before for *you*, the tiny difference in *you*, or *friend*. The timing, hardly noticeable in the moment but unmistakable in sound. Somewhere through the enchantment of deep vibrations floating out over the warm, close evening air, another voice breaks through. Just past the word, *friend*.

Help us Lord . . .

Is this the first? Second? That old panic starts to surface. My father's warning ring of a sure confrontation to come, alien and cold, rising as it does through sultry air. For a second the fear rattles me, then quickly, I'm recovered. I set aside his threat. Breathe. Continue.

There's room at the cross . . . for you.

Quiet continues after the last note.

Entirely unusual. Nobody moves, shouts, or prays. There's one more dark, growled *Help Us Lord* cut short by Minnibee, oldest woman in the county from what I've heard, her low moan hardly audible at first, then soaring. Her voice comes out larger, grander than she is, a howling wind. "Holy, ho o ly, ho o o ly, ho o o ly, ho o o o oly, ho o o o oly . . ." a prayer urgent as the air that moved waters across the earth before creation. Others join the irresistible siren song, drawing heart, soul, spirit into one vast wave covering us. Healing me. Anxiety melting away in the immensity.

If I had to recite the Preacher's topic, even a word of what he says tonight, or be lynched? I'd be lynched. Not a single phrase sticks.

Altar call, the Preacher switches an earlier plan for me to sing *Softly and Tenderly*, instead he and mother perform, *I Am Coming, Lord.* Folks streaming toward the front touch my shoulder where I sit on the aisle as they pass by. Then, kneeling, head in my hands as my parents sing. After I rise, there's such a flood of folks jumbled in the first three rows extending the altar area, my place is nudged for space and I move closer and closer to the side door. Observing where everybody's located, I slip into the friendly dark beyond the steps, headed to the rooms around back.

James materializes again, this time like magic at the back door, whispering, "Hey Girl—ya shor sang 'im ta heav'n t'night . . . wheweee!"

I say nothing.

"You OK, Shug?" touching my arm tentatively.

I nod.

"Lookee heah—ah gotta scrimmage t'morrah? Satiddy?—can ya meet up w'me fer a walk, ya know at ole bridge up aroun a bend . . . under a bridge? Mebbe walk inna creek."

I'm still silent, but emit a "hmmmmm" sound. Thinking. He adds, "Brang at list, a one fer a Poss Of'ss, huh?"

"I'll try. Gotta go." Then I take the two steps in one, going through the door and into the bathroom. Pull the chain on the dangling light bulb and sit on the lid of the toilet until I can regain my senses that are flopping around wildly, panicked rabbits in a sack.

Flashes of my younger self come up, fairly trembling on a church bench after one *Help Us Lord* was tossed out for my benefit. Doesn't matter what town: Florence, Alabama, Williamsport, sitting with Peggy? Columbus or Beaverton. Scratch Ankle, Nell whispering to me. If I'm distracted or turn my head away more than once from full attention, or swing my legs, the instant voice correction either takes or there's a whipping with the belt later on. That's after the third *Help Us Lord*. Thought I grew out of it since I haven't heard those threatening words this time on the road. Maybe not.

Slowly, those who are kneeling, praying, and pleading, rise and drift away. I'm back in the front, sitting on the first bench. Sister Agnes lingers next to me, dabbing at the moist smile on her face, "Least three sinnahs welcome on home," Sister Agnes tells me, patting my arm, "that's some sangin, praise Jayzus!" I manage a weak smile in response.

One of those sinners is Hattie Marshall's nephew, here on leave from the army. His red hair and freckles wet with sweat and earnest tears, he takes my hand just as I stand to leave, thanking me "fer sangin." Fresh snuffles, he looks away, "touch m'heart." That's mutual. I murmur, "Well, thank the Lord, Brother."

Althea and mother mosey back to the platform after everyone has gone, working out different chords for something that was sung tonight. I don't know what. Just noise, everywhere.

Instead of going on out of the church like I'm headed, I sit on the steps of the side entry staring into the dark. Lightening bugs flashing, a cricket chorus humming through the woods turn into the most comfort I've had today. All week I've played the part of a Negro shadow, walking. Attempting invisibility, wanting no comment. No trouble.

I failed.

And now I can't dawdle any longer. My body heavies to lead weight walking the few steps back to the dreaded confines of the trailer house. A dim circle of light falls through the screen door. As I step inside, the sound of my father's throat being cleared comes from where he's sitting on the back settee underneath my bed that's still hooked to the ceiling. He says not a word, but the container called *home* is charged. Never felt so tight.

"Humph, use ta be a Spark Plug," first words.

Staring straight ahead at the opposite wall from where I've walked in, poised with my hand on the table. He escalates, "What's this, now. *Hollywood?*"

I start to look toward the back where he is but pause instead. Glance at the end of the seat where I'm standing and consider sitting down. Decide it's a time to stand up instead.

"Who do you think you are? Entertainer? Singer? Huh? *Who do you think you are?*" Standing now, belt whipped off, winding it around his hand.

"We're here to serve the Lord, not Hollywood. Not the Devil."

The girl's body stills, her face stiffens in stark white hot rage burning through two blue flames, half turned to face her Judge and Jury. Her silencer. She starts to open her mouth but the voice—her voice—has been snuffed, nothing more than a child's birthday candles extinguished in a breath.

But the Evangelist, fueled by his own outrage bellows again, louder, "You're *nobody.* You're nothing. Hear me?" Followed by a low growl, No-body. Nothing. Brandishing the leather whip and advancing the few feet, standing almost eye to eye.

She's straight up to attention, private before commanding officer. Her stance holds insistence. Eyes, once trained to be his own, turn to annealed and tempered steel, now hardened to resolve: her eyes go straight through him. His weapon hand wilts.

Ashes to ashes.

From the church house sounds the vibra harp and accordion, her mother singing, but to the girl's ears the music reaches and wails.

> *You can have all this world*
> *But give me Jesus . . .*
> *Dark midnight was my cry*
> *Give me Jesus . . .*

12

Wildwood, Florida 1956
Some Like It Hot

- *Tension mounts in Montgomery, Alabama, where the arrests of 115 Negroes on charges of boycotting the city's buses trigger protests.*

- *Reverend Martin Luther King Jr., found guilty of organizing the Montgomery bus boycotts.*

- *The University of Alabama enrolls its first Negro, Autherine Lucy; the University accused of succumbing to mob rule when it suspends her after riots erupt over her initial admittance; she's re-enrolled. "That girl sure has guts," says Thurgood Marshall.*

- *President Eisenhower states, "It is incumbent on all the South to show some progress" toward integration.*

- *Elvis Presley has #1 hit with Heartbreak Hotel.*

- *Suburban housing boom underway in US with war veterans marrying and seeking security in fresh air and sunshine for their families, a land of perfect lawns and swing sets.*

- *A nationwide network of highways linking major cities—bypassing small towns—in the US being planned, creating an estimated 150,000 construction jobs.*

- *President Eisenhower wins a second term in the White House, a landslide over Adlai Stevenson, with Richard Nixon, Vice president.*

- *Audrey Skondeen is fourteen.*

CAIN'T MISTAKE A PENTECOSTAL Assemblies a God Church in Wildwood, Florida, fer at romantic place sung so sweet in ole timey music. One at has

Sabbath bells ringin an wild flowrs bloomin roun a door? This here church house's built a cinderblocks, unpainted, narrow add on of a kitchen, bedroom an sittin room across a back, an makes a home fer a pastor, too.

Now these perticlar cinderblocks do claim a molded, decertive design less you think folks neglect artiness or fine looks roun this town. Why, even a outhouse makes a statement a decency, harborin a possibility a being hid like it do? Built the other side a the clothesline, see.

Holiness peoples herebouts have Bill and Doris Skondeen on ther minds since they in town agin. Memberin when they come up from Key West, jus youngins then, an Wildwood Assembly brought them as pastor an wife. Yes, Lord. Live in a back a ouvr church house, they did. Iss week, they at a Brown's house, an ats usul. But nothin else bein usul like when they in revival. When they in revival, then they keep close up atta church house, park at lil ole trailer home right ther. Things has changed.

Skondeen's girl Althea arrives while they livin here back in 19 an 37 an she's name fer a local woman. Audrey, youngun, borned five yar later when they liven in Calfornia, reckon Bill has kin out ther. Agin! they name her for an Audrey livin right here in Wildwood, good friend a Sister Doris. Seems this here town got a holt on em.

Keep coming on by. When they travel up and down Florda? Always park aside Theodore an Pauline Brown, owners of at grocery in town. Pullin ther trailer to Miami fer December an Janyary, months when revivals don't work so good. Hear tell Bill Skondeen makes a perty penny upholsterin fer fancy hotels onna beach. No wonder they drive a *De*Soto, mostly. Dodge iss time aroun. Course he points out a trailer house needs powr, pullin it up an down an all roun like at. Need a hefty car, reckon.

Man can preach, yes he can. Praisa Lord. Poured God's precious Word all over us las time he's here, April iss yar. Things as change, like a said, fer at famly since then. We'll git ta that. Any rate, he preached at las night a revival like I never heared him er any other preacher. Preached his own funerl service! Yes he did. Now I mean to tell you, that will get everbody in the church house down to bidness.

Them girls, includin mother Doris—face looks like a sixteen yar ole hersef—sang so perty that final night. "I Know Who Holes Tomorry." No angels in heaven, which we wer all thinking on aplenty, sound any sweeter than Althea, Audrey an ther mama. Altar call spoke to near ever one. Sister Stella took ta dancin in a Holy Ghost and got so wore out, she slain in a Spirit. Went down, flat out on a floor stretched atta altar, an a rest of us tarried atta altar hopin Jesus'd come carry us on to heaven right then an ther but it were not ta be. We still here.

Railroad come through Wildwood near the end a the las centry an makes iss here town crossroads ta ouvr whole world, stop an think bout it. Course most of us call it "rayroad." Proper spellin sometimes goes right on by me, but iss here a tied down on account a the importance ta ouvr town.

Train's hotter than hades, as we say, stoked-wood fire poundin at engine along em rails like nobodys bidness. Soot covered wash lines took over back yards, course, an when folks ain't workin a railroad, they workin round it. Know what a mean.

Famous folks includin President Roosevelt bin known a ride through here. Yep, gives lil ole Wildwood life an work an all manner a noterity. My, what a time.

Cain't be no easy thang, bringin a giant to a halt when a steam goes shooosh. Negro porters bustin brass buttons on ther black suit, hat on jus proper, jumps out, bringin a step down fer folks a leavin or a boardin. When it's time ta pull out, they announce, lookin straight ahead at no one in perticler, "All aboarrrd!" An them lookin proud, itsa sight.

Brown's younger boy, Kenny? loaded him some peanuts at his grandpa's farm, boiled em, sacked em an when a train smokes inta town he gits on board. Runs a length a them cars sellin boil peanuts. Smart one. Takin what you got an makin a wage. Yes, Lord.

Highway 44 brings Skondeens ta roost at Browns place, naturly, not them rails. Yars back, older boy Albert workin atta grocery waitin on custmers, toll everbody who'd listen when Skondeens was acomin. Talkin how Browns er totin a coupla bottles ginger ale—holiness folks champagne!—home cause a Skondeens on a way ta town. He's grinnin ear ta ear like as if Christmas comes when they do.

Albert Brown aint one ta moon over any thang, no, he busts out his roller skates, bicycle er whatever ya got an goes after it. Perdiction roun here, he's gonna be big success. He's oppsit a his daddy. That ther's acertain. More like is mama, Pauline, not seen so much out front a ther store, but busy as can be ever wher else. An worry? Have mercy. Don't know what she'd do thout a Lord. Some needs ta go ta prayin more 'n others an ats his daddy. Theodor Brown takes care a that. Good famly, littlest one's a girl. Carlyn.

Accordin to a latest news, at boy Albert Brown? He got last tag on Skondeen's girl Althea. No secert, an Wildwood holds secerts aplenty, at boys been sweet on iss here girl since youth camp when he's forteen yar old. He toll Althea someday he's gonna marry her. An that's a reason Skondeens landed up here iss week. Not fer revival er jus a visit, but plannin a weddin! Yep. Nex spring.

Preparin ta lose his girl, a guess, Skondeens buyed em a house on a busy road in Orlando. An right out front, hangs his sign fer fixin furnture. No need fer advertisin. Smart man. Apostle Paul made tents ta keep body an soul together. Skondeen makes furnture. Besides his girl Althea bein married off, a littler one's goin ta school. Mebbe college, too, ats what a hear.

Al, he's called, he's gone an growed up, works fer Western Union Telegraph. Says praying fer a Skondeen's photograph which stands on a Brown's piana sure did impress him ta pray like his daddy, one thing, and love Skondeens like we all do cept he loves one of em a lot more, know what a mean.

Even Sister Stella at ouvr church house loves Doris an Bill, perferrin as she does vangelists at turn up a sound. Not on music, mind you, but on a shoutin. Skondeen don't do that much. He specially keeps a volume down when he's apreachin. Volume of a shouters, that is, like Sister Stella. Understan, he breaks inta loud on his own, Vangliss Skondeen, he jus don't want a crowd ta out shout him. Hard line ta hold fer a Pentecostal preacher I will say. But Sister Doris or Brother Bill, either one don't make a public show aspeakin tongues. Never seen or heard neither one dancin in a Holy Ghost or speakin tongues as a Holy Ghost gives em uttrance.

Sister Stella warms at church house inna coldest winter when smudge pots er busy wipin frost away by turnin uppa heat in citrus groves onna outside. Onna inside, she out-blasts a pot belly stove we got inna corner with her dancin inna Ho-ly Ghost. An speakin in tungs whilst flame's lit up over yer head, a body can feel it! At tells ya somthin bout how hot em words might be. Things git ta movin.

Stella knows more'n she lets on, up dancin stead a sittin on a straitback hard bench, know whatta mean! Some people pack stories bout her life outside a church house, but it don't matter. Not when she steps thru a door mark *Holiness*.

Course Brother Skondeen surely does identfy with a likes a us "holy rollers" as we called roun here. But pentecost insis on a fire fallin, ya know? How can ya keep quiet when somethin like ats a goin on? Folks Jesus left ahind when He went on up ta God a Father, they all together an gone ta prayin. Sure like at part. Ats how it starts up ever time. All together an gone ta prayin!

"And when the day of Pentecost was fully come, they were all with one accord in one place. And suddenly there came a sound from heaven as of a rushing mighty wind, and it filled all the house where they were sitting. And there appeared unto them cloven tongues like as of fire, and it sat upon each of them. And they were all filled with the Holy Ghost, and began to speak with other tongues, as the Spirit gave them utterance." Now at's Apostle Paul writin in a book a Acts, chapter two, purely from a King James Bible. How can a person sit still an be quiet when ats agoin on? Praise Jesus.

A frien a my best frien toll me at youngest Skondeen girl Audrey was taken down ta altar at Wimamma camp meetin, Pentecostal Holiness Church of God, after some prayin sisters ask her if she receive since she believe. Like we do when we not sure? An her a shakin her head *no* leadin em ta be moved ta pray her threw ta baptism a Holy Ghost an fire. Says they fine prayin wimmins but close as at girl come, cryin real hard, red face n all, a frien a my frien, personal, did not hear that girl utter one word inna unknowed tongue. No sirree. She specks a prayin sisters in Christ went on ta others thinkin Audrey's all prayed through but a frien a my best frien says she don't think so.

Younger chiles' a handful anyways, you can jus tell. But never saw her act ugly, mus say. When she's a wee thing, she's a spit image a her daddy, dark curls bouncin and blue eyes sparklin, reminds a body a Shirley Temple, a declare—but bright a star as she is, folks guess she's a heartache fixen a happen. So a baptism a Holy Ghost'd be right helpful. Give er a fire onna inside wher she can store at spark, know what a mean.

But na, how cain ya be serprise when er folks don't make speakin tongues, prophesyin, an dancin in a Holy Ghost a priorty. What can they speck? They raisen her up. On a platform ever night fer yars an atta altar. Ever night. Cute as can be slappin at bass fiddle, but that don't count much in a long run. Fourteen, na, ya might say they loss at battle ta break'r spirit so a Holy Ghost taken on over.

Well, cain't judge no way, no how. Course Skondeen says if ya sees a black hog cross a road, ya know its a black hog. No judgin to it! My point bein ther's a conneck, yes Lord, twixt an tween parent's attude an kid's attude.

What a can say fer sure is at boy Albert Brown, tall dark an handsome as he is, itsa truth! Black hair, brown eyes an 6'2". He done chose a right Skondeen girl, praisa Lord. His mama, Pauline, don't need no more headaches than she already has got, keepin books fer a grocery like she do.

Anyways, High school kids roun here, Al Brown run with some a them hooligans, been actin smart aleky bout holiness. Sister Stella has bore up under lotsa laughter. Course she never paid it no mind. Them youngins sneekin up an lookin inna winders at Wildwood Pentecostal like its a peep show fer ther benfit. Stead a gettin right with a Lord an learnin a closer walk with Jesus at a age when at can make a differnce ta yor life, know what a mean.

Here's wher Brother Skondeen comes in real handy with sayins at stick to a body. Take Jonah, "Thers always a boat down atta dock waitin to take you to Tarsus," uh huh. Stead a Nineveh like God the Father Almity says ya got to go? Ats purely a truth. And "thers always a Deelila happy ta give you a hair cut!" Taken your power plum outta you likes a what she done to poor ole Samson. Have mercy. Skondeen has somethin ta say. Talk about a ugly actin woman.

Preacher Skondeen knows how to vangelize all right. Welcomes folks, glad hands strangers and friens all a same, but you won't find him kissin babies er old ladies er huggin em up like some preachers do. Keeps a fair distance. An nobody dares declare what at man's athinkin. They be wrong, garantee. Too deep in ther ahind what's plum outta sight, hid away. Not sayin ennythings wrong, just mean t'menshun theys mystry aplenty.

But ever so often a body who listens close t' at man will hear im say, with that big grin a his, "Life gets teejus, don't it," like at song a guy sings onna radio? Somebody intersted might figger Brother Skondeens a man at gets low, time t' time. Heres other words fer at song,

> *The sun comes up and the sun goes down*
> *The hands on the clock keep goin round*
> *I jus git up and its time to lay down*
> *Life gits tee-jus, don't it?*[1]

B'lieve he means a be funny like? But even at crooked grin, half a smile, ya still hear a guard standin out back while ya hava Gospel-says asmilin out front. Its Bill Skondeen's *v*ilin tells em sad songs, less he's a playin it fer a fiddle. Fiddles er always happy.

Sister Doris she don't say hardly ennything, but she smiles an thanks a Lord fer everthing. That's er way. Hear tell er health wavers twixt strong an frail. Don't know why, really. Mebbe has ta do with er heart? Might could say she's a good balance for Bill Skondeen, onna one hand, er he's a burden fer Doris Skondeen on a other hand. It's heart trouble all right.

Not yet noon, but hot in these here parts, spite a oak trees spreadin wings over us fer perfect shade all up a street. Limbs shelterin us mus be wings steada open arms like some says, on a counta moss strung thru branches bein wavy angel hair. Ats how a sees em. Perty as can be. Magnolias nod from yards, flowers openin up white, lookin like flyin saucers bout ta take to a sky. Ah declare. Crepe myrtle, too, shockin pink. An a fig tree at ever

1. Carson J. Robison, MCA Music, 1948.

August fills a air with fragrance an fils yer hands with fruit. Jesus'd bless iss here tree fer sure.

Over all? Its em orange trees come May, June, at beats all. Em blossoms give everbody reason ta prais God ouvr Father, creater of a universe. Thank God He made iss worl s'wonderful.

Trees is how Wildwood come to be named as it is. Back in 18 an somethin, a surveyer fer a telgraph line? Radios a boss, an boss asks wher is he? Says, Dunno. Wild woods . . . ats alla can see. Ats us. *Wild woods.*

We run thru at bit a true down atta grocery today? Lollygaggin, drinkin cole cocolas, one thing goes right on ta 'nother. Know what a mean. After while we all fromma Holiness. We goes out back with our cocolas, talkin over ole times. Skondeens name what brot it up fo'ward, how ever revival meetin we pray s'hard, iss one'll be ouvr las? Jesus comin ta carry us home! Theodor's with us, Albert able to runna store when is daddy's pre-occpied, an Theodor's thinkin bout a Lord an not sellin groceries. Not like Pauline who's totin up a numbers bout how they better be a sellin groceries.

Any rate, ever revival might be a las one, but when it come clear we gonna git on up tomorra an do a same as we did afor revival started up, we go to praisin Jesus at it aint gonna be jus like no other day. Tomorry? We been *revived*, praisis Name. Been set on a Glory road after fallin in a ditch a doubt an fear, er a pond plum full a dispond. Uh huh. We bran new Christians all over agin. Yes Lord! Bran new Christians all over agin.

We havin a prayer meetin right inna middle a our a lollygaggin, then it come out at Brother Skondeen done toll some body er other bout havin the trailer house hauled away. Weeds growin roun it parked inna yard like it was in Orlando. Watched a truck haul it off. Says Skondeens voice nearly broke ta tears. No body can say a word after at.

Walkin back under oak trees, pass magnolias, recollectin orange blossoms, a got ta hearin words fromma Lord's Supper. ". . . In Rememrance a Me" halluyah! Brought a tear to ma eye as a tarried, goin a long way home. Sittin onna stump, hearin Jesus joy playin in a breezes. Trans-lated, like at *Cowboy Paul*, Skondeen calls im, Paul a fallin off his horse an all. Yes, Lord. Bein purely translated takes me back ta at las revival. Not jus a thinkin an lollygaggin with a cocola, but fer *real*.

Sister Stella s'fulla Jesus, dear saint a God rattlin a rafters inna lil church a Wildwood. What a mean ta say here, Sister Stella bein s'real, at made a whole sperience a bein translated true as m'hand afor me.

Skondeen family all here, not jus ages in a present day, but all at time we known em. Littlest girl a Spark Plug afore this here las revival, but this time they inna church house, Vangelist only calls er Audrey if he talks about er at all. She din't lead a singin not s'much. Slaps a bass fiddle, like a said, an at sounds good fer singin an looks real cute. But in m'trans-latin, she's a *live wire* like she use'ta was. *Spark Plug.*

Sister, Althea, never give nobody any trouble, sayin hardly a thang, purely normal like er mama. She's a playin iss chimin harp at vibrates? Its a heavnly kinda sound. It's Glory, pure Glory.

At music—*I Dont Know Bout Tomorry, At the End a the Trail*—we takin it in. We feelin a Skondeens with all a sweetness we learnt in life. Raisin' us higher n higher. Lord, Lord. Las song afore Brother Skondeen preaches, duet with him an Sister Doris, bless'er heart.

> *Some day face to face I shall see Him,*
> *And oh, what a joy it will be*
> *To know that His love, now so precious,*
> *Will forever grow sweeter to me!*[2]

Then a Vangliss goes ta preachin an from a git go we know ther aint no more sermins a likes a this'n. Some times a mus confess, gittin saved makes me thinka drownin, despert plee an waitin onna lifeline? Know what a mean. But such a night cain't see me goin enny wheres but up. Praisis Name!

> Since I'm going to die—
> one of these days wakin up in Glory—
> *It Is Appointed,* we're told!
> And all funerals are preached by some one else,
> they might not give an accurate pitcher—fix things up a little,
> color it pretty.
>
> But I know my self and
> here is one I can talk about
> with *no* body accusin' me a gossip!
>
> With the Psalmist I can say
> You have proved my heart:
> visited me, tried me!
> What's the verdict?
> What have you found!
> To find nothing inside, that's my greatest fear.
> Or discover deep, hidden revenge, no no.
> Has to do with *Final Exams.*
> Keeping books up to date, right Sister Pauline?
> Never know when the books are closed . . .

2. Chas. H. Gabriel, "Growing Dearer Each Day" (R.G. Excell, owner), 1907.

Reaper comes knockin on a door
Please go 'way.
I'm come after you.
Take my money.
But I've come for *you* . . .

Right about then Preacher has me s'full a leave takin, I pitcher im atta Golden Gates witha Angels in Glory. An alla folks from his preachin come to greet im: cain't ya see Adam still shakin is head. Confuse? Standin in a cool garden, sweet pea blossoms gone ta seed. An right ther in at outta season garden, Eve says ta Skondeen, ya sure true when ya tell folks, Don't get in no argument with a snake. He'll win ever time.

Like Skondeen says, You can live with a wooden leg, but cain't live with no wooden head. Looks like Eve bin a thinkin with a wooden head an she can see it? Too late, a course.

But a seen'er in heaven, Eve. Mus be pure mercy.

Then here comes Samson—hugs Skondeen's neck real careful like, realizin is power's back—an he tells Bill Skondeen, Brother at theme you sung in yer preachin, *one more time*, ya know. An he pauses jus a spell, how cinders come inta eyes a strong guys? Yep. Samson, too. An he shakes is long golden locks with alla luxry a lion shrugs when he's a roarin, an he tells a Preacher at ever time Skondeen comes over at song *one more time*, again. Pleadin. *One more time.* He sees folks stop. Consider.

Samson says ever time a person gives way, says I'm not awaitin fer one more time, Preacher, "Ya give m'life back ta me agin. Agin. An agin. Ever time ya tell m'story ya give m'life back to me."

Lil servant girl ta Naaman's wife neva had no name inna Bible, but thanks a Skondeen, roun here she's well knowed.[3] How she's snatch from er home, bloody battle, my Lord, dragged inna chariot and took away. Family gone but she's personal with'r God. Halluyah. Makes me smile, hearin Skondeen preach on at girl, sayin how he knows a little bout girls. Had two a his own an they not alla time sugar an spice! Have sweet moments, course, but also,

Serious
Resentful
Revengeful
Rightous Indignation? *Full of it.*

But here's is lil ole girl took outta her home. Na she cain't choose er mood. Know what a mean. 'Magine, bein a slave, but when everthang gone, cain't nobody take what you got onna inside.

3. 2 Kgs 5:1–19.

This girl has Compassion when she heared her owner got leprosy. Commander, loaded up n medals, doncha see. An she's such a sweet chile at when she talks, er big shot officer-owner goes n listens. He meets up with a prophet Elisha as she toll him. Does what Elisha says do. Dips seven times inna muddy Jordan river. Comes up clean praisa Lord. Cause at lil girl stands alone. Her names not put inna Bible, but she's *Compassion*.

Well a course ya'd reconize at chile anywher. She come ta stand, real 'specful like near Bill Skondeen wher he's a restin inna shade. Reckon at hug from Samson nearly wore him out. Preacher turns ta her an she does a little bow, em fine manners, says his preachin, pointin up her personal frienship with God a givin her compassion? Ats better an havin a name her parents give her writ down inna Bible. Better by far, she says. Rather be known as Compassion, my *true* name.

At lil ole girl always bring a tear ta my eye.

Astonishin as it may seem, lil boy Blue come along, chile a Spark Plug sings about? He's out astrollin with a baby, a one at mama nearly wep er self ta death at a casket, um hm. Skondeen talks about an prays fer at famly fer yars. Brot em afor a throne a grace a know. Boy Blue puts at lil chile in Skondeen's arms an ther he is, *kissin a baby*. Praisa Lord.

Jesus joins em bout then. They go ta walkin, takin turns holdin a baby.

Wouldn't ya know David shows up, harp under is arm. Wants to be sure Skondeen knows that blot's been wiped on out. They go ta speakin bout meadows up yonder, still waters no motor boats like our Lake T'sala Apopka. Satisfy yer soul ever minute. Course Skondeen asks David won't he play on his harp?

That's what sets David off ta laughing, strumming at lil ole harp. You can tell he's recallin a detail? And Brother Skondeen just cain't hep his self, he laughs, too, even tho he's not sure why. Perty soon ya have angels flutterin around. Happy draws em in, much as sad. Some kinda commotion. David keeps a laughin, words pressed twixt n tween. Goodness an Mercy? He stops fer a breath. Starts up a strummin agin, says, Namin kids Goodness and Mercy. Havin'm chase a preacher to prove how they follows a person all a days a ther life?

By now a crowds gathered, hearin David tell how Evangelis Skondeen names two childern, one Goodness n one, Mercy, when he's apreachin Psalm 23? An toll em ta foller him, not let im outta sight. An just like at, he takes off a runnin.

Them kids hardly knows what ta do at first, then they go on an grab ther senses an runs after him! Straight outta at church house front door, roun about park cars, inna back door, crashin over choir chairs. Bout at time he slows on down atta altar, yep. Skondeen stops is runnin an lets em catch up. He turns roun ta face Goodness an Mercy in a middle a all at laughin.

An right here's wher Skondeen's story ends.

Epilogue

How swiftly the strained honey
of afternoon light
flows into darkness

and the closed bud shrugs off
its special mystery
in order to break into blossom:

as if what exists, exists
so that it can be lost
and become precious

In Passing
Lisel Mueller

FINDING MY WAY TO the Porter's Gate, Christ Church, proved easy enough, but having missed the actual porters meant steering my luggage through swarms of visitors in Sir Christopher Wren's Tom Quad and on through the cloisters before settling into the Meadows Dormitory. Oxford University's school of theology summer session would begin the next morning. Meantime, the view alone from the small balcony outside my windows where placid cows grazed over the Christ Church Meadow convinced me I had made the right choice to be here.

An ad in one of my professional journals announcing the overall title of the class selections, *Religion, Ethics, and Public Theology* had convinced me to apply. Peering into Chaucer's village in *Canterbury Tales* for a look at morals or lack thereof and visiting the world's religions for lessons in *Ethical Issues Across the Faiths* intrigued me as much as *Mammon's Revenge: the Last*

Six Years of the Global Financial Crisis where questions of integrity loomed. Gnarled ideas of creation, the physiology of life—beginnings and endings— would be argued in *Ethical Issues in Science and Religion,* according to the readings we'd been assigned.

Oxford uses the tutorial system, students digging into original texts rather than textbooks. And, classroom guides, however brilliant and holders of higher degrees, are simply referred to as *tutors.*

Every day I thought of how my father would love Oxford as I studied, debated, or walked along the Rivers Isis and Cherwell that border the meadows or absorbed her gardens. First of all for her natural beauty: seasons of planting, growth and harvest whether on a farm in Canada, California, or the Deep South, ever drew him into their vitality. But he craved education as well. He was a confirmed student of music, story—Tolstoy and Dostoevsky read in Russian—preaching and poetry throughout his life. When my father's hands were too arthritic to do the fingering for the violin he learned as a teen at the San Francisco Conservatory of Music, he took up piano lessons. Perhaps even World Religions and the advances of science, medicine, and global warming discussed in my classes might have intrigued rather than infuriated him as they would have in his earlier years.

Christ Church classrooms gathered us in for God talk using the lens of our particular disciplines from lawyers to bishops, financiers to psychiatrists. All, students. The various professions added texture to the colors of our cultural hues and accents—I heard a lot of *southern*—from all over the world. Disagreements were usually approached with courtesy. Our dislocation allowed greater care in hearing each other, certainty of footing and one's usual lean toward left or right wobbling on new territory.

But by midday I often needed to get away. Escaping the words whirling through lunch hour in the magnificent dining hall where prime ministers, cardinals and kings peered over us, I descended wide stone steps worn to a downward slant into an enchantment of roses, lavender and hollyhocks tall as a cottage roof. Alongside the meadow, an arched wooden gate provided an open invitation into the Master's Garden. I'd head for the sequestered bench at the far end beneath an espaliered fig tree trellised over a rock wall. Dad sat with me in this corner filled with self sown sun brushed panicles of lady's mantle mingling with the delicate blue of love in a mist. Whirring hummingbirds dipped for sips of nectar, butterflies alighted and lifted off. I was quickly lost in wonder. Restored.

The Rev'd Dr. Shaun Hensen, author of *God of Natural Order: Physics, Philosophy and Theology* (New York: Routledge, 2013) was our tutor for Ethical Issues in Science and Religion, using the definition for the scientific method as a systematic practice of *doubt that leads you closer and closer to the truth.* Who knew that *gift of suspicion* received from my father was scientific? Henson assured us as well that in our evolution, we do inherit ancestral ways of thinking.

But toward the end of the class, ruminating about conclusion of life decisions, we found new information—at least it was for me—in considering the heart not only a muscle for distributing blood to our vital organs, but as a repository of memory. Informing and influencing the brain with collected data. This connects to my following the trail our family traveled: many towns and country churches no longer exist, and yet, without an idea of which dirt road went where, or a set of instructions, I'd go to the exact spot.

No current map has the name *Sayreton* on it. But I found a soul food shack in the general area and, crashing my way through a nearly unhinged screen door, inquired *Sayreton?* A time-worn man over in the corner hunched over his black eye peas and corn bread glanced up and said, "Yer standin innit." Or, crossing railroad tracks, turning right, and, a couple of miles down the country lane finding the Beaverton church full of broken, dusty furniture. A mailbox next door bore a name I instantly knew, but could not have said until that moment.

During the hours I spent in the presence of the Master's Garden at Oxford, I never saw people weeding, watering, or working fertilizers into the soil, yet the gifts of their hands were evident in this wild patch of miracles. I imagined tools with imprints of fingers that recognize the difference of second and third sets of leaves on reseeding perennials from that of weeds, allowing blossoms to flourish more abundantly year after year. Instruments used for creating paradise.

After my father's death, Clarice, a daughter of the woman he married when my mother died, called me to say his violin had been found in a hiding place between walls of a loft he'd built. An instrument that bears my father's fingerprints, embodies the stories of life before my birth and could have been my guide to every place we ever traveled. When I brought it home, I discovered a stash of small, black and white photos circa 1947 to 1948 tucked under the crushed blue velvet lining of the case. Photos of our family, standing outside the open trailer door looking into the sunshine, smiling through all the years since then, telling my father with every view, and now telling me, too: *It's true. This is you. Happy. Working for your Lord exactly as you chose among beloved people.*

Wherever I was, late afternoons, chimes from the carillon called me into the Christ Church cathedral. Within her grandeur abides an intimacy that is never more serene than in the liminal hour of day's slipping into night. Evensong. Traditionally constructed in the twelfth century, participants face each other across a long aisle; candles are lighted in the lamps in front of the choristers. First the silence, then the singing never failed to move me. In their blended voices, I experienced what is for me a ringing truth: all questions meet and dissolve in the human heart. Whether in a cathedral or a cement block church house, a cotton field or Irene's talks with Jesus at the mill, it's in the simple complexity of our hearts that true religion rests and rises to the need.

Devoted people of the southern woods and meadows of my child-hood, along with my mother and father, lived their hope that all would be well however their earthly stories ended. They tutored me in generous love, mercy, and forgiveness, original texts developed by some of whom could not even read. Yet they effectively communicated the raw simplicity of their faith in heart language, connecting generations. More powerful than any printed work.